The Occult & Subversive Movements

Tradition & Counter-Tradition in the Struggle for World Power

By

Kerry Bolton

The Occult & Subversive Movements

Tradition & Counter-Tradition in the

Struggle for World Power

By

Kerry Bolton

ISBN-13: 978-1-910881-92-7

Black House Publishing Ltd
Kemp House
152 City Road
London
United Kingdom
EC1V 2NX

www.blackhousepublishing.com
Email: info@blackhousepublishing.com

Contents

The Occult & Subversive Movements, provides an excellent overview of the conspiratorial view of history and the role of the occult therein. It also does so without the often heavy-handed, ideological baggage that affects many works in the genre. You allow the source materials, which are ample and well-cited, to speak for themselves.

One thing that I strongly agree with is your assertion that the objective reality of doctrines and theories discussed is not the issue, but whether or not people were motivated to act on them or affected by those who did. I emphasize the identical thing in my class on Conspiracies and Secret Societies in History. In that respect I think your work is a worthwhile tool indeed.

Dr Richard Spence

Chair, Department of History
University of Idaho.

Dr Richard Spence Honors Program courses include: 'Secret Societies and Conspiracies in History', and 'The Occult: Its Presence and Influence in History'.

He is the author of :

Secret Agent 666: Aleister Crowley, British Intelligence, and the Occult - Feral House. 2008

Trust No One: The Secret World of Sidney Reilly - Feral House. 2003

Boris Savinkov: Regade on the Left - Columbia University Press 1991.

Foreword

Dr Mark L. Mirabello

Conspiracies and secret societies are older than recorded history. The late great Professor Joseph Campbell, the mythologist and scholar of religion, wrote in his classic work, *The Masks of God*, that many hunting nomads, such as the Ona people from Tierra del Fuego, have a story of a more primitive time when women were in sole possession of the magical art. In those days, women ruled because they could bring sickness and death to all who dared to displease them.

According to the legend, the older women taught the magic to young girls at the time of "first blood," the time of the mystery and terror of puberty. The men were vexed by their subordinate position, however, and they secretly plotted to gain power. The male plan was so simple – and so ruthless – that success was guaranteed.

Striking without warning, the men murdered all the women. Only the little girls – the prepubescent ones who had not yet been initiated into the mysteries – were spared. Still wet with blood, the men then formed a secret society to keep the females in subjection forevermore.

• • • •

I am from a different tradition than Dr. Kerry Bolton – he is a prominent right-wing thinker – whereas I am a student of all traditions, left as well as right, but Dr. Bolton understands the power of conspiracy and secrecy in history.

All readers, from all traditions, will find this book worthy of attention.

Foreword

Mark L. Mirabello, Ph.D., Professor of History, Shawnee State University (USA), author: *Death & Other Worlds: A Skeleton Key; Handbook for Rebels and Outlaws: Resisting Tyrants, Hangmen, and Priests; The Odin Brotherhood; The Cannibal Within,* etc.

Preamble

'Occult conspiracies,' including conjecture on the continuing influence of the 18th century Illuminati, excite the popular imagination, particularly with a proliferation of such theories on the internet since '9/11'. There are often biases according to religious perspective, or a focus on a variety of pet-theories such as reptilian extra terrestrials, Nazi-UFO-Bush and /or British Royal Family connections, the Vatican, Opus Dei, Priory de Sion, Jews, bankers, and any one of a muddle of combinations thereof. Commercial interests, which one would expect, from the 'conspiratorial' perspective to be part of some vast conspiracy, are nontheless cashing in on this interest, with movies such as 'National Treasure', and books such as the 'conspiracy' series of volumes published by Collins & Brown, and the best-selling books by Dan Brown.

This book attempts to approach the subject with the use of scholarly methodology combined with the perspective of Tradition versus Counter-Tradition. The focus is here on a 'spiritual' or 'occult war', with the emphasis being on the primary esoteric current of the past several centuries, from which many others have emerged: Freemasonry.

What compounds the difficulty in dealing with this subject is that what Perennial Traditionalists describe as the 'Counter-Tradition' and 'Anti-Tradition', are 'counterfeits' of Tradition, and – like counterfeits in general – are therefore difficult to recognise from the genuine article. It is an analogous situation to that warned of in the Bible where 'false prophets' and the 'Antichrist' were prophesied as arising to fool many of the faithful. This 'Antichrist' would appear performing many miracles and be thought of as the returned Christ to set up a world government.

The Christian prophesy is not too far removed from what is today happening with 'false prophets', 'gurus' and 'messiahs' proclaiming a 'new age' of peace, joy and unity for all mankind under a centralised authority.

Another seeming anomaly is that many of these occult societies were at the forefront of promoting rationalism and scientism using the language, rituals and symbols of the occult while proclaiming their opposition to all religions and superstitions. From a Traditionalist perspective, these 'rationalists' in mystical garb were the 'Anti-Traditionalists' performing the work of the 'Counter-Tradition'. This is a dialectic in which rationalism and materialism are used as a means of destroying all Faiths that pose a barrier to what some have called the 'Black Adepts' who aim to impose their own authority over the world and set up their own religion on the ruins of the old beliefs. Hence rationalistic, atheistic, materialistic, and communistic doctrines are a means to an end, and not the end.

What must be emphasised from the start is that it matters not whether YOU believe in such metaphysics, or regard it as utter nonsense and primitive superstition. What matters is that there are – and have been for centuries – those who regard themselves as Adepts in the service of what are often called 'Hidden Masters', who believe they are chosen to usher a new form of government and ultimately a new form of humanity.

As a contemporary authority on such matters, Dr Richard Spence, of Idaho University, remarked on an early MS of this book: 'One thing that I strongly agree with is your assertion that the objective reality of doctrines and theories discussed is not the issue, but whether or not people were motivated to act on them or were affected by those who did'.

Introduction

The reality of the matter is that magic is basic to the modern mentality, to our politics and science, and we cannot understand our present-day world without a knowledge of what magic is.[1]

Socio-psychological explanations reduce beliefs in occult conspiracies down to a symptom of neuroses during periods of change and uncertainty. Such an explanation is insufficient. While beliefs in the occult and mysticism might arguably themselves be delusional, such delusions impact upon reality no less than when the paranoid delusions of a psychotic murderer impact upon the reality of his victims.

The power of myth is important in its own right, outside of any rational or empirically proven historical factors. Myth, whether ultimately based on the embroidering of an actual individual or event over the course of a long duration, or entirely grounded in superstition, instinct and the irrational, shapes history, and is of greater importance in doing so than empirical 'truth'. It is the foundation of religions, of faith, 'the holy lie', the subjective way of looking at the world, whether caused by instinct, intuition, or some mystical connection – or perceived connection – with the divine, that turns the wheels of history in the great cycles of rise and fall. The German philosopher Hans Vaihinger considered in his primary work *Philosophy of 'As If'* the vital role of 'fictions' – what he called 'fictionalism' - in both individual and collective life. Hence the world was not governed by 'truth' but by the impact of an idea. For example, we might say that the 'value' of Darwin's evolutionary theory is not that it has been 'proven' but that it served the Zeitgeist or the ethical outlook of 19th century

---

1   Rushdoony, p. 54.

materialism and English economic theory in interpreting life as 'struggle'; a doctrine that met the requirements of English capitalism.

The 'occult war' that has taken place for at least several centuries, in an empirically discernible line of history that will be examined here, relies for its sustenance not on 'facts' but on myth, or 'fictionalism', that nonetheless becomes real when applied to the shaping of events to accord with these 'fictions'. One might say that making such fictions into reality is itself 'magic'.

The historical impact has significantly centred around a conflict between Catholicism and Freemasonry. Some occult theorists such as Eliphas Levi trace the origins of Masonry back to the Knights Templar, whose Order was suppressed by the Church for heresy. Here is a primary example of the influence of myth and legend, whether having any historical basis or not, as an important influence on secret societies. Occultism by definition is based on myth and it is how this myth is perceived that is important. In this instance, what is important is not so much whether a direct Templar connection with Masonry is historically accurate, but that it is perceived as such by Masonry and its derivatives.

It is something of a paradox (or a dialectical process) that the secret societies and revolutionary thinkers that heralded the Enlightenment and the triumph of liberal-humanism resorted to occult societies and occult allegory. In the same vein, rationalism itself became a substitute for traditional religion, as the 'Goddess of Reason' was worshipped on the altar of Notre-Dame Cathedral during the French revolutionary regime, hymns were sang and baptisms performed in the name of 'Reason' and of the 'Unknown Deity', upon the wreckage of the Church. Current generations have witnessed the same irrational phenomenon under atheistic communism, which manifested in forms of mass religious worship, and placed the mummified body of Lenin within a stepped pyramid.

What can be concluded from this is that man has an inherent religious nature and need for spirituality that cannot be fulfilled by rationalistic or economic interpretations of history. Man needs to worship something beyond himself and believe in something other than processes of production and consumption. Hence, religion is more than an 'opiate of the people', a prop for the maintenance of a ruling class, but can be perverted into serving such an end.

The hatred of established religion often assumed the form of outright Satan and Lucifer adulation, especially during the 19th century, when these figures were given heroic proportions as the archetypes of rebellion against tyranny. Such Luciferic rebellion was established within certain occult degrees of initiation, and the 'Light-Bringer' also became a god of the 'Enlightenment' and of 'Rationalism', supposedly against superstition. It is an example of what Traditionalists such as Rene Guénon recognised as the façade of Anti-Tradition working for the goals of Counter-Tradition in the name of 'science' but for the ultimate purpose of establishing something quite different. The aim, whether with the use of myth and superstition or with 'reason' and 'science, is world power.

Anti-Tradition & Counter-Tradition

To Traditionalists, the great faiths of mankind that have remained true to their original beliefs share a common – perennial – core, which maintains humanity's nexus with the Divine; sees the duty of the individual, from peasant to king and priest, as being that of manifesting the Divine order, and society as being the terrestrial re-presentation of the cosmos. Perrenial Traditionalists such as Julius Evola and Rene Guénon, regarded the 'modern world' as not being a product of a lineal, progressive ascent or Darwinian-type evolution of humanity, but as being the product of a cultural cycle of decline, where humanity had been divorced from its spiritual, cosmic nexus. Into this 'dark age', prophesied in the holy texts and oral lore of the traditional faiths, from Hopi to Norse, from Hindu to Muslim and The Revelation of John of Patmos; come to the fore the forces of Counter-Tradition, which aim to bind humanity to crass matter. Hence the doctrine of materialism that is propagated by Anti-Tradition posing in the guise of religion and mysticism; hence the use of Marxism, for example, by occultic initiates.

Anti-Tradition was stated by Guénon to be 'pure negation and nothing more', and was the prelude of Counter-Tradition.[1] Within this Counter-Tradition there is a 'counter-initiation',[2] representing what Guénon called a 'satanic' current of those who seek the severing of the nexus between the terrestrial and the divine. Guénon wrote of this:

> After having worked always in the shadows, to inspire and to direct invisibly all modern movements, it will in the end contrive to 'exteriorise', if that is the right word, something

1   Guénon, 2001, p. 260.
2   Guénon, 2001, p. 261.

that will be as it were, the counterpart of a true tradition, at least as completely and as exactly as it can be so within the limitations necessarily inherent in all possible counterfeits as such.[3]

Of these Counterfeit-Traditions, Guénon stated that they can never be anything other than a 'parody', an 'inverted spirituality' involving organisations of 'counter-initiation.'[4] Guénon regarded these movements as being of supernatural origin, and believed that a figure analogous to 'The Antichrist' will manifest at the head of a world order.[5]

Guénon described the strategy of Counter-Tradition which first uses the doctrine of 'egalitarianism' as a means of overthrowing faith and tradition. On the ruins of the traditional social and spiritual order will be erected, in place of the divinely-sanctioned hierarchies, a 'counter-hierarchy', atop which sits an individual that again seems analogous to 'The Antichrist' which Guénon described as nearest to the 'very bottom of the "pit of hell"'.[6] Of the numerous orders that were emerging especially in France during the 19th century, Guénon referred to them, regardless of their spiritual pretensions, as 'anti-tradition', and as reflecting the Zeitgeist or 'spirit of the age, of the present epoch of Western decline. He here specifically refers to the numerous Orders that claimed to be 'Rosicrucian'. [7] We shall return to this when considering the French Revolution.

Following Guénon, the Traditionalist Baron Julius Evola stated in similar vein in regard to the subversive activities of the Counter-Tradition represented by Anti-Tradition:

---

3   Guénon, 2001, p. 261.

4   Guénon, 2001, p. 267.

5   Guénon, 2001, pp. 271-273. Guénon draws on both Islamic and Christian traditions here.

6   Guénon , 2001, p. 271.

7   Guénon, 2001, p.251.

I wish to mention one more instrument for the secret war, though it refers to a very particular domain; the tactic of the replacing infiltrations. It is when a certain spiritual or traditional organisation falls into such a state of degeneration that its representatives know very little of its true, inner foundation, or the basis of its authority and prestige. The life of such an organisation may then be compared to the automatic state of a sleepwalker, or living body deprived of its soul.

In a sense a spiritual 'void' has been created that can be filled, through infiltrations, by other subversive forces. These forces, while leaving the appearances unchanged, use the organisation for totally different purposes, which at times may even be the opposite of those that were originally its own. We should also not rule out the case where such infiltrated elements work for the destruction of the organisation that they now control, for example, by creating new scandals, liable to give rise to serious repercussions.

Having mentioned Masonry, it must be stated that the genesis of modern Freemasonry as a subversive force is due to this tactic of replacement and insertion that is exercised within some of the oldest organisations, which Masonry retained as mere vestiges, structures, symbols, and hierarchies, while the effecting guiding influences have a different nature altogether.[8]

In this manner the Counter-Tradition infiltrated and redirected the guilds of the Medieval stone masons to effect totally different purposes from those that were bound by Faith and craft. Evola described this as part of an 'occult war', defined as 'a battle that is waged imperceptibly by the forces of global subversion, with means and in circumstances ignored by current histiography'.[9]

---

8   Evola, 2002, pp. 250-251.

9   Evola, *Ibid.*, p. 235.

Black & White Adepts

The 'infamous' British occultist Aleister Crowley, scourge of respectable English society during the 1920s, portrayed by the tabloid press as a 'Satanist' and as 'the wickedest man in the world', was also an operative for the British secret service in both World Wars[10] and far from being a 'Black Magician' sought to oppose the 'Black Adepts' in the occult war. The reference to the 'occult war' to which he referred was the same as exposed by Guénon and Evola. Indeed, Evola, as a seminal spokesman for the Traditionalist school, also regarded Crowley as essentially a Traditionalist. Crowley's doctrine when applied to the political and social and even the economic spheres, is contrary to that of the Anti-Traditionalist and Counter-Traditionalist currents, and is aristocratic rather than communistic.[11]

Crowley explained that while the Yellow School 'stands aloof', 'the Black School and the White are always more or less in active conflict'.[12] He wrote of the nexus between the Black School and Freemasonry, and that Masonry had been taken over and redirected by the Black Masters and their adepts, a complaint also of the 19th century French occult theorist Eliphas Levi.

Crowley also referred to English Masons being 'in official relationship with certain masonic bodies whose sole *raison d'etre* is anti-clericalism, political intrigue and trade benefit', despite English Masonry supposedly eschewing such motives.[13] English Masonry, or United Grand Lodge (UGL), in which we can include all Lodges of so-called 'Regular' Masonry, is at pains to point out that any nefarious activities ascribed to Freemasons, are not those of 'genuine' Masons. The argument is disingenuous, and in the same category as the claims by factional Marxists that Marxism fails because it is not the 'genuine' variety. It is from the UGL that much of the 'Black School' emanated, and to those

---

10   Spence, 2007, pp. 25-30.

11   Bolton, 2011a, pp. 5-27.

12   Crowley, *Ibid.*, p. 66

13   Crowley, 1986, p. 697.

looking at the many aspects of the occult war, UGL objections mean little.

Rudolf Steiner and The Ahrimanic Deception

Rudolf Steiner, founder of Anthroposophy, whose influence has gone far beyond 'occult' circles for his prominence in alterative education, architecture, and organic gardening, also believed in the existence of an 'occult war' between contending schools of Adepts. Steiner, like Guénon, Evola, et al, sought to expose a Dark current at work within the secret societies, and in particular within Freemasonry, whose influence Steiner saw being directed in the world politically.

In a 1919 lecture delivered in Zurich, entitled 'The Ahrimanic Deception', Steiner stated that 'a great part of mankind today is already under the control, from one side or another, of Ahrimanic forces of a cosmic nature which are growing stronger and stronger'.

Steiner had an unusual perception of what he called the 'Luciferic Impulse', which he stated had manifested on Earth in 3000BC. The Luciferic Impulse prepared the way for the 'Christ Impulse' in Steiner's cosmology. Both 'Impulses' began to fade and mankind has therefore become increasingly materialistic. Steiner stated that this Ahrimanic Deception emanates from an actual being:

> The Ahrimanic impulse proceeds from a supersensible Being different from the Being of Christ or of Lucifer. … The influence of this Being becomes especially powerful in the Fifth Post-Atlantean Epoch. If we look at the confused conditions of recent years we shall find that men have been brought to such chaotic conditions mainly through the Ahrimanic powers.[14]

---

14   Steiner, 1919.

Rudolf Steiner (1861-1925) Austrian philosopher, architect and esotericist.

While the 'Lucierifc Impulse' pushed humanity into what the philosopher Nietzsche might have called the Dionysian passion that gives birth to arts and brings humanity outside of itself, albeit, according to Steiner, with a 'false spirituality', 'Ahriman is the power that makes man dry, prosaic, philistine – that ossifies him and brings him to the superstition of materialism'.[15] Ahriman would seem to equate with the Christian perception of the Antichrist. The 'Christ Impulse' balances the two poles:

> And the true nature and being of man is essentially the effort to hold the balance between the powers of Lucifer and Ahriman; the Christ Impulse helps present humanity to establish this equilibrium…. [T]he Ahrimanic influence has been at work since the middle of the fifteenth century and will increase in strength until an actual incarnation of Ahriman takes place among Western humanity.[16]

15   Steiner, 1919.

16   Steiner, 1919.

Preparing the Way for Ahriman

The relevance of this concept of the Ahrimanic Deception in regard to an 'occult war' for world rule, is that:

> Now it is characteristic of such things that they are prepared long in advance. Ahrimanic powers prepare the evolution of mankind in such a way that it can fall a prey to Ahriman when he appears in human form within Western civilization… Ahriman will appear in human form and the only question is, how he will find humanity prepared. Will his preparations have secured for him as followers the whole of mankind that today calls itself civilized, or will he find a humanity that can offer resistance?[17]

The way in which humanity looks at the cosmos under the Ahrimanic Deception is not with the spiritual awe and cosmic sense of place of those of past Civilisations, including Western Civilisation until the Reformation, but as merely part of a mechanical and mathematical process, or what I have referred to here (see below) as 'chaining man to matter'. Steiner said of this:

> Today man gazes from his earth up to the star-world and to him it is filled with fixed stars, suns, planets, comets, and so on. But with what means does he examine all that looks down to him out of cosmic space? He examines it with mathematics, with the science of mechanics. What lies around the earth is robbed of spirit, robbed of soul, even of life. It is a great mechanism, in fact, only to be grasped by the aid of mathematical, mechanistic laws. … [18]

Steiner warned that the Ahrimanic Deception aims to imbue Man with the 'scientific superstition', an 'external illusion', that while necessary (it was far from Steiner's intent to repudiate the sciences) has made rationalism and materialism into a dogma, and it this dogma that was fermented and conveyed by

---

17   Steiner, 1919.

18   Steiner, 1919.

secret societies that – ironically – claim to be part of a 'spiritual tradition'. The second method of the Ahrimanic Deception is to split society into contending factions. Steiner aptly identified Marxism as a primary method of the Ahrimanic Deception. Since the times of the Reformation and the Renaissance the economist has emerged as the new priest into the increasingly materialistic world, while Steiner also pointed out that Christian religion had become desacralised:

> Since that time the economist has been in command. Rulers are in fact merely the handymen, the understrappers of the economists. One must not imagine that the rulers of modern times are anything but the understrappers of the economists.[19]

Steiner next alludes to a very important matter; the power that the bankers have assumed:

> In the nineteenth century the 'economical' man is replaced for the first time by the man thinking in terms of banking, and in the nineteenth century there is created for the first time the organization of finance which swamps every other relationship. One must only be able to look into these things and follow them up empirically and practically.[20]

This statement provides the key to the history of the 'modern world' for the past several hundred years, and the human agency pushing for a world state – a 'New World Order' – enchained to the dead weight of matter. The power of the international banking cabals prepares the way for an Ahrimanic World Order by reorienting the spirit of Man. Steiner explains: 'If men do not realize that the organism of the Spirit must be set against the economic order called up through the economists and the banks, then again, through this lack of awareness, Ahriman will find an important instrument for preparing his incarnation'.[21]

---

19   Steiner, 1919.

20   Steiner, 1919.

21   Steiner, 1919.

Role of Secret Societies

The 'Ahrimanic Deception' equates with what Guénon and Evola referred to as the 'Counter-Tradition'. The secret societies it uses are the 'Anti-Tradition'. Steiner lectured on the role of these secret societies in the occult war. While referring to both the 'humanitarian works' and the spiritual evolution that is supposedly at the foundation of Freemasonry,[22] Steiner, like Evola and Guénon, also spoke of the manner by which the 'Ahrimanic Deception' operates through Freemasonry. Steiner even went further than most anti-Masonic 'conspiracy theorists' such as Nesta H Webster[23] and Professor John Robison,[24] since they accepted the English-derived United Grand Lodge Masonry's innocence of intrigue. Steiner, to the contrary, made a point of discussing the origins of Continental Masonry within the English Lodges. Despite its repudiation of 'irregular' Grand Orient Masonry that predominates in Continental Europe and Latin America, United Grand Lodge Masonry, stated Steiner, was also involved in a struggle for world power. He stated that the British Government was subverted by the secret societies, and that in particular foreign affairs was taken over by 'an inner committee'.[25] Steiner, in tracing the origins of Grand Orient Masonry to the United Grand Lodge, wrote that:

> But everywhere in a different way, in many places outside the actual British realm, Freemasonry pursues exclusively or mainly political interests. Such political interests in the most palpable sense are pursued by the 'Grand-Orient de France', but also by other 'Grand Orients'. One might now say: what has that to do with the English? … But view this in conjunction with the fact that the first High-degree Lodge in Paris was founded from England, not France! Not French people but Britons founded it; they only wove the French into their Lodge …[26]

---

22   Steiner, 1904.

23   Webster, 1964, Chapter 6, 128-129.

24   Robison, 'Introduction', 6.

25   Steiner, 1916.

26   Steiner, 1917.

After listing the Lodges that were founded under the auspices of the United Grand Lodge, from Spain to Russia, Steiner states that 'these Lodges were founded as the external instruments for certain occult-political impulses'. These impulses included the 'fury of the Jacobins', Weishaupt's Illuminati and the Italian Carbonari. Although Steiner states that these began without 'evil' intent (which I would dispute), they 'continued their underground work in many different forms', after being driven underground. Steiner alludes to the disingenuousness of United Grand Lodge Masonry in being able to say:

'[L]ook at our Lodges, they are very respectable – and we are not concerned with the others'. But if one can see through the historical connection and the driving forces in an interplay of mutual opposition to one another, then it is indeed high British politics that is concealed behind it.[27]

Of the 'occult-political' societies Steiner observed that they serve a materialistic aim behind the façade of spirituality: what Guénon and Evola called 'Anti-Tradition', and Eliphas Levi (see below) called 'profanity'. These 'various Orders' are 'not spiritual, because of their purposes and goals'. They are the secret societies that work in the name of 'democracy' and a 'universal republic'. Steiner warned:

If one wants as a person of modern times to see clearly in order to meet the world openly and understand it, then one should not let oneself be blinded by democratic logic, which is justified only in its own sphere, or by phrases concerning democratic progress etc. One would have also to point to the interposing of something that reveals itself in the attempt to give rulership to the few through the means available within the Lodges – namely, ritual and its suggestive effect.[28]

---

27   Steiner, 1917.

28   Steiner, 1917.

While genuine mystical lodges exist(ed), and Guénon, Evola and Steiner sought initiation in them, they pointed out that one must be cognisant of those Orders with mystical trappings and claims to ancient pedigree as a mask for other motives, as they are 'often nebulous, maybe even fraudulent'… 'For power is of special importance for these secret societies, not insight'.[29]

Enchaining Man to Matter

The aim of these 'Black Adepts' of what Crowley called the 'Black School of Magick' and what Guénon called the Counter-Tradition, is to enchain humanity to the dead weight of matter; hence the use of materialistic ideologies, epitomised by the dialectical materialism of Karl Marx. Such theories postulate that man is nothing other than 'matter in motion' and that history is nothing more than a struggle for material interests. Hence, the 'Black School of Magick' by such means seeks to detach humanity from its nexus with the Divine. Such a nexus is the foundation of all Traditional societies, where each individual 'knows his place' in the cosmic order. Marxism, with its doctrine of 'class struggle' where the cosmic hierarchy reflected on earth as 'castes' is turned upside down, is a method by which the 'Black Adepts' wreck the cosmically based foundations of a traditional culture, upon which can be erected their own edifice of material enslavement.[30]

Students of the Western Mystery Tradition will readily see what this aim is by its representation as 'The Devil' trump of the Major Arcana of the Tarot. Paul Foster Case provides a meaning of 'The Devil' that is particularly relevant:

> In its most general meanings, it signifies Mammon and thus big business, the conventions of society, the injustice and cruelty of a social order in which money takes the place of God, in which humanity is bestialised, in which

---

29   Steiner, 1920.

30   Evola, *Revolt Against the Modern World*.

war is engineered by greed masquerading as patriotism, in which fear is dominant. Students of astrology will have no difficulty in seeing how this corresponds to Capricorn, the sign of big business, and the sign of world fame.[31]

Case, founder of the occult order, The Builders of the Adytum, in this description of 'The Devil' cogently describes all the key aspects of the Counter-Tradition. The key point is the 'bestialisation' of humanity, represented by a male and female, which, reduced to an animal state by being robbed of its spirituality, is chained to a solid block mass, while the Devil is enthroned. Like the Devil, the human pair is depicted with tail and horns. One does not have to be an adherent of the esoteric to appreciate the significance of this symbolism and the manner by which humanity is being reduced to a bestial state, in the name of 'progress' and science. This goal of bounding humanity to the tyranny of matter – and one does not have to be a Christian or Muslim to call it 'satanic'– is the reason why ostensibly mystical and esoteric bodies have promoted rationalistic and materialistic doctrines.

31   Case, *Oracle of The Tarot: A Course on Tarot Divination*.

Are There 'Conspiracies'?

Much of what has been considered so far already sounds like 'conspiracy theory'. The allegation that someone is a 'conspiracy theorist' is supposed to shut down a discussion immediately, having a similar effect as alleging that someone is a 'nazi', an 'anti-Semite', 'holocaust denier', 'racist', and so forth. The instant ridicule of 'conspiracy theories' especially from academia is fairly predicable given that 'scholars' tend to be narrowly focused and quite incapable of synthesising knowledge from a variety of disciplines. There is also the pull of conformity and respectability within academia. There are noteworthy exceptions such as Dr Richard Spence, Chair of the History Department of the University of Idaho, who teachers an honours programme on the role of secret societies in history; and Dr Mark Mirabello, Professor of History at Shawnee State University, who teaches on many subjects relevant to this book, including: legend, myth and folklore; intellectual history; gnosticism; alternative religions and cults, revolutionary Europe, etc.

The law courts hear evidence for criminal conspiracies every day. There are financial conspiracies, such as 'insider trading'. The Mafia is generally accepted as a centuries old international criminal conspiracy whose tentacles starting from families in the hills of medieval Sicily, have come to encompass many states, to have influenced politicians, and to have had the rich and powerful in their entourage or on their payroll. The same can be said of the Chinese Triads, which have been a major political influence. There have been conspiracies that have been both religious and criminal in nature, such as the Thuggee in India. The Ku Klux Klan is a secret society that achieved immense political influence during the 1920s. Yet if someone suggests that there might be political conspiracies involving Freemasonry, occult societies or banking dynasties, this is laughed out of court by orthodox academia. There is nothing particularly extraordinary about the existence of conspiracies. A conspiracy is defined by the Oxford English Dictionary as:

> a secret plan by a group to do something unlawful or harmful: *a conspiracy to destroy the government.*

A 'criminal conspiracy' is defined in US law as 'conspiracies against the public, or such as endanger the public health, violate public morals, insult public justice, destroy the public peace, or affect public trade or business.[1]

That such conspiracies exist is obvious enough, but we are expected to disregard any such notion when it comes to secret societies, bankers, political lobbies, etc. Comparatively recently, the widespread conspiracy of Lodge P2, deriving from the Italian Grand Orient, exposed a colossal conspiracy that reached into the highest levels of Government and the Vatican. Presumably we are expected to regard this as an anomaly.

Was Dwight Eisenhower a crank 'conspiracy theorist' when in his 1961 Farwell presidential address to the American people, he warned of a 'military-industrial complex' of wide-ranging implications, reaching throughout US society:

> Until the latest of our world conflicts, the United States had no armaments industry. American makers of plowshares could, with time and as required, make swords as well. But now we can no longer risk emergency improvisation of national defense; we have been compelled to create a permanent armaments industry of vast proportions. Added to this, three and a half million men and women are directly engaged in the defense establishment. We annually spend on military security more than the net income of all United States corporations.

1   Free Legal Dictionary.

This conjunction of an immense military establishment and a large arms industry is new in the American experience. The total influence – *economic, political, even spiritual* – is felt in every city, every State house, every office of the Federal government. We recognize the imperative need for this development. Yet we must not fail to comprehend its grave implications. Our toil, resources and livelihood are all involved; so is the very structure of our society.

In the councils of government, we must guard against the acquisition of unwarranted influence, whether sought or unsought, by the military industrial complex. The potential for the disastrous rise of misplaced power exists and will persist.

We must never let the weight of this combination endanger our liberties or democratic processes. We should take nothing for granted. Only an alert and knowledgeable citizenry can compel the proper meshing of the huge industrial and military machinery of defense with our peaceful methods and goals, so that security and liberty may prosper together.[2]

While I have written extensively of this 'military-industrial complex' elsewhere[3] we are here dealing specifically with occult societies, but the principle remains. Eisenhower's warnings on hidden and pervasive agendas are as applicable to secret societies as they are to the often hidden agendas of transnational corporations. Dr Mirabello, an academic of rare independence of mind, has stated of such secret societies, in a manner that is directly in accord with the purpose of this book:

'Secret Societies' are conspiracies working covertly to achieve a hidden agenda. For members, secrecy is a sanctuary and a source of power. Secret societies often

2   Eisenhower, 1961.

3   Bolton, *Revolution from Above.*

claim to be ancient and they claim direct 'initiatory descent from a fabled founder or group of founders. By definition, no secret society can appear to be a novelty.

Secret societies have various functions, usually esoteric, political, or charitable in nature. Secret societies may plot world domination, subvert legal or financial institutions, enlighten the world, distribute charity, protect a secret, or 'attempt to rewrite history by circulating certain literature'.[4]

Mirabello defines six types of secret society:

1. In the first type, the existence of the group is known and the membership is public knowledge, but the rituals and the meetings are secret. This describes the Freemasons.

2. In the second type, the membership and the objectives are public knowledge, but all meetings are private. This describes the Bilderberg Group.

3. In the third type, the existence of the group is known, but the membership and the objectives of the organization are secret. This describes the Hellfire Club.

4. In the fourth type, the existence of the group is rumored, but few, if any, concrete facts are known about the group. This describes the Illuminati.

5. In the fifth type, the existence of the group is rumored, the identities of the members are secret, but the rituals and the objectives are known. This describes the Odin Brotherhood.

6. In the sixth type, the existence of the group is denied, but the identities of the members and the objectives of the group are known. This describes the Mafia.[5]

---

4   Mirabello, p. 1.

5   Mirabello, pp. 2-3.

Mirabello lists secret societies of various types, including the Order of the Assassins, Black Hand, Broederbond, Illuminati, Knights of the Apocalypse, Ku Klux Klan, Leopard Society, Luddites, Mafia, Odin Brotherhood, Order of the Skull & Bones/Lodge 322, and the Cult of Thuggee.[6]

Conspiracy Theories and Epochal Events

There has been a significant rise in interest in 'conspiracy theories' during times of epochal turmoil. Sceptics respond that 'conspiracy theories' are simplistic answers to complex questions. These turning points in history, marked by social, political and religious uncertainties have included:

- The French Revolution,
- The 1905 Russian Revolution,
- The 1917 Russian Revolutions and World War I.
- September 11.

A prolific genre of literature on Bolshevism, Jews, and Masons arose in the wake of the Bolshevik Revolution, particularly from the Right and from Catholic clerics looking for a directing hand behind the death of the traditional order. With World War II, while this literature continued in the Axis states and in neutral states such as Spain and Portugal, it was suppressed as being of fascist inclination among the Allied states. The aftermath of World War II tended to discourage a revival of such literature, because it has been associated with the 'extreme right-wing', anti-Semitism and Nazism.

The current revival of occult conspiracy literature has been prompted by the uncertainties of the post-Cold War era and the collapse of the Soviet bloc, bringing increased instability and insecurity rather than the elusive hope of universal peace and brotherhood, that was supposed to be the harbinger of a

---

6   Mirabello, pp. 5-13.

'new world order'. The wars against Iraq and the 'global war on terrorism' have also contributed to a revival in conspiracy theories, in part because of the Bush family's long association with Lodge 322.

The Beginnings of Conspiratorial Theory

The French Revolution

The allegation of an occult conspiracy to establish a Universal Republic on the ruins of altars and thrones arose during the tumult of the French Revolution. The Grand Orient de France, with Grand Orient branches spreading throughout Europe, and distinct from the English form, had an anti-clerical and radical political orientation, bringing Masonry into conflict with the Catholic Church. Catholic responses to Freemasonry have included many books by Cardinals and laymen alike.

The French cleric, the Abbé Augustin Barruel was among the first writers to ascribe occult influences to the French Revolution, and his views have remained seminal. In 1797 he wrote the five volume Memoire pur servir a l'histoire du jacobinisme ('*Memoirs Illustrating the History of Jacobinism*'), tracing the origins of revolution and subversion to the Knights Templar. This Templar theme has continued to the present with such popular books as *The Temple & the Lodge*. Barruel wrote:

> At an early period of the French revolution, there appeared a Sect calling itself Jacobin, and teaching that all men were equal and free! In the name of their Equality and disorganising Liberty, they trampled under foot the altar and the throne, they stimulate all nations to rebellion aimed at plunging them ultimately into the horrors of anarchy [sic]…. It was under the auspices of this Sect, and by their intrigues, influence, and impulse that France beheld itself a prey to every crime; that its foil was tainted with the blood of its pontiffs and priests, of its rich men and nobles, with the blood of every class of citizens, without regard to ranks, age or sex![1]

---

1   Barruel, Vol. 1, i.

The Beginnings of Conspiratorial Theory

Jesuit Augustin Barruel wrote of the role that Freemasonry played in the French Revolution of 1789.

Barruel warned that this conspiratorial sect had spread throughout Europe and that it was essential that its nature be known before the thrones and altars of all Europe were brought down in blood. This bloodlust upon Tradition had been represented by the intelligentsia under Voltaire, Diderot, et al. Its doctrinal achievement was the Encyclopedie, described by Barruel as 'a vast emporium of all the sophisms, errors or calumnies, which have ever been invented against religion… artfully concealed' so that the reader would imbibe the sciences without suspecting that the purpose was one of subversion and destruction.[2] Behind Voltaire, Diderot et al, according to Barruel, stood Freemasonry and behind that the Illuminati. It is notable however that Barruel emphasised that these 'occult Masons', as he calls them, are not to be identified with the bulk of the 'brethren' who are 'too virtuous' to be initiated into 'the occult mysteries';[3] specifically the 'English Lodges'.[4]

2   Barruel, Vol. 1 p. 75.

3   Barruel, Vol. 2, i.

4   Barruel, Vol. 2, p. 148. My own experiences with United Grand Lodge Masons in New

It is Barruel who seems first to have traced an inspiration for the French Revolution to the Knights Templar, alluding to Louis XVI being taken in 1792 to 'the Tower of the Temple', 'so named because it formerly belonged to the Knights Templar.[5] Barruel then gives his personal testimony as having heard and witnessed the declaration of the revolutionaries that 'France is no other than an immense Lodge. The whole French people are freemason, and the whole universe will soon follow their example'.[6]

> I witnessed this enthusiasm; I heard the conversations to which it gives life. A few Masons, till then the most reserved, who freely and openly declared, 'Yes, at "length the grand object of Free-masonry is accomplished, Equality and Liberty; all men are equal and brothers; all men are free'. That was the whole 'substance of our doctrine, the object of our wishes, the whole of our grand secret'. Such was the language I heard fall from the most zealous Masons, from those whom I have seen decorated with all the insignia of the deepest Masonry, and who enjoyed the rights of Venerable to preside over Lodges. I have heard them express themselves in this manner before those whom Masons would call the prophane, without requiring the smallest secrecy either from the men or women present. They said it in a tone as if they wished all France should be acquainted with this glorious achievement of Masonry; as if it were to recognize in them its benefactors and the authors of that Revolution of Liberty and Equality of which it had given so grand an example to all Europe.[7]

Zealand, in regard to academic corruption at Waikato University by one of their number, and to a corrupt Kapiti Coast councillor and lawyer, who is a local eminence in Masonry, are that UGL Masonry is morally bankrupt, and cares nothing for its lauded 'virtues'. UGL in Britian was exposed as a corrupt network in local councils, police and elsewhere, amidst well-publicised scandals during the 1970s. See: Stephen Knight, *The Brotherhood*.

5   Barruel, Vol. 2., p. 148.

6   Barruel, Vol. 2, p. 149.

7   Barruel, vol. 2, p. 150.

Barruel, again alluding to what he witnessed in the French lodges, states of the degree of the Rose Cross or Rosicrucian that this is accompanied by an explanation to the initiate of the Templar connection and the birth of the revolutionary character of Masonry as a means of avenging the death of the last Templar Grand Master Jacques de Molay, for which the Papacy and the French Monarchy were responsible:

> Many circumstances relating to this degree made us believe at first sight that it was connected with Illuminism; but on examination we find it to be only a farther explanation of the Masonic allegory. Here again the candidate is transformed into an assassin. Here it is no longer the founder of Masonry, Hiram, who is to be avenged, but it is Molay the Grand Master of the Knights Templars, and the person who is to fall by the assassin's hand is Philippe le Bel, King of France, under whose reign the order of the Templars was destroyed.[8]

It is notable that, many years later, Albert Pike, in codifying the system known as the Scottish Rite, described the 18° of the Rose Cross precisely as Barruel claimed, yet the exiled cleric is still the subject of ridicule and slander and is called a liar. Barruel maintained the attitude that is the premise of this book, that it is not necessary for a myth to be empirically 'true'; the significance is how it is acted on:

> Nor is it necessary in this place to examine whether Molay and his order were innocent or criminal,[9] whether they were the real progenitors of the Free-masons or not; what is incontestable is sufficient; it is enough that the Masons recognize them for their ancestors; then the oath of avenging them and every allegory recalling that oath decidedly points out an association, continually threatening and conspiring against Religion and its Pontiffs, against Empires and their Governors.[10]

---

8   Barruel, Vol. 2, p. 175.

9   That is, innocent or criminal of the Church's charge of heresy.

10   Barruel, vol. 2, p. 203.

As will be shown, Freemasonry claims Templar descent, and incorporates supposedly Templar degrees into its initiatory system. Barruel began to trace associations and activities of the Order of the Illuminati which he characterised as 'Anarchy against every religion natural or revealed; not only against kings, but against every government, against all civil society, even against all property whatsoever'. In this description we might recognise Communism as promulgated by Karl Marx the following century. He also draws a connection with the Rosicrucians appearing in Germany the previous century, which called themselves Illuminees. Again, however, although present-day smug 'scholars' disparage Barruel and others such as his Scottish counterpart, Professor John Robison, Masonry itself calls its 18° 'Rosicrucian'.

The aims of the Illuminati were known because of the documents that had been found by authorities in the residence of members. Barruel states of these documents:

> The first is a collection entitled *Some of the Original Writings of the Sect of Illuminees*, which 'were discovered on the 9th and 12th of October, '1786, at Landshut, on a search made in the House of 'the Sieur Zwack, heretofore Counsellor of the Regency; and printed by Order of His Highness the Elector. Munich, by Ant. Franz, Printer to the Court'.

> The second is a supplement to the Original Writings, chiefly containing those which were found on a search made at the castle of Sandersdorf, a famous haunt of the Illuminees, by order of His Highness the Elector. Munich, 1787.[11]

Professor John Robison drew on much the same material as Barruel in writing *Proofs of a Conspiracy*. This work has remained in print, having been republished by the publishing arm of The John Birch Society, Western Islands, in 1967. The books by

---

11   Barruel, Vol. 3, vi.

Barruel and Robison have been seminal in writings critical of Masonry and discussing the Illuminati. Both have therefore drawn the brunt of sneers and condemnation from sceptics, whose critiques are more notable for their vitriol than as sober assessments of the evidence Barruel and Robison marshalled. What is more, their basic premises are supported by the 19th century occultist, Eliphas Levi, who had been both a prominent Left-wing propagandist and who seems to have been initiated into the 18° of Freemasonry, that of the Rose Cross, which, based on the description of the Degree by Scottish Rite Masonic authority General Pike, is the Degree in which the Masonic initiate does indeed, learn for the first time that Masonry is both of a revolutionary nature and is descended from the Templars.

1905 Russian Revolution & the Appearance
of the *Protocols of the Learned Elders of Zion*

The Russian Revolution of 1905 gave renewed impetus to theories of an occult conspiracy that had been postulated by Robison and Barruel. It is around this time that the widely termed 'infamous' *Protocols of the Learned Elders of Zion* make their appearance, first given public circulation by Sergei Nilus as part of his book *The Great in the Small*.[12] Although *The Protocols* have generally been regarded as a primary cause of anti-Semitism, having been taken up with enthusiasm by the Nazis after their introduction to Germany by Russian émigrés following the 1917 Revolution; their theme is not primarily Jewish, but is Masonic. Least of all does the document describe any Zionist programme, although Nilus came to believe *The Protocols* came from the First Zionist Congress of 1887.[13] Neither of its doctrines are an expression of Orthodox Judaism, but are universalistic and seem more akin to the doctrines that emerged during the Enlightenment, and during the revolutionary ferment throughout Europe in the mid 19th century when there were 'large numbers' of Jews entering 'the secret societies which were the fighting force of the Revolution;

12   Cohn, p. 74.
13   Cohn, p. 74.

[who] made their way into the Masonic lodges, into the societies of the Carbonari, [where] they were found everywhere in France, in Germany, in England, in Austria, in Italy'.[14] Among these Masonic Jews was Adolphe Cremieux, founder of the Alliance Israelite Universelles, who became head of the Grand Orient de France, Mizraim-Memphis, and Scottish Rite Masonry, and whom Lazare states was among those Jews who were 'the most ardent adherents of the liberal, social, and revolutionary parties.'[15]

The Protocols is a document dismissed out of hand by most academics, especially in the Western world, as a 'forgery' of the Okhrana, the Czarist secret police, working in France. The aim was supposedly to undermine the influence of the revolutionary movements by exploiting traditional Russian anti-Semitism among the masses, claiming that revolution was a Jewish plot. Another aim is said to have been as a reactionary means of discrediting modernist influences on the Czar, by stating that they were also part of a Jewish plot.[16]

The repudiation of *The Protocols* centres on the allegation that Czarist agents plagiarised most of the text from a political satire, Dialogues in Hell, written by Maurice Joly against Emperor Napoleon III,[17] for which Joly was arrested. The Joly association however raises further questions. Joly was a leading French radical propagandist. He was a protégé of Adolphe Cremieux, who was a prominent critic of Napoleon III, and served as Minister of Justice in the Second Republic. It seems reasonable to ask, then, whether Joly's polemic against Napoleon III, from which *The Protocols* were supposedly plagiarised, was drawn from Masonic sources directed by his mentor Cremieux, or at least followed a general line of thinking from those quarters? Having failed to secure a position in the regime of Napoleon III, Cremieux became a Minister in the Gambetta Government.[18]

---

14   Lazare, p. 155.

15   Lazare, p. 174.

16   Cohn, pp. 113-114.

17   Cohn, p. 80.

18   Miller, pp. 411-420

Despite the importance attached to the alleged plagiarism of *The Protocols* from Joly, academic debunkers such as Cohn fail to mention the association between Joly and Cremieux, and the latter does not merit a single mention in Cohn's book.[19]

The Protocols are signed by 'the representatives of Zion, of the 33°'.[20] The 33° refers specifically to the Scottish Rite rather than to any known – or alleged – specifically Jewish organisation, and happens not only to have been headed by Cremieux, but also to be revolutionist in doctrine. Coincidence?

The Mizraim Rite was founded by the well-known 18th century charlatan, healer, alchemist, libertine, and occultist Cagliostro (Guiseppe Balsam), as the supposedly genuine form of Masonry derived from Egypt. Cagliostro ingratiated himself with High Society throughout Europe and especially at the Royal Court of France. Cagliostro had been initiated into the Strict Observance of Baron von Hund, serving as an emissary of the Order throughout Europe. In 1780 he was initiated into the Illuminati at Frankfurt, having been sponsored by two prominent adepts of the Strict Observance. Taken for the initiation into an underground chamber at a house three miles from Frankfurt, Cagliostro swore his oath of destruction against the Church and monarchy, signing a document that he claimed also bore the signatures of the grand masters of the Knights Templar.[21] Disgraced in Europe for his roguery, Cagliostro found a warm reception among the English Masons, including George, Prince of Wales; Edward, Duke of Kent, and William, Duke of Clarence, who found Masonry to be a useful vehicle for opposing their father, King George III.[22] Cagliostro had been recommended by the Duc d'Orleans, Grand Master of the Grand Orient de France, who was to play a major role in the preparation and funding of the French Revolution. Cagliostro had initiated d'Orleans and his mistress into the

19   Cohn, pp. 66-83.
20   *The Protocols*, p. 89.
21   McCalman, pp. 103-104.
22   McCalman, p. 144.

Egyptian Rite shortly before.[23] It becomes evident that English Freemasonry was very much involved in political and occultist intrigues, despite the claims of innocence for English Masonry even by Robison and Barruel. Occultism had from the 1770s made inroads into English Masonry, introduced by occultic charlatans from the Continent.[24]

In 1786 Cagliostro wrote a propaganda tract directed at the French Throne, Count Cagliostro's Letter to the French People, which was widely circulated in France and England. Here Cagliostro predicted that a revolution would topple the Throne: 'It is a fitting purpose for your parliament to work [for] the necessity of revolution... this revolution, so much needed, will be brought about, I prophesy it for you'.[25] He referred to a 'prince' who would assume power and restore the 'true religion'. This prince was his Masonic brother, Duc d'Orleans, who did indeed provide crucial backing for the revolution, albeit, one that did not see him assume the power for which he had plotted. With death, Cagliostro assured his adepts that this would elevate him to 'the highest grades of Egyptian Masonry to become one of twelve immortals ruling over mankind's destiny for the rest of time'.[26] This means that Cagliostro believed he would become what in occult societies to the present time, became a predominate belief that the world is governed by 'Hidden Masters'. It is supposed communication with these 'Hidden Masters' that is used by occultists to legitimise their authority or to found new esoteric Orders.

Originally, the origins of *The Protocols* were ascribed not to the World Zionist Congress, or to a secret conclave of Rabbis, but to having been taken from a lodge of Mizraim in France.[27]

---

23   McCalman, p. 145.

24   McCalman, pp. 145-146.

25   McCalman, p. 153.

26   McCalman, p. 233.

27   Miller, *Lady Queenborough,* p. 408.

While the claim was made in 1921 in the *London Times,* by an anonymous source, who 'conclusively proved *The Protocols* to be a forgery'[28] that he had found the origins of *The Protocols* to be the Joly book, nothing is said by Cohn, et al in regard to Joly having been a protégé of Cremieux. Is it not at least as likely that Joly was drawing from the same sources as those from which *The Protocols* emerged? If that is so, then there would of course be parallels between Joly's Dialogues in Hell and The Protocols. However, there are also salient parallels between passages in *The Protocols* and the stated aims of the Illuminati:

[THE END JUSTIFIES THE MEANS]: The result justifies the means, Let us, however, in our plans, direct our attention not so much to what is good and moral as to what is necessary and useful. Protocol # I.

We must first gradually explain away all our preparatory pious frauds. And when persons of discernment find fault, we must desire them to consider the end of all our labour. This sanctifies our mean. Spartacus.[29]

[INFORMERS]: In our programme one-third of our subjects will keep the rest under observation from a sense of duty… It will then be no disgrace to be a spy and informer, but a merit. Protocol # XVII.

And in particular, every person shall be made a spy on another and on all around him. Nothing can escape our sight. Spartacus to Cato, 6 Feb. 1778.

[THE PRESS]: Not a single announcement will reach the public without our control. Even now this is already being attained by us inasmuch as all news items are received by a few news agencies, in whose offices they

---

28   Cohn, p. 78.

29   Illuminatists adopted pseudonyms: Spartacus was Weishaupt; Cato was Zwack, professor of law; Philo was Baron Knigge.

are focussed from all parts of the world. These agencies will then be already entirely ours and will give publicity only to what we dictate to them. ... We shall have a sure triumph over our opponents since they will not have at their disposition organs of the press in which they can give full and final expression of their views.... Not a single announcement will reach the public without our control. Protocol # XII.

In like manner we must try to obtain an influence in ... the printing houses, booksellers shops, chapters, and in short in all the offices which have any effect, either in forming or managing, or even in directing the mind of man: painting and engraving are highly worth our care. If a writer publishes anything that attracts notice, and is in itself just, but does not accord with our plan, we must endeavour to win him over, or decry him. Instructions for the Degree of Regent.

[SECRET SOCIETIES, MASONRY]: Who and what is in a position to overthrow an invisible force? And this is precisely what our force is. Gentile masonry blindly serves as a screen for us and our objects, but the plan of action of our force, even its very abiding-place, remains for the whole people an unknown mystery. Protocol # IV.

The great strength of our Order lies in its concealment, let it never appear in any place in its own name, but always covered by another name, and another occupation. None is fitter than the three lower degrees of Free Masonry; the public is accustomed to it, expects little from it, and therefore takes little notice of it. Instructions for the Degree of Regent.

[RELIGION, ARISTORCACY]: We have long past taken care to discredit the priesthood of the goyim and thereby to ruin their mission on earth, which in these days might still be a great hindrance to us. Day by day its influence on the peoples of the world is falling lower. Freedom of conscience has been declared everywhere, so that now only years divide us from the moment of the complete wrecking of that Christian religion.... We shall set clericalism and clericals into such narrow frames as to make their influence move in retrogressive proportion to its former progress. In all corners of the earth the words 'Liberty, Equality, Fraternity' brought to our ranks, thanks to our blind agents, whole legions who bore our banners with enthusiasm. As you will see later, this helped us to our triumph: it enables us to grasp, among other things, the master card – the destruction of... the very existence of the aristocracy of the goyim, that class which as the only defence peoples and countries had against us. Protocol # I.

But in the meantime while we are re-educating youth in new traditional religions and afterwards ours, we shall not overtly lay a finger on existing churches, but we shall fight against them by criticism calculated to produce schism. Protocol # XVII.

We must consider the ruling propensities of every age of the world. At present the cheats and tricks of the priests have aroused all men against them, and against Christianity. But at the same time superstition and fanaticism rule with unlimited dominion, and the understanding of man really seems to be going backwards. Our task therefore is doubled. We must give such an account of things, that fanatics shall not be alarmed, and that shall, not withstanding, excite a spirit of free enquiry. We must not throw away the good with the bad, the child with the dirty water; but we must make the secret doctrines of Christianity be received as the secrets of genuine freemasonry. But further we have to deal with the despotism of the Princes. This increases every day. But the spirit of freedom breathes and sighs in every corner; and, by the assistance of hidden schools of wisdom, Liberty and Equality, the natural and imprescriptible rights of man, warm and glow in every breath. We must therefore unite these extremes we must proceed in this manner. Philo to Cato.

[JESUITS]: In this respect the Jesuits alone might have compared with us, but we have contrived to discredit them in the eyes of the unthinking mob as an overt organisation, while we ourselves have kept our secret organisation in the shade. Protocol # V.

By the activity of our brethren, the Jesuits have been kept out of all the professional chairs at Ingolstadt, and our friends prevail. We have been very successful against the Jesuits and brought things to such a bearing that their revenues are now under the management of our friends…. Cato.

The purpose here however is not to argue for the authenticity of *The Protocols*. Whatever the origins of *The Protocols*, the document served as a further impetus to conspiratorial theories involving Freemasonry, while they also continue to serve to divert and undermine any examination of esoteric and Masonic programmes as being anti-Semitic and based on a forgery.

From a Traditionalist perspective, Evola wrote that *The Protocols* could have been the work of someone who had contact with the secret societies (which, in regard to Joly, was indeed the case), but in any event should not be dismissed as 'a vulgar mystification, forgery and work of plagiarism'.[30] Evola rejected *The Protocols* as being the blueprint of a 'Masonic-Jewish plot', however.[31]

---

30   Evola, *Men Among the Ruins*, p. 239.

31   Evola, *Men Among the Ruins*, p. 242.

1917 Russian Revolutions
Nesta Webster

In the wake of the 1917 Bolshevik Revolution, like the French Revolution and the 1905 Russian Revolution, there was an upsurge in conspiratorial literature, tracing connections between the Russian revolutionary movements and Masonry.

The most prominent of this literature in the English speaking world was by Nesta H Webster. Mrs Webster's books gained influence during the 1920s. She was invited to lecture on subversive movements to several branches of the British military and to repeat her lecture to the officers of the Secret Service. At their request she wrote *World Revolution – The Plot Against Civilisation*. Winston Churchill cited her in his article on the rivalry for Jewish loyalty between Zionism and Bolshevism.[32] Lord Kitchener described her as 'the foremost opponent of subversion'.[33] In *World Revolution* Webster traces the origins of Communism from the Illuminati, through the French Revolution and the revolutions of 1848. An update based on her notes brings the reader to the 1970s in the final two chapters written by Anthony Gittens of the Britons Publishing Society.

However, it is in *Secret Societies & Subversive Movements* that Mrs Webster not only traces an ongoing occult agenda to the Templars, but to the Assassins and to more obscure Gnostic sects and heresies within both Christianity and Islam. The Knights Templar served as the nexus between these currents fermenting in the Middle East and their introduction to Europe. Webster also extensively cited *The Protocols* leaving her open to the predictable allegations of 'anti-Semitism'. Although little recognised today, Jewish involvement in revolutionary movements was widely commented on in diplomatic, intelligence, military and ruling class circles, in the aftermath of the Bolshevik Revolution, as indicated by the article by Winston Churchill.[34] Webster's opinion

---

32   Churchill, 1920.

33   Webster, *World Revolution*, 'Introduction'

34   Winston Churchill, *'Zionism vs. Bolshevism'*, 1920.

of *The Protocols* was one with which this writer concurs; that the document represents one element in a line of revolutionary programmes paralleling the doctrines of the Illuminati.[35]

Other widely read books from the time of the Bolshevik Revolution until the outbreak of World War II, associate Bolshevism with occult and Masonic societies. *Trail of the Serpent* by 'Miss Stoddard' became a classic of the type, circa 1935. Miss Stoddard had previously written *Light Bearers of Darkness*, detailing her experiences in the occult, where she had been 'Ruling chief of the "Mother Temple" of the occult body Stella Matutina'. Like Webster, Stoddard traces a conspiratorial line of descent from the ancient Mystery Schools through the Gnostic sects, to the Rosicrucians and the Illuminati, the French Revolution, the revolutionary movements in Europe during the 1840s such as the Carbonari in Italy, Grand Orient Masonry, Theosophy, and secret societies in the USA and Asia. Warren Weston's Father of Lies had as its theme the destruction of Christianity by occult societies and the substitution of the worship of man for the worship of God. Lady Queenborough's *Occult Theocracy* is a single volume encyclopaedia of occult and subversive movements.

---

35   Wesbter, *World Revolution*, pp. 288-295

Christian Responses to Masonry

Catholic

We have seen something of the conflict between Traditionalists in opposing what Guénon described as Anti-Tradition and Counter-Tradition and what Crowley called the Black School of Magick. The Catholic Church has been the other primary institution that has been involved in this spiritual conflict and is therefore another significant source.

The Catholic Encyclopedia, and Catholic sources in general, are of a higher scholarly standard than the anti-occult literature of Fundamentalist pastors. The Church has a long history of dealing with Freemasonry and its many derivatives, which often regard themselves as sworn to avenge the deaths of their supposed Templar forefathers, with the toppling of the Papacy being a primary aim. As we have seen, the Catholic cleric, the Abbé Barruel, a refugee from the French Revolutionary terror, is the father of this genre of literature. *The Catholic Encyclopedia* is therefore a good source in tracing the associations between Masonry, claimed Templar survivals or revivals, and the emergence of the Rosicrucians. From this milieu Masonry assumed revolutionary forms:

> The revolutionary spirit manifested itself early in French Masonry. Already in 1746 in the book *Les Francs-Maçons écrasés*, an experienced ex-Mason, who, when a Mason, had visited many lodges in France and England, and consulted high Masons in official position, described as the true Masonic programme a programme which, according to Boos, the historian of Freemasonry, in an astonishing degree coincides with the programme of the great French

Revolution of 1789. In 1776 this revolutionary spirit was brought into Germany by Weishaupt through a conspiratory system, which soon spread throughout the country. Charles Augustus of Saxe-Weimar, Duke Ernest of Gotha, Duke Ferdinand of Brunswick, Goethe, Herder, Pestalozzi, etc., are mentioned as members of this order of the Illuminati. Very few of the members, however, were initiated into the higher degrees. The French Illuminati included Condorcet, the Duke of Orleans, Mirabeau, and Sieyè.[1]

While revolutionary and anti-clerical doctrines were – and still are – particularly manifested in the Grand Orient, *The Catholic Encyclopedia* considers the origins of another revolutionary form of Masonry, the Scottish Rite:

> The principal system in the United States (Charleston, South Carolina) is the so-called Ancient and Accepted Scottish Rite, organized in 1801 on the basis of the French Scottish Rite of Perfection, which was established by the Council of the Emperors of the East and West (Paris, 1758). This system, which was propagated throughout the world, may be considered as the revolutionary type of the French Templar Masonry, fighting for the natural rights of man against religious and political despotisms, symbolized by the papal tiara and a royal crown.[2]

Although the predominant Anglophone form of Masonry, the United Grand Lodge, attempts to understate the influence of the Scottish Rite, this form of Masonry assumed worldwide ramifications in alliance with the Grand Orient. *The Catholic Encyclopedia* states of this:

> It strives to exert a preponderant influence on the other Masonic bodies, wherever it is established. This influence is insured to it in the Grand Orient systems of Latin

---

1   *Catholic Encyclopedia*, 1910.

2   *Catholic Encyclopedia*, 1910.

countries; it is felt even in Britain and Canada, where the supreme chiefs of craft Masonry are also, as a rule, prominent members of the Supreme Councils of the Scottish Rite. There are at the present time (1908) twenty-six universally recognized Supreme Councils of the Ancient and Accepted Scottish Rite.[3]

After considering Masonry's role as a philanthropic association, the *Catholic Encyclopedia* states that there was a progression to revolutionary agitation:

> Even with regard to the most recent Turkish Revolution, it seems certain that the Young Turkish party, which made and directed the Revolution, was guided by Masons, and that Masonry, especially the Grand Orients of Italy and France, had a preponderant role in this Revolution.[4]

The assumption that the revolution in Turkey was under Masonic direction proves to be correct. Masonic historian Celil Layiktez traced the development of the Masonic revolutions in Turkey, stating that the revolutionary Union and Progress Party was 'a Masonic political party':

> After the model of Young Italians, Young Germans, Young Swiss, the Young Turks organized in Paris with the aim of bringing back the constitutional monarchy. But the Young Turks talked a lot but did not act. Freemasons, military students in the faculty of medicine started a revolutionary party, which later took the name of Union and Progress. Their model was the Italian paramasonic revolutionary society, the 'Carbonaries'.[5]

Because foreign nationals were immune from police interference, the Turkish revolutionaries held their meetings in the Masonic

3   *Catholic Encyclopedia*, 1910.

4   *Catholic Encyclopedia*, 1910.

5   Layiktez, 2001.

lodges of foreigners in Thessalonica. Layiktez states that Sultan Abdulhamit felt he could not take action because 'Most of the European powers were governed by freemason kings and ministers'. The threat of an invasion of Istanbul by the revolutionary army officers obliged the Sultan to declare a constitutional monarchy but in March 1909 fundamentalists staged a revolt:

> The freemasons in the Thrace, mainly from Thessalonica, organised an army of reservists. Almost all officers were Freemasons. There were too many officers; some joined the expeditionary force as ordinary soldiers. The army took back Istanbul from the fundamentalists, there were bloody battles and hangings, and Abdulhamit was dethroned by a committee of 5 deputies, all of them Freemasons.[6]

According to the French historian Thierry Zarcone, the period from 1908 to 1918 could be called 'The Masonic State'. The Union and Progress Party in power used Freemasonry in its foreign relations.

Are we then to dismiss such historical revelations from well-placed Masonic sources as conspiratorial delusions, 'Papist propaganda', the legacy of the 'liar' and 'fabricator', the Abbé Barruel? The Catholic researchers were correct in at least this example of Turkey. We see here also that this Masonic secularist revolution was aimed at a Muslim state. It is an example of Anti-Tradition in operation, aiming to subvert and destroy all Traditional societies, whether Christian, Muslim, Hindu, Buddhist or Shinto, etc., to erect a world state in the name of 'Liberty, Equality, Fraternity', as happened in France and Russia. Returning to *The Catholic Encyclopedia*:

> In conducting this work Freemasonry propagates principles which, logically developed, as shown above, are essentially revolutionary and serve as a basis for all kinds of revolutionary movements. Directing Masons to find out for themselves

6   Layiktez, 2001.

practical reforms in conformity with Masonic ideals and to work for their realization, it fosters in its members and through them in society at large the spirit of innovation. As an apparently harmless and even beneficent association, which in reality is, through its secrecy and ambiguous symbolism, subject to the most different influences, it furnishes in critical times a shelter for conspiracy, and, even when its lodges themselves are not transformed into conspiracy clubs, Masons are trained and encouraged to found new associations for such purposes or to make use of existing associations. Thus, Freemasonry in the eighteenth century, as a powerful ally of infidelity, prepared the French Revolution.

The alliance of Freemasonry with philosophy was publicly sealed by the solemn initiation of Voltaire, the chief of these philosophers, 7 February, 1778, and his reception of the Masonic garb from the famous materialist Bro. Helvetius. Prior to the Revolution various conspiratory societies arose in connection with Freemasonry from which they borrowed its forms and methods; Illuminati, clubs of Jacobins, etc. A relatively large number of the leading revolutionists were members of Masonic lodges, trained by lodge life for their political career. Even the programme of the Revolution expressed in the 'rights of man' was, as shown above, drawn from Masonic principles, and its device: 'Liberty, Equality, Fraternity' is the very device of Freemasonry. Similarly, Freemasonry, together with the Carbonari, cooperated in the Italian revolutionary movement of the nineteenth century. Nearly all the prominent leaders, and among them Mazzini and Garibaldi, are extolled by Masonry as its most distinguished members. In Germany and Austria, Freemasonry during the eighteenth century was a powerful ally of the so-called party of 'Enlightenment' (Aufklaerung), and of Josephinism;[7] in the nineteenth

---

7 'The Church-State policy of Joseph II (1741-90), Emperor of Austria, which advocated secular interference and state supremacy in ecclesiastical affairs. He consolidated almost the entire property of the Church and merged all the religious funds into one

century of the pseudo-Liberal and of the anti-clerical party.

Such attitudes expressed in Catholic literature were given official sanction by the encyclical of Pope Leo XIII written in 1884, entitled Humanum Genus[8] in which Masonry is charged with being the revolutionary advocate of a 'naturalistic' religion. This 'naturalism' manifested in the 'Deism' of Masons and others among America's Founding Fathers; in the cult of nature and science of the Masonic Encyclopaedists, Diderot et al; and in the 'Cult of Reason' during the French Revolution.

Among the numerous books associating Freemasonry with subversion written by prominent Catholics, the Cardinal of Chile, Caro y Rodriguez, Archbishop of Santiago, wrote *The Mystery of Freemasonry Unveiled*. The Cardinal ranges over topics from the oaths and organisation of Masonry to the involvement of Masons in atheistic and anti-clerical agitation, and revolutionary movements in France, Germany, Italy, Spain, Portugal and elsewhere.

The attitude of the Church to Masonry underwent a dramatic change during the 1980s, albeit rejected by Catholic Traditionalists. In a paper published by the Quatuor Coronati Lodge in 1991 on Masonry and the Church by Will Read, it is noted that there is no mention of Masonry in the 1983 codification of canon law. According to this United Grand Lodge (UGL) paper, the Church now recognises a distinction between 'regular' and 'irregular' Masonry, 'irregular' being defined by UGL as, 'those jurisdictions which require no profession of faith from their candidates, and which may also be anti-Christian or anti-civil authority, or both'. Hence, even the UGL admits to

---

great Religionsfund for the requirements of public worship. To achieve his purpose, he suppressed all the monasteries and secularized them. For meddling in Church affairs, even to the regulation of candles, he was called the "Sacristan Emperor."' 'Josephinism', Catholic Dictionary, https://www.catholicculture.org/culture/library/dictionary/index.cfm?id=34386

8   *The Catholic Encyclopedia*, 1910, cites encyclicals by 17 Popes condemning Masonry, from Clement XII in 1738 to Leo XIII in 1890.

there being forms of 'irregular' Masonry that are 'anti-Christian', subversive and revolutionary. Why then are there UGL apologists and others who attempt to ridicule such notions of 'conspiracy' as simplistic and delusional, or as outright fabrications? It seems that Masons, including those of the UGL, want things both ways, boasting of the Masonic role in secularising society and overthrowing the supposed tyrannies of Altar and Throne, while on the other hand condemning with outrage those who question whether the work of Masonry in such matters is really for the betterment of humanity.

According to current Church law a Catholic can join a Lodge upon the advice of a Bishop or priest as to whether the Lodge is part of 'regular' Masonry. However, clerics are still prohibited from any Masonic membership.[9] With Vatican II a revolution in Faith was wrought within the Church, lauded by Masons for its liberalising and secularising tendencies. This new, liberal Catholicism has seen the Church in recent decades moving closer to the syncretic religion that is being formulated as a foundation for a new world order. Masons have seen glad tidings in the radical shift of the Church away from Tradition, making reasonable the question as to whether Masonry had an influence in the Church councils, and whether the remaining ban on clerics being initiated has been covertly circumvented? One name for this process of formulating a new syncretic religion is Ecumenism, in which the Church has since Vatican II been avidly involved. Yves Marsaudon 33°, a member of the Scottish Rite Supreme Council, stated of this in *L'oecuménisme vu par un franc-maçon de tradition* (Ecumenism Viewed by a Traditional Freemason): 'We can say that ecumenism is the legitimate son of Freemasonry Maçonnerie'.[10]

---

9   Read, 1991.

10   Marsaudon, p. 119.

Protestant

Christian criticism of Masonry and the occult influences in politics now comes increasingly from Christian Fundamentalists, in the aftermath of the liberalisation of the Catholic Church, post-Vatican Council II, although Masonry had affiliations with early Protestantism via the Rosicrucian society. Ironically, there have been allegations that Freemasonry is a 'Catholic conspiracy', or a Jesuit conspiracy, and it is still stated by some conspiracy theorists that Illuminati founder Adam Weishaupt was working for Jesuits. Such allegations have an early pedigree, Cagliostro's onetime protégé Elisa von der Recke claiming in 1786 that she suspected her late guru had been a crypto-Jesuit trying to undermine Protestantism by the use of the Strict Observance.[11]

Fraternitatis Rosae Crucis, the mysterious Rosicrucian fraternity that anonymously circulated its manifestos in Europe during the early 17th century, can be directly traced to the Lutheran revolt against the Church. From here Rosicrucianism became one of the esoteric currents that coalesced to form Freemasonry the following century. This is acknowledged with the 18°, that of Knight of the Pelican & Eagle & Sovereign Prince Rose Croix of Heredom.[12] Hence the anti-clericalism emanates from at least two sources, that of Lutheranism via Rosicrucianism, and that of the heretical Knights Templar. Later Judaism entered the scene.

The anonymous Rosicrucian manifestos were revolutionary in character. The first Rosicrucian manifesto to appear was Fama Fraternitatis of the Meritorious Order of the Rosy Cross (1614), followed by the Confession of the Rosicrucian Fraternity (1615) and finally, The Chemical Wedding of Christian Rosencreutz (1616).[13]

According to Rosicrucian legend, the founder was the mysterious Christian Rosenkreuz, born in 1378. He studied the magical arts and sciences in North Africa and learned magic and the

---

11   McCalman, p. 234.

12   Knight, p. 40.

13   Redd, p. 8.

18th century print depicting the first part of the initiation into the third degree.

Jewish mysticism of the Cabala at Fez. Rosencreutz returned to Germany, where he assembled seven disciples, and they founded the Fraternity of the Rosy Cross. It was determined that they would live in separate countries where they might influence learned people. 'Before dispersing, they agreed to profess nothing but to cure the sick, without payment; not to distinguish themselves by any particular costume; to meet annually in Germany; to nominate their successors before dying; to adopt the initials R.C. as their seal; and to keep their fraternity secret for one hundred years'.[14]

This description of the Fraternity resembles that of the Illuminati, the first aim being to 'influence learned people', from which a revolution could proceed. The Rosicrucian Manifestos 'announced the dawn of a 'New Age', and proclaimed a universal reform of science, religion, and society'. The Confession of the Rosicrucian Fraternity condemned both Catholicism and Islam.[15]

14   Vaughn, p. 16.
15   Redd, p. 9.

That Lutheranism was instigated by Rosicrucianism is indicated by the symbolism having been adopted from Luther's own coat-of-arms. Luther's seal appeared on the third Rosicrucian Manifesto, The Chemical Wedding of Christian Rosenkreutz.

This Lutheran ingredient to the founding of the Anti-Tradition and Counter-Tradition currents that have come down to us today through Masonry and its offshoots, places the anti-clerical pastors of Protestantism and Fundamentalism in a predicament. When describing what they regard as an anti-Christian conspiracy, their writings are therefore generally insufficient, and tenuous associations are established while major ones are ignored. Following are some examples of such literature, which nonetheless usually contain something of interest.

Don E Stanton attempts to draw together disparate conspiratorial strands linking Masonry, the Illuminati, bankers, communism, Satanism, the United Nations Organisation, and others. He cites numerous conservative works on conspiracy theories, such as those published by The John Birch Society, including Gary Allen's *The Rockefeller File* and *None Dare Call It Conspiracy*, which became best sellers in the USA. [16] In attempting to trace 'Satanic' origins to these various conspiratorial threads Stanton resorts to the most visible form of 'Satanism', the Church of Satan', founded by Anton LaVey in San Francisco in 1966. Stanton claims phenomenal growth for LaVey's Satanism, whose Satanic Bible had 'sold more than a million copies by 1975'.[17] While Stanton follows his chapter on Satanism with a review of Pastor Richard Wurmbrand's *Was Karl Marx a Satanist?*[18] he fails to establish a direct relationship, or indeed any relationship, between LaVey and the various conspiratorial agencies and events he has considered. Since the basis of Stanton's book is that there is an international conspiracy to establish a world state

---

16   *None Dare Call it Conspiracy* lists the printing runs for three editions from February to April 1972 as totalling 5,600,000.

17   Stanton, p. 140.

18   Early edition of Wurmbrand's fuller exposition, *Karl Marx – Prophet of Darkness*.

led by international bankers, and stemming partially from the Illuminati, his resort to LaVey in this context is unconvincing.

LaVey's Church of Satan was established as an overt attempt to affront American conventions and Christian morality. LaVey was also during the 1960s as much opposed to the hippie sub-culture as to Christian morals. More a polemical philosophy than a magical order, LaVey's doctrine owes much to Friedrich Nietzsche. At its most basic level it is an inversion of the Sermon on the Mount. The Nine Satanic Statements include 'Blessed are the strong', etc.[19] While LaVeyan Satanists might like to present themselves as a commanding influence over lesser mortals in a scenario out of The Omen, there is no evidence that the Church was or is anything other than theatrics. The rhetoric of the Hollywood-style Satanist who 'stands proudly in his secret places of the earth and manipulates the folly-ridden masses through his own Satanic might, until that day when he may come forth in splendor proclaiming "I AM A SATANIST! BOW DOWN, FOR I AM THE HIGHEST EMBODIMENT OF HUMAN LIFE!"'[20] is far from reality.

Nor does LaVey's doctrine reflect the occult doctrines being perpetrated by those promoting a New World Order. However, LaVey, because of his overt satanic imagery has served as a convenient reference point for some Christian conspiratologists. But what is actually 'satanic' is being missed. Traditionalists such as Guénon and Evola called the occult currents of Anti-Tradition and Counter-Tradition 'satanic' because they aim at reversing the Divine or cosmic order upon which Traditional cultures are founded. Crowley likewise referred to these as the 'Black Adepts' and the 'Black School of Magick', as we have seen. They will just as often operate under a 'Christian' guise as representing the 'true Jesus' or the 'Christ within'. Even the Illuminati claimed in the lower grades to be following 'true Christianity', just as one might meet a Leftist theologian claiming that 'Jesus was a Communist'.

---

19   LaVey, 1969, p. 25.

20   LaVey, 1969, p. 45.

As we have seen, the Rosicrucians operated under the mantle of Lutheranism. In his correspondence, Weishaupt explained how he used the cover of Christianity to slowly secure a conversion to his revolutionary cause – literally – by degree, writing to 'Cato':

> One would almost imagine, that this degree [Priest], as I have managed it, is genuine Christianity. My explanation of the hieroglyphics, at least, proceeds on this supposition; and as I explain things, no man need be ashamed of being a Christian. Indeed, I afterward throw away this name, and substitute Reason.[21]

While Satan and Lucifer came into vogue as romantic rebels among the decadent literati of the late 19th century, including those within Freemasonry, as will be shown, the 'satanic' currents of the Anti-Tradition and Counter-Tradition that do possess genuine influence to shape history, must for the most part be sought among those who eschew the label 'Satanist'.

Another contemporary Christian conspiratologist who cites LaVey to bolster his argument of a Satanic basis for an international conspiracy is Texe Marrs, an American evangelical writer. Marrs' book, *Codex Magica*, is a production of 620 pages and 1000 illustrations, many drawn from Masonic sources. However there tends to be a lot of supposition in attempting to relate every hand-sign, handshake and stance performed, consciously or not, by sundry celebrities and politicians to Masonry and *ipso facto*, to the Illuminati.

A well-known preacher and writer in New Zealand, with international repute among Fundamentalists, the late Barry Smith, wrote a series of books on conspiratorial themes including Masonry and the occult. *Final Notice*, like Stanton's *Mystery 666*, attempts to unite disparate strands in an all-embracing conspiracy to establish a New World Order. The connections that such Fundamentalist authors attempt to make are often

---

21   Robison, p. 85.

unnecessarily tenuous, although they enjoy a wide audience among Fundamentalist Christians.

Revival of Interest

Conspiratorial books tracing the origins of revolutionary and subversive upheaval to occult societies enjoyed widespread readership in the aftermath of the French Revolution and the Russian Revolution. World War II brought such theories into disrepute, as they were often associated with anti-Semitism and Fascism. Alternative small press publishers such as Britons Ltd., the Christian Book Club and Omni Christian Book Club kept the works of Nesta Webster et al, in print for a limited audience.

With the renewed upheavals in the Middle East, 9/11, and the widespread suspicion of globalisation, books on conspiracy theories, including those on Freemasonry and the occult, are again enjoying success via mainstream publishers and distributors.

Baigent, Leigh and Lincoln's bestseller, *The Holy Blood & the Holy Grail*, postulating a conspiracy by a crypto-Masonic society called the Prieure de Sion, published in 1982, began the revival in the mainstream. Although their theories on the Prieure will not be within our scope, the possibility of such occult or mystical conspiracies has caught the imagination of a large audience.

Within this revival there have been an increasing number of books associating Freemasonry and even the Illuminati with revolution and subversion. Baigent and Leigh have contributed directly to this literature with *The Temple & the Lodge*, which traces the origins of Masonry to the Knights Templars. John J Robinson's *Born in Blood* also traces the Templar origins of Freemasonry.

A unique dimension to conspiracy theory relative to occult societies is the work of David Icke: reptilians from outer space who have assumed human form. Their conspiratorial brotherhood goes back to Sumeria. Incorporated into this conspiracy are the

Illuminati, Masonry, globalist think tanks such as the Council on Foreign Relations and Bilderbergers, Communists, UNO, NATO, etc. controlled by reptilian international bankers and statesmen. Icke is aware of the ridicule this contention will bring to him but in a chapter entitled 'Don't mention the reptiles' (Icke, pp. 19-49) states 'what the hell?', in the interests of 'truth'. Among the reptilian lineage is the Rothschild dynasty.[22]

The best-selling novelist Dan Brown has contributed to the revival of interest with *Angels & Demons*, made into a motion picture. This novel is a thriller about the Illuminati. Although the historical background bares little relation to verifiable historical fact, the novel has spawned two non-fiction books, which include chapters on Masonic and Illuminati conspiracy theories, and are credible efforts. *Secrets of Angels & Demons* edited by Dan Burstein and A Sura, includes a chapter entitled 'The Illuminati Illuminated', which comprises an anthology of interviews with journalists and researchers on their views regarding Illuminati conspiracy theories.[23]

The Down Brown Companion by Simon Cox has a chapter entitled 'Illuminati' where Cox presents a succinct account of the Order.[24] Cox's references include Webster's *Secret Societies & Subversive Movements* and Robison's *Proofs of a Conspiracy*, thereby making these now largely forgotten writers known again. Cox concurs with the conspiratorial view that Karl Marx's doctrines are similar to those of the Illuminati, and with the possibility that the precursor of the Communist League, the League of the Just, of which Marx was a member, was likely to have been descended from the Illuminati. We shall consider more precisely the often-stated but seldom documented contention that Marx was intiated into illuminatist Masonry. Cox sees the influence of the Illuminati in the French Revolution. Considering the possibility of the continuing existence of the Illuminati, Cox writes:

---

22   Icke, p. 215.

23   Burstein and Sura, pp. 191-248.

24   Cox, pp. 139-76.

The break up of the Order of the Illuminati in 1785 is unlikely to have been the end of the secret organisation. It is much more probable that its members simply went even further underground and that the ideas were disseminated through Europe.[25]

Cox considers several globalist think tanks such as the Bilderberg Group and the Trilateral Commission, as well as the so-called 'neo-conservative' think tank, the Project for a New American Century, that was influential in the Administration of President George H W Bush. Of particular significance is that Cox considers Lodge 322 (also known as The Order of the Skull & Bones) and the similarity of its initiation rituals to the rituals of the Illuminati.

Such is the interest in 'conspiracies' and Masonic plots that the entertainment and publishing industries have cashed in on these. While the sceptic might sneeringly quip that the wire-pulling abilities of such conspiracies must be meagre if they cannot stop their plots from being made into best-selling novels and motion pictures, from a scholarly viewpoint there are variables in any given situation. One such variable is that the entry of such plots into the realm of popular fiction is likely to induce a blasé public attitude. One becomes familiarised with something to the extent that it no longer appears to be a problem. In recent times the revelations about the P2 Lodge, which operated under the auspices of the Grand Orient of Italy, and which reached the highest circles of politics, banking and the Church, brought down the Forlani Government in 1981. P2 had infiltrated the Christian Democrats, Socialists and Republicans.[26] Attention was focused on the ultra-secret organisation when Michele Sindona, 'Italy's most influential private banker, had fled to the United States leaving financial chaos behind him'.[27] A Prosecutor's report stated: 'Lodge Propaganda Due is a secret

25   Cox, p. 146.

26   Knight, pp. 269-278.

27   Knight, p. 272.

sect that has combined business and politics with the intention of destroying the country's constitutional order'.[28] In a scenario reminiscent of the discovery of the Illuminati papers during the 18th century by the Bavarian authorities, the Italian magistrates, examining the huge corpus of P2 files from Grand Master Gelli's villa, commented that he had 'constructed a very real state within a state'.[29] Despite the P2 revelations that rocked Italy in the early 1980s, academia continues to ridicule notions that such things exist, and the mass public have become familiar with these subjects as a mere form of entertainment. 'Conspiracy theorist' continues to be a term of ridicule.

Hence when the publisher Chrysalis Books Group runs a series of volumes under the heading 'Conspiracy Books', despite several of these volumes being very well done, the revelations are not going to cause a major disruption in the agendas of the various power groups and lobbies that are examined. Indeed, there is something surreal about the very title given to the series, 'Conspiracy Books'.

One of the books in the series in particular is notable for its discussion of the Illuminati and Freemasons, while focusing on the Bilderbergers, Trilateral Commission, and the Council on Foreign Relations (CFR). *Who Really Runs the World?* by Thom Burnett and Alex Games, attempts to answer the question by considering several candidates. Burnett is the pseudonym for a British security and military analyst. Games is a columnist for the *Financial Times* and former associate media editor for the London *Evening Standard.* The book starts with several chapters looking at contenders for the question of 'who really runs the world?' However, most of the book thereafter becomes a fairly standard, although well researched, work on globalisation.

Having considered and disposed of several groups for the contender, Burnett's technique of reductio ad absurdum in

---

28   Knight, p. 273.

29   Knight, p. 274.

eliminating the Illuminati from the scene does not do justice to the mostly well-researched book. For example, Burnett ridicules the notion popularised during the 18th century by the eminent scholar John Robison in *Proofs of a Conspiracy* that the Illuminati survived its outlawing by the Elector of Bavaria, through the expedient of re-organising as book clubs. Burnett finds it laughable that a sinister conspiracy for the establishment of a new world order could continue in such a manner. However the importance of what was at the time subversive literature was a feature not only of Weishaupt's Illuminati but also of other revolutionary societies, and it was this literature that paved the way for the French Revolution. Books and pamphlets at the time were as influential as television and the internet are today. The owner of a printing press was as potentially subversive as today's Rupert Murdoch and other media barons. One needs only recall Benjamin Franklin as a printer for example. The French Revolution itself was fomented by a coterie mostly of Masons, The Encyclopaedists. It is naïve to think that the Illuminati was obliterated by a decree and police action, any more than a Communist party apparatus is eliminated by a state order and police raids. It was the Illuminati that created the cell structure upon which Communist parties were modelled, as were numerous Masonic-type revolutionary societies such as those of Babeuf, Blanqui, Mazinni, et al. Burnett offhandedly dismisses the contention of Professor Robison (and previously the much-maligned Abbé Barruel) that the Illuminati continued via book clubs: 'A reading society? Are we to be believe that members of some book club were now the hidden manipulators of history?'[30]

Burnett then arrives at Lodge 322, also known as The Order of the Skull & Bones, of which both former presidents Bush and rival presidential contender John Kerry are initiates. Lodge 322 is widely believed by conspiratologists to be a continuation of the Illuminati. Burnett again resorts to ridicule to eliminate Lodge 322, not only as a continuation of the Illuminati but even as a contender as a major power group, despite the elite

30   Burnett, p. 25.

of industry, banking, politics, and education being among its initiates. Lodge 322 has the type of influence that was once welded by Lodge P2 in Italy. Burnett cites only one work on Lodge 322, Ron Rosenbaum's 1977 article for *Esquire*, 'The Last Secrets of Skull & Bones'.[31] Rosenbaum points to a common initiatory feature of the Illuminati and Lodge 322, the initiate arising from a coffin and being confronted with a line from the Masonic German dramatist Lessing: 'Wer war der Thor, wer Weiser, Bettler oder Kaiser? Ob Arm, on Reich, in Tode gleich?' ('Who was the fool, who was the wise man, beggar or king? Whether poor or rich, all's the same in death'). Burnett dismisses this as an inconsequential coincidence, while accepting a vague Masonic connection from Germany.[32] He states that the skull and bones symbol of Lodge 322 probably represents a pirate symbol. It seems odd that Burnett would not know the importance of the symbol in Masonry. As evidence of the unimportant nature of Lodge 322, Burnett states that it is merely a Yale fraternity, ignoring the significance that prospects are not 'tapped' until their final year at Yale, and that the old boy network continues to hold meetings for its 'patriarchs' on an island resort, Deer Island, purchased for that purpose. It is not until after Yale graduation that one becomes a 'patriarch' of the Order. Burnett concludes that it is the influential think tank, the Council on Foreign Relations, that is the winner for the contender 'who really runs the world', a subject which is outside the scope of this book but which is examined in detail in this writer's book *Revolution from Above*.

One of the most interesting books to be published recently is *The Secret Founding of America: The Real Story of Freemasons, Puritans & The Battle for The New World*, by the eclectic scholar Nicholas Hagger, who concludes that both Puritans and Masons had a common interest in thwarting the advance of Catholic Spain and France in the Americas:

---

31   Burnett, p. 20.

32   Burnett, p. 18.

Because the English saw off the French and Spanish, the Catholic legacy influenced the Founding Fathers less than a secret society that gathered influence among the Protestants: Freemasonry. Despite the efforts of Catholics, Anglicans and Puritans, the founding of America owes more to this fourth group: the Freemasons in the Anglican-Puritan north.[33]

There was also a convergence between Puritanism and Rosicrucian-Masonry. Hagger suggests that the Rosicrucian-Masonic interest in the Americas was to establish a Utopia in the New World based on the ideas in *New Atlantis* (published posthumously in 1626) by English scholar Francis Bacon, who is regarded as the founder of Rosicrucianism and Masonry in England.[34] Hagger claims:

> Rosicrucian Freemasonry may have established itself in America in 1635 when missing works by Bacon were reputedly taken to Jamestown. These may have included the sequel to New Atlantis Bacon is thought to have written. This is believed to have included a timetable for fulfilling the Masonic plan for America.[35]

Hagger states that Puritan doctrine was Rosicrucian, continuing: 'So it could be that some of the post-Mayflower Puritans who joined the Plymouth settlement as reinforcements brought Rosicrucianism with them and over a period of time it passed into Freemasonic lodges'.[36]

---

33   Hagger, p. 81.

34   Hagger, p. 85.

35   Hagger, p. 95.

36   Hagger, p. 97.

Debunking Debunkers

As one would expect in the age of banal scepticism, the debunkers of such 'conspiracy theories', as they are dismissively called, rely on the illogical while posturing as the champions of scholarly empiricism, logic, and rationality. 'Conspiracy theories' on Masonic plots make for good entertainment at the movies and as the theme for Dan Brown novels, but should not be confused with serious history. Hence, McCalman, after writing an excellent biography on Cagliostro, showing the escapades of this con man, mystic, Mason and Illuminatus across the royal courts of Europe, concludes by ridiculing the enduring notion that the founder of Mizraim Masonry was really serious about anything. McCalman writes:

> One legend about Cagliostro that proved particularly enduring was the idea that he led a Masonic conspiracy against Europe's old order. Cagliostro never was a revolutionary, but many will see him no other way…

> Other enemies of Cagliostro enriched this black legend. No single source was more important than Giovanni Barberi's compendium, which claimed that Cagliostro had confessed to joining the leadership of the revolutionary and atheistical German Illuminati, who also operated under the cover of masonry. Several Catholic victims of the French revolution added their support. In 1792, a French Catholic priest, Abbé Augstin Barruel, managed to escape to London, where he would spend the next five years assembling a massive document of lies, half-truths, and errors, which he published as a multivolume opus, *Memoirs of the History of Jacobinism*.

Apart from his massive documentation, Barruel's original contribution to the conspiracy theory was to trace it origins back to the suppression of the Knights Templar in 1312. He claimed that a remnant of the Templars had formed as Masonic underground in Scotland dedicated to undying vengeance against the church. His Knights Templar lodges linked up with the anticlerical salons of French philosophers and the republican cells of German Illuminati. Out of this toxic blend came a plan of world terror, whose first success was the French revolution. [1]

Yet it is McCalman who alludes to Cagliostro having stated that he was initiated into the Illuminati under the sponsorship of two high initiates of the Strict Observance.[2] Interestingly, Adam Weisphaupt had been initiated into the Strict Observance in 1777.[3] McCalman further states that the Strict Observance, founded in 1754 by Saxon nobleman Baron Charles von Hundt, 'whose lodges had then spread through much of Germany, Eastern Europe and southern France… drew on the legend of the Templars'. McCalman states that it was Strict Observance lore that claims the Templars survived in Scotland and 'resurfaced as Freemasons', having magical secrets that were directed by an 'unknown Master'. McCalman adds that the Strict Observance had also incorporated Rosicrucianism into its system.[4] In 1780, according to McCalman, Cagliostro had been initiated into the Illuminati, which McCalman adds, had been founded by Adam Weishaupt as 'a tough disciplined cadre of republicans dedicated to the overthrow of established religion and monarchy. The Illuminati then fostered their political mission by gradually infiltrating the German Masonic movement. Always on the lookout for new recruits, the officials in Frankfurt were pleased top welcome the rising Masonic star Count Cagliostro'. McCalman states that according to Cagliostro's account he

1   McCalman, pp. 234-235.
2   McCalman, p. 36.
3   Roberts, p. 125.
4   McCalman, pp. 38-39.

signed a parchment upon which were eleven other signatures; those of the 'grand masters of the Templars'.[5]

Hence, McCalman, in his biography, confirms all the primary assertions of the much-maligned Abbé Barruel, who is supposedly a 'liar' for having presented his evidence in *Memoirs of the History of Jacobinism.* Barruel, like his scholarly contemporary, John Robison, was merely marshalling evidence from Masonic and Illuminatist sources; especially the latter which had been made public by the Bavarian authorities, after raids on Illuminati had secured the papers and correspondence of the Order.

If Masonic apologists now object that they are being misrepresented then it is only because their own lore – as manifested in their Degrees – connects them not only to Templars and Rosicrucians, but the Grand Orient de France boasts of its associations with the French Revolution and revolutionists such as Bakunin.

However it is with Lindsay Porter's *Who Are the Illuminati? Exploring the Myth of the Secret Society,* published in 2005 as part of the above mentioned 'Conspiracy Books' series that we come to a particularly good example of attempts at 'conspiracy debunking' that are of unsound research. Porter, described as an author and researcher who specialises in secret societies, takes the position that not only is the Illuminati a myth outside a brief existence as a harmless society of intellectuals who didn't outlast the 18th century, but that any notion of a long running political conspiracy is mere paranoia or the simplification of history by yokels.[6]

Porter's book is probably one of the few that reads like an apologia for Adam Weishaupt, founder of the Illuminati. While drawing on accounts that show Weishaupt to have been paranoid, dictatorial, and amoral, Porter, like Thomas Jefferson during the anti-Illuminati scare in America in the 18th and 19th centuries, nonetheless portrays Weishaupt in sympathetic terms

---

5   McCalman, pp. 103-104.

6   Porter, pp. 10-11.

as a misunderstood philanthropist persecuted by reactionaries. Likewise, the Illuminati are portrayed as professing ideals that are nothing more than the democracy that we are all now presumed to thankfully take for granted.

While those who have traced the Illuminati and Masonry back to the Knights Templar are ridiculed by Porter, she attempts to form a lineage of her own of 'conspiracists', starting with Barruel, closely followed by Dr John Robison, to British historian Nesta Webster, who was the first and most prominent to revive the idea in the early 20th century, then on to Robert Welch of The John Birch Society whom she claims was the first to revive the Illuminati theory after World War II to explain the rise of Communism.[7] Into this Porter mixes anyone and everyone who ever so much as mentioned the Illuminati, along with many who didn't but just opposed some subversive tendency such as Communism. Hence melded together in what seems to be Porter's suggestion of a centuries-long anti-Illuminati conspiracy by reactionaries, are the anti-Communist Senator Joseph McCarthy, always good to slander; Father Charles Coughlin, the popular Depression era 'radio priest' who is susceptible to allegations of being 'anti-Semitic' and pro-Fascist; and Henry Ford the automobile manufacturer, who published a long series of articles on the Protocols of Zion and Jewish influence, in his newspaper *The Dearborn Independent*, which were subsequently published as a series of volumes called *The International Jew*.[8] It is doubtful whether any of these latter sources ever so much as mentioned the Illuminati, but they have all been smeared as 'anti-Semites', hence Porter is able to insinuate that conspiracy theories per se are anti-Semitic, latently if not blatantly. But Porter particularly relishes the chance to give special attention to David Icke who has added an extraterrestrial dimension by claiming that the Illuminati are hybrid humanoid-reptilian aliens, that include the Bush, Rothschild and Rockefeller families.[9]

---

7   Porter, pp. 11-12.

8   Porter, pp. 12-13.

9   Porter, p. 10.

While Porter scathingly attacks Professor Robison's seminal *Proofs of a Conspiracy,* republished by The John Birch Society, she is obliged to draw on the work of the eminent Scottish scholar where she actually attempts to describe the Illuminati. She must therefore concede that Robison is a definitive source. Indeed, Porter states that Robison was an 'esteemed scientist', and a Mason who wanted to distinguish between Continental Masonry and the English version; but this just means to Porter that it gives Robison a 'dangerous respectability'.[10]

In a chapter on what Porter calls the anti-Illuminati 'hysteria' in the USA during the 18th century, when the doctrines of the French Revolution were being introduced via Jefferson's Democrats, she claims that Robison's work was finally repudiated when a letter arrived from a Dr Ebeling in Germany, who claimed that Robison had been exposed in Europe as a fraud and a bankrupt.[11] Who this Ebeling was is not stated. Ebeling's allegations are not examined further by Porter, who declines to cite any primary sources. Robison was one of the foremost scientists of his day, the first general secretary of the Scottish Royal Society, and was eulogised by James Watt. Porter claims that Robison was not sufficiently acquainted with German to translate the Illuminati papers found by the Bavarian authorities. Yet the website of Edinburgh University describes Robison as an eminent linguist. In describing Dr David B Wilson's history of Scottish science, *Seeking Nature's Logic*, Penn State University states of Robison:

> As professor of natural philosophy at Edinburgh University from 1774 to 1805, John Robison taught the premier science of the day at the premier science university of the time. He discovered experimentally that electrical and magnetic forces were, like gravity, inverse square forces, and he wrote influential treatises on electricity, magnetism, mechanics, and astronomy. By articulating a particularly Scottish approach to physics, he was the main conceptual

10   Porter, p. 75.
11   Porter, p. 111.

link between Newton and those Scottish geniuses of Victorian physics, Lord Kelvin and James Clerk Maxwell.[12]

While the motives of Robison in exposing Masonry and the Illuminati seem to remain a puzzle for Porter, apparently unable to accept that Robison was applying his scientific methodology to the question, particular venom is reserved for Nesta Webster, whose influence on 'conspiracists' continues. Webster is scorned as 'pseudo-scholarly', for having been little heeded in her own time, and for being an 'anti-Semitic fantasist'.[13] However, Lord Kitchener, a Mason, called Webster 'the foremost opponent of subversion'.[14] Even H G Wells, the famed historian and novelist, who as a Fabian socialist and internationalist on the opposite political spectrum to that of Webster, commended her 1924 book *Secret Societies & Subversive Movements* as being 'a book that all serious people interested in the British situation should read and think about.... I believe that Mrs Webster's influence has spread beyond the circle of her actual readers'. Other tributes at the time came from *The Daily Express, Chicago Tribune, NY Herald Tribune, Daily Mail, The Spectator* and many more. Webster was asked to lecture to the British Military as an expert on subversion, and these lectures formed the basis of her book *World Revolution*. Winston Churchill another Mason, commended Webster for having 'ably shown' the origins of 'this worldwide movement for the overthrow of civilisation', as being traced to Weishaupt and the Illuminati, through to the French Revolution and to the Bolshevism of his day.

Porter seems to have commented much about authors whose books she does not appear to have read. At one point in attempting to associate Illuminati conspiracy theories with *The Protocols of Zion*, and ipso facto with 'anti-Semitism' and 'forgery', Porter claims that *The Protocols* purport to expose 'secret Jewish rituals'. This is nonsense; there is no allusion to 'secret Jewish

12 Penn State University Press.

13 Porter, pp. 13-15.

14 Webster, *World Revolution*, back cover.

rituals'. As has been considered previously, The Protocols, insofar as they express a doctrine, are more akin to Illuminism, than to Orthodox Judaism or to Zionism. However, Porter even states that *The Protocols* are now believed to be a forgery perpetrated by the 'Soviet secret police' in order to incite anti-Semitism,[15] whereas what she means to say is that debunkers of *The Protocols* regard them as being faked by the Czarist secret police, the Okhrana, in Paris.[16] To be charitable, perhaps this is a typing or editorial error (?).

Robert Welch, who founded the once formidable anti-Communist lobby, The John Birch Society, comes in for much condemnation as an individual who revived the Illuminati conspiracy theory after World War II to explain Communism. Porter quotes from Welch's booklet *The Truth In Time*,[17] yet we find that according to the Bibliography, not only has Porter apparently not even read *The Truth In Time*, but the only book she records there by Welch is The Blue Book of The John Birch Society, the founding document of the society, which does not deal with conspiracy themes.[18]

Others brought together into a 'conspiracist' conspiracy of Porter's imagination include the Ku Klux Klan; Pat Robertson, the evangelist; The Militias, and UFOlogy, welded together with Nesta Webster, Senator McCarthy, Henry Ford, Robert Welch, John Robison, et al.[19]

If the neglect of Burnett to mention Dr Antony Sutton's books on Lodge 322 in *Who Runs the World?* is a bad oversight, then Porter's neglect is nothing less than appalling. For a book that purports to trace – and debunk – theories on the Illuminati not to mention Sutton's research, even for the purposes of scorn, is

---

15   Porter, p. 13.

16   Cohn, pp. 87-96.

17   Porter, pp. 166-168

18   Porter, Bibliography, p. 247.

19   Porter, p. 190.

odd; especially given that his final book in the series on Lodge 322, *The Secret Cult of the Order,* was specifically written to show links between the Illuminati and the Lodge.

Of course there are many Masonic writers who seek to repudiate the accusations against Masonry as vile smears. Their strategies appear to be of three types:

1. To state that the accusations do not involve 'genuine Masons', but those of 'irregular' Masonry, such as the Grand Orient.

2. To ridicule claims about Templar and Rosicrucian origins for Masonry, despite these being part of Masonic lore.

3. To repudiate the notion of widespread Masonic influence when the claims are being made by anti-Masons, yet to boast of those same influences when lecturing to fellow Masons (examples: Masonic influences in the revolutions of the Americas, Turkey, Spain, the role of Masonry in creating the European Union, etc.).

Lineage of Secret Societies

Order of the Knights Templar

The Knights Templar are considered an occult society within the context of this study because:

1. The Templars, rightly or wrongly, were accused of secretly adhering to heretical doctrines.

2. There is evidence that the Templars incorporated Gnostic teachings, as indicated by the presence of pentagrams and other symbols.

3. Most importantly for this subject, the Templars are considered by occult societies as having been their forerunners. Such mythic perceptions are more important in this context than the historical reality.

Eliphas Levi, the nom de plume for Alphonse Louis Constant, the famous late 19th century French occult theorist whom, on the basis of his descriptions of certain occult societies, we may regard as being a Traditionalist at war with the Counter-Tradition, stated of Templarism in Masonic lore.

> Masonry has not merely been profaned but has served as the veil and pretext of anarchic conspiracies descending from the secret influence of the vindicators of Jacques de Molay, and of those who continued the schismatic work of the Temple. In place of avenging the death of Hiram[1] they have that of his assassins. The anarchists have resumed

---

1   Hiram Abif, one of the mythical architects of the Temple of Solomon whose murder Masons are sworn to avenge; a central motif of Masonic ritual.

The Knights Templar escort Christian pilgrims to Jerusalem

the rule, square and mallet, writing upon them the words Liberty, Equality, Fraternity – Liberty, that is to say, for all the lusts, Equality in degradation and Fraternity in the work of destruction. Such are the men whom the Church has condemned justly and will condemn forever.[2]

Levi is, then, in accord in his description of the Anti-Tradition of Masonry, with the opinions of Guénon, Evola, Steiner, and Crowley. Levi was here referring to the legend of the curse of the last Grand Master of the Order of Knights Templar, Jacques de Molay, upon the King of France, Philip IV, and Pope Clement V

---

2   Levi, p. 310. As for Levi's condemnation of Freemasonry, we can deduce that he had been a Mason of the 18°, that of the Rosicrucian Degree. This is indicated in a footnote to his *History of Magic*, where he states: 'Having attained by our efforts to a grade of knowledge which imposes silence, we regard ourselves as pledged by our convictions even more than by an oath. ... and we shall in no wise fail to deserve the princely crown of the Rosy Cross....' (Levi, p. 286). Levi was here stating that he was staying true to what he considered the genuine Tradition of Masonry, whilst condemning what he saw as the perversion of Masonry by the Counter-Tradition. His reference to the Masonic oath attached to the 'Rosy Cross' indicates that he had reached as far as the 18° of Knight of the Pelican & Eagle & Sovereign Prince Rose Croix of Heredom.

as de Molay was about to be burned at the stake for heresy. This curse, whether real or entirely mythical, was adopted as the cause of subsequent secret societies claiming the Templar legacy. The curse broadened into the destruction of the Catholic Church and all monarchies and continued through the revolutionary societies of the 19th century and into the present. The Knights of the Temple of Solomon was an Order founded in 1119 to protect pilgrims to the Holy Land from Muslim attack. They played a prominent part in the Crusades. Their primary goal was the rebuilding of the Temple of Solomon. This work of rebuilding also happens to be the primary goal of Freemasonry, which will be examined later. The Templars amassed tremendous wealth as the financial middlemen between the commerce of Europe and the Middle East. Dr Peter Partner states: 'The financial dealings of the Templars led them straight to the royal treasuries, of which they were frequently keepers. This financial influence lasted right up until the dissolution of the Templars in the 14th century'.[3]

Accusations of Heresy

Charges of heresy centred on the worship of an idol called Baphomet that, according to some Templar confessions, was described as a head.

While such charges of heresy have generally been dismissed as having been based on confessions under torture, the description of the alleged idol as a head is quite specific and could relate to the cult of John the Baptist, the Johannites. This is a heresy that the Templars could plausibly have adopted from their long stay in the Holy Land. The Bible relates that since the time of Jesus there were those among the followers of John the Baptist who regarded Jesus as a usurper, but were rebuked by John. The Biblical account states that disciples of John the Baptist came to him complaining, 'he that was with thee beyond Jordan, to whom thou barest witness, behold, the same baptizeth, and all men come

---

3   Partner, pp. 16-17.

to him'.[4] John the Baptist, according to the Biblical accounts, had been emphatic that he was not the Messiah, nor even a reborn prophet, but was preparing the way for the Messiah, replying to his disciples: 'Ye yourselves hear me witness, that I said, I am not the Christ, but that I am sent before Him…. This my joy is therefore fulfilled, He must increase, but I must decrease'.[5] The Baptist was imprisoned by Herod and beheaded.[6]

The worshipping of a head as an idol becomes plausible if the Templars were influenced by the cult of John. According to Eliphas Levi the Johannites claimed that John, contrary to the Biblical account, had identified Jesus as a fraud. Levi states that the first Templar Grand Master Hugh de Payens was initiated into the Johannites by the sect's 'grand pontiff', Theoclet: 'Thus was the order of the Knights of the Temple tainted from the beginning with schism and conspiracy against kings'.[7] Again, whether this is true or not is of less singifance as to it being part of Masonic lore. It is therefore plausible that Templars confessed to the Inquisition that at their initiation they were obliged to declare Jesus to be a 'thief'. This accords with the teachings of the Johannites. Occult authority Lewis Spence states: 'When we read over the numerous examinations of the Templars, in other countries, as well as in France, we cannot but feel convinced that some of these charges had a degree of foundation, though perhaps the circumstances upon which they were found were misunderstood'.[8]

The examination of the Templars began in 1316 in Paris. The accusations included that the Templars had to deny Christ at their reception into the Order, declaring that he was a 'false prophet', and was punished for his crimes, and that the Templar had to spit and trample upon the cross. Baphomet is described as

---

4   John, 3: 26.

5   John, 3:30.

6   Mark 6: 17-28.

7   Levi, p. 210.

8   Lewis Spence, p. 406.

having three faces, being a skull, or a head with a long beard and sparkling eyes, made of wood or metal. A French Templar stated that he had been shown the idol and told: 'You must adore this as your saviour and as the saviour of the order of the Temple'. Another was told: 'adore this head. This head is your God and your Mahomet'.[9]

Because Baphomet is possibly a corruption of the name Mohammed, sceptics claim that this was an attempt to smear the Templars as being in alliance with Islam. For example, Dr Partner writes of this:

> The name given to the idol, 'Baphomet' (once or twice the form Mohamet is actually used by the witnesses in the trial), is one of the most persuasive pieces of evidence that the charges were used to 'smear' the Templars. It was impossible for the Templars to have 'picked up in the East' the practice of worshipping an idol bearing the name of the Prophet Muhammed, since no such idol existed anywhere in the Levant...[10]

However, Lewis Spence[11] points out that Christians at the time used the word Mohammed to signify any idol. According to Spence, so-called 'heads of Baphomet' had been found in 1818 among forgotten antiquaries at the Imperial Museum of Vienna. Spence stated that one of these 'gilded heads' had long been preserved at Marseilles, having been seized when the Templars were fleeing the authorities.[12] Regardless of the circumstances of the confessions by the Templars, many of the accusations in regard to denying Christ as a 'false prophet' are in keeping with the Johannite sect. An example of this Johannite tradition that Jesus is an 'impostor' having endured in the teachings of Masonry is indicated by the statement of Senator Auguste

9   Spence, *ibid.*
10   Partner, p. 78.
11   Spence p. 407.
12   Spence, p. 203.

Delpech, president of the French Radical Party, and head of the Grand Orient de France,[13] who in announcing 'the death of the impostor God, the Galilean', said in a speech of 20 September 1902:

> The triumph of the Galilean has lasted twenty centuries. But now he dies in his turn. The mysterious voice announcing (to Julian the Apostate) the death of Pan, today announces the death of the impostor God who promised an era of justice and peace to those who believe in him. The illusion has lasted a long time. The mendacious god is now disappearing in his turn; he passes away to join in the dust of ages the divinities of India, Egypt, Greece, and Rome, who saw so many creatures prostrate before their altars. Bro. Masons we rejoice to state that we are not without our share in this overthrow of the false prophets. The Romish church, founded on the Galilean myth, began to decay very rapidly from the very day upon which the Masonic Association was established.[14]

Albert Pike, head of the Scottish Rite Southern Jurisdiction (USA), who codified the rites and doctrine of the Scottish Rite, used words similar to those of Delpech in abjuring Christianity and Jesus, indicating that Delpech's views were more than the rhetoric of a radical politician in the tradition of the revolutionary and humanistic doctrines of Grand Orient de France. Pike, in his celebrated magnum opus on Scottish Rite Masonry, explained what doctrines are taught on initiation to the 18°:

> More than eighteen centuries have staggered away into the spectral realm of the Past, since Christ, teaching the Religion of Love, was crucified, that it might become a Religion of Hate; and His Doctrines are not yet even

---

13 According to his Senatorial biography, Delpech was 'a founding member of the League of Human Rights, and Chairman of the Order of the Grand Orient of France', whose books included those of an anti-Catholic nature. (Jolly, 1977).

14 Delpech, p. 381, cited by *the Catholic Encyclopedia*.

nominally accepted as true by a fourth of mankind. Since His death, what incalculable swarms of human beings have lived and died in total unbelief of all that we deem essential to Salvation!

What multitudinous myriads of souls, since the darkness of idolatrous superstition settled down, thick and impenetrable, upon the earth, have flocked up toward the eternal Throne of God, to receive His judgement? The Religion of Love proved to be, for seventeen long centuries, as much the Religion of Hate, and infinitely more the Religion of Persecution, than Mahometanism, its unconquerable rival.[15]

These Johannite doctrines had found their way into Masonry via Templarism, and were to be manifested in the de-christianisation of France, Mexico, Portugal, Spain and other states where Masonry instigated revolution in the name of 'Liberty, Equality, and Fraternity'. As for the Johannites, they became known as the Sabeans, and prior to these, the Mandaeans, a Gnostic sect living in Iraq, whose rites resemble that of Freemasonry. Helena Blavatsky, founder of the Theosophical Society, through which much of the Counter-Tradition has been conveyed from Freemasonry as a Counterfeit Tradition, into the present 'New Age' movement, writes of the Johannites:

Mandaeans. Also called Sabians, and St. John Christians. The latter is absurd, since, according to all accounts, and even their own, they have nothing at all to do with Christianity, which they abominate. The modern sect of the Mendæans is widely scattered over Asia Minor and elsewhere, and is rightly believed by several Orientalists to be a direct surviving relic of the Gnostics. It was Norberg who was the first to point out a tribe belonging to the same

---

15   Pike, p. 294. Pike's chapters in Morals & Dogma correspond to each of the 33 Degrees of Scottish Rite Masonry. Hence the 18th chapter corresponds to the 18°, that of Knight Rose Croix.

sect established in Syria. And they are the most interesting of all. This tribe, some 14,000 or 15,000 in number, lives at a day's march east of Mount Lebanon, principally at Elmerkah, (Lata-Kieh). They call themselves indifferently Nazarenes and Galileans, as they originally come to Syria from Galilee. They claim that their religion is the same as that of St. John the Baptist, and that it has not changed one bit since his day. On festival days they clothe themselves in camel's skins, sleep on camel's skins, and eat locusts and honey as did their 'Father, St. John the Baptist'. Yet they call Jesus Christ an impostor, a false Messiah, and Nebso (or the planet Mercury in its evil side), and show him as a production of the Spirit of the 'seven badly-disposed stellars' (or planets).[16]

It seems that the Mandaean doctrine of Jesus as an 'impostor' is part of a 'sacred tradition' coming down from the Johannites and has been maintained by the Grand Orient and other Masonic revolutionaries.

Templars & Masonry

While the pioneering works of John Robison and the Abbé Barruel draw much criticism, largely centered around the slandering of those authors, for having postulated the associations between the Knights Templar and Freemasonry, recent authors have arrived independently at similar conclusions, yet still manage also to condemn Barruel. Baigent and Leigh state that Barruel triggered 'a wave of hysteria', his book being 'a veritable bible for conspiracy theories'.[17] For example, Baigent and Leigh's largely commendable book tracing the origins of Freemasonry to the Knights Templar also documents the Freemasonic 'conspiracy' surrounding the American Revolution, while pointing out – justifiably – that Freemasons have included both reactionary monarchists and revolutionists such as the anarchist Mikhail Bakunin.[18]

---

16 Carson, 'Gnostics & Mandaeans'.

17 Baigent and Leigh, 1989, pp. 263-264.

18 Baigent and Leigh, *Ibid.*, p. 265.

Whether Freemasonry stems directly from surviving Templars in a literal manner is not crucial. What is significant is that Freemasonry claims the legacy of the Templars. It is the way in which the Templar legacy is perceived which is of consequence. Pike states:

> Therefore, it was that the Sword and the Trowel were the insignia of the Templars, who subsequently, as will be seen, concealed themselves under the name of Brethren Masons. This name, Freres Macons in the French, adopted by way of secret reference to the Builders of the Second Temple, was corrupted in English into Free-Masons.[19]

There are obvious indications from Scottish Rite symbols and Degrees: 15° Knight of the East, 17° Degree Knight of the East & West, 27° Degree Commander of the Temple. There is a Masonic youth affiliate called the Order of DeMolay, founded in the USA in 1919 in honour of the last Templar Grand Master.[20] There is also the Knights Templar of English Grand Lodge Masonry, open only to Royal Arch Master Masons and higher. The emblems of this incorporate the skull and crossbones motif of the Knights Templar, which is an important symbol of Masonry in general. Some examples are depicted by Baigent including an English Masonic Templar apron, circa 1800,[21] and two English Masonic Templars jewels, circa 1830.[22]

Baron Karl von Hund, initiated into Masonry in 1742, established his version of 'Templar Masonry' in Germany after having been initiated in Paris where he claimed to have been dubbed a 'Chevelier Templier' by an 'unknown superior' bearing the title 'Knight of the Red Feather'[23]. Hund's Masonry became

---

19   Pike, p. 816.

20   Pick, p. 298.

21   Baigent and Leigh, 1989, First plate between pp. 258-59.

22   Baigent and Leigh, *Ibid.*, last plate between pp. 194-95.

23   Baigent & Leigh (p. 197) identify the 'unknown superior' as Alexander Seton, Tenth Earl of Eglinton, a descendant of original Templar survivors in Scotland.

known as the Strict Observance, claiming direct descent from the original Templars.[24] When Weishaupt created the Illuminati, several important Strict Observance Templars were involved, such as Baron Adolf von Knigge.[25] Cagliostro, having been initiated into the Esperance Lodge of the Strict Observance in London in 1776[26] was introduced to the Illuminati by two high initiates of the Strict Observance.[27]

Rosicrucians & the 'Society of Unknown Philosophers'

We have previously considered Rosicrucianism as an anti-Catholic secret society linked to Lutheranism, as well as the overt association with Masonry acknowledged by the 18°, Knight of the Pelican & Eagle & Sovereign Prince Rose Croix of Heredam, where the Mason first hears an explanation of the revolutionary character of Masonry.[28] Freemasons acknowledge the historical link between Freemasonry and the Rosicrucians, the prominent Masonic historian Albert G Mackey writing of this:

> Many writers have sought to discover a close connection between the Rosicrucians and the Freemasons, and some, indeed, have advanced the theory that the latter are only the successes of the former. Whether this opinion be correct or not, there are sufficient coincidences of character between the two to render the history of Rosicrucianism highly interesting to the Masonic student.[29]

Manly P Hall, the Masonic adept who sought to revive Rosicrucianism in the 20th century,[30] confirms that the

24   Baigent& Leigh, 1989, p. 74.
25   Robison, pp.117-18.
26   McCalman, p. 36.
27   McCalman, pp. 103-104.
28   Pike, Chapter 18.
29   Mackey, 1912, Vol. II, p. 639.
30   Manly P Hall was founder of the Rosicrucian Fellowship, and the Rosicrucian Philosophical Research Society (1934).

Rosicrucians were advocating a democratic, secular revolution against the Church and monarchs of Europe. As such they appear as the forerunners of the Illuminati and the communistic doctrines that were to emerge during and after the French Revolution. Hall states that Sir Walter Raleigh was a member of the same 'secret society' dedicated to the overthrow of Catholic dogma and the divine right of kings as that of Sir Francis Bacon, who was regarded as the head of the Rosicrucian fraternity. Hall also states that Raleigh was beheaded for his refusal to divulge the other members of the fraternity who were plotting rebellion.[31] Hall is unequivocal in describing Freemasonry and its Rosicrucian origins as a revolt against the established order of Europe, in seeking to establish a 'universal order'. He states that Freemasonry is just the outer order of something deeper:

> The modern Masonic order can be traced back to a period in European history famous for its intrigue both political and sociological. Between the years 1600 and 1800, mysterious agents moved across the face of the Continent. The forerunner of modern thought was beginning to make its appearance and all Europe was passing through the throes of internal dissension and reconstruction. Democracy was in its infancy, yet its potential power was already being felt. Thrones were beginning to totter. The aristocracy of Europe was like the old man on Sinbad's back: it was becoming more unbearable with every passing day. Although upon the surface national governments were seemingly able to cope with the situation, there was a definite undercurrent of impending change; and out of the masses, long patient under the yoke of oppression, were rising up the champions of religious, philosophic, and political liberty. These led the factions of the dissatisfied: people with legitimate grievances against the intolerance of the church and the oppression of the crown. Out of this struggle for expression materialized certain definite ideals, the same which have now come to be considered peculiarly Masonic.[32]

---

31 Hall, *Rosicrucian & Masonic Origins,* p. 406.

32 Hall, *Ibid.,* p. 405.

Hall lauds Cagliostro as one of the great Masonic revolutionaries of his time, whose depredations at the hands of nobles and clerics were prompted by what Hall is describing as Masonic leadership of the French Revolution.

> Tried by the Inquisition for founding a Masonic lodge in the city of Rome, Cagliostro was sentenced to die, a sentence later commuted by the Pope to life imprisonment in the old castle of San Leo. Shortly after his incarceration, Cagliostro disappeared and the story was circulated that he had been strangled in an attempt to escape from prison. In reality, however, he was liberated and returned to his Masters in the East. But Cagliostro—the idol of France, surnamed 'the Father of the Poor', who never received anything from anyone and gave everything to everyone— was most adequately revenged. Though the people little understood this inexhaustible pitcher of bounty which poured forth benefits and never required replenishment, they remembered him in the day of their power.[33]

Note that Hall ascribes Cagliostro's 'return' to 'Masters of the East'. Another of the Brethren who was instructed in the occult, states Hall, was Benjamin Franklin, yet to play a leading role in the American Revolution. Here Hall ascribed a 'definite organisation of political and religious thought', including some of the most prominent thinkers of the time, stemming from the Rosicrucian fraternity and manifesting in Freemasonry, with the aim of establishing 'philosophic government upon the earth':

> Then appears that charming 'first American gentleman', Dr Benjamin Franklin, who together with the Marquis de Lafayette, played an important role in this drama of empires. While in France, Dr Franklin was privileged to receive definite esoteric instruction. Through all this stormy period, these impressive figures come and go, part of a definite organization of political and religious

33   Hall, *Ibid.*, p. 408.

thought—a functioning body of philosophers represented in Spain by no less an individual than Cervantes, in France by Cagliostro and St-Germain, in Germany by Gichtel and Andreae, in England by Bacon, More, and Raleigh, and in America by Washington and Franklin. Coincident with the Baconian agitation in England, the Fama Fraternitatis and Confessio Fraternitatis appeared in Germany, both of these works being contributions to the establishment of a philosophic government upon the earth. One of the outstanding links between the Rosicrucian Mysteries of the Middle Ages and modern Masonry is Elias Ashmole, the historian of the Order of the Garter and the first Englishman to compile the alchemical writings of the English chemists.[34]

These societies were revolutionary and included the Illuminati. Hall describes their role on history as being seminal, having 'undermined in a subtle manner the entire structure of regal and sacerdotal supremacy':

The foregoing may seem to be a useless recital of inanities, but its purpose is to impress upon the reader's mind the philosophical and political situation in Europe at the time of the inception of the Masonic order. A philosophic clan, as it were, which had moved across the face of Europe under such names as the 'Illuminati' and the 'Rosicrucians', had undermined in a subtle manner the entire structure of regal and sacerdotal supremacy. The founders of Freemasonry were all men who were more or less identified with the progressive tendencies of their day. Mystics, philosophers, and alchemists were all bound together with a secret tie and dedicated to the emancipation of humanity from ignorance and oppression. In my researches among ancient books and manuscripts, I have pieced together a little story of probabilities, which has a direct bearing upon the subject. Long before the establishment of Freemasonry as a

34   Hall, *Ibid.*, p. 409.

fraternity, a group of mystics founded in Europe what was called the 'Society of Unknown Philosophers'. Prominent among the profound thinkers who formed the membership of this society were the alchemists, who were engaged in transmuting the political and religious 'base metal' of Europe into ethical and spiritual 'gold'; the Cabbalists who, as investigators of the superior orders of Nature, sought to discover a stable foundation for human government; and lastly the astrologers who, from a study of the procession of the heavenly bodies, hoped to find therein the rational archetype for all mundane procedure. Here and there is to be found a character that contacted this society. By some it is believed that both Martin Luther and also that great mystic, Philip Melanchthon, were connected with it.[35]

The Anti-Tradition Hall is describing, controlled by a Counter-Traditionalist cabal of 'unknown philosophers' is more far-reaching than anything described by Barruel or Robison, but comes from a high adept of Masonry. This higher initiatory body of occult adepts continues to exist, according to Hall:

The whole structure of Freemasonry is founded upon the activities of this secret society of Central European adepts. The outer body of Masonic philosophy was merely the veil of this cabbalistic order whose members were the custodians of the true Arcanum. Does this inner and secret brotherhood of initiates still exist independent of the Freemasonic order? Evidence points to the fact that it does.[36]

Just how seriously Hall is taken by other Masons is indicated by his having been initiated into the 33° in 1973, the highest Degree of the Scottish Rite being conferred on him by the Supreme Council.[37] In 1985 he was awarded The Grand Cross of Scottish

---

35   Hall, *Ibid.,* pp. 409-410.

36   Hall, *Ibid.,* p. 412.

37   Manly P Hall Archive.

Rite Freemasonry, Southern Jurisdiction, Washington, D.C. Hall is, whatever objections might be raised as to his historical claims, recognised as an honoured authority by a leading body of the Counter-Tradition.

Freemasonry

The parent body of Freemasonry, the United Grand Lodge (UGL), regards as 'irrregular' the Grand Orient de France (GODF), Scottish Rite, Universal Co-Masonry, etc. These 'irregulars' however are the basis of the Anti-Tradition and the vehicles of the Counter-Tradition; the 'Black Adepts'. Furthermore, all these 'irregular' rites trace their origins to the Grand Lodge which, as we have seen, was itself conceived as a subversive movement from Rosicrucians or what Hall called the 'Society of Unknown Philosophers'. Furthermore the Grand Lodge Masons, although the best known form of Masonry in the English-speaking countries, are far from being the dominant form of Masonry in the world.

The Grand Orient de France, although not recognised by Grand Lodge, nonetheless gives a succinct account of the origins of Freemasonry in Britian in explaining its own origins, which will be examined in the section following.

> Modern freemasonry is an institution, which will soon be 300 years old. It descends directly, or in a symbolic way, from the medieval stonemasons who, for several centuries, travelled throughout the whole of Europe putting up religious or non-religious buildings, most of which are still in existence today.[38]

The secret – and sacred - bond between these guild craftsmen appealed to the imaginations of ambitious bourgeois and debased nobility and a coterie of scientists who formed the Royal Society. The craft guilds were a genuine sacred Tradition, whose

---

38   Grand Orient de France, *'History'*.

purposes were corrupted by the Counter-Tradition. To the idea of craft guilds was grafted a complexity of ritual and allegory based around the myth of the stone masons involved in the building of the Temple of Solomon. These ancient masons were held to possess the secrets of sacred geometry. Other influences from gnostics, alchemists, Rosicrucians, the ancient mystery religions, and sundry varieties of occultism combined with scientific enquiry. This synthesis of mysticism with rationalism was to form the revolutionary illuminist secret societies that led to both communism, and the liberal-democratic creed we now take for granted in the modern West. It explains how atheists could unite with occultists, in the same underground movements to overthrow the Traditional social order. The Grand Orient description continues:

> They used to gather together on the evening to prepare their work for the following day and teach their apprentices their art, the art of building; in a communal house they called a lodge. In England, in 1717, when the great period of building of this type was over and the masonic builders grew scarcer, people who had been in contact with them although they themselves were not builders by trade and who called themselves Accepted Masons, particularly members of the Royal Society, a learned society of the time, took up the tradition and created the Great Lodge in London.

> After the Freemasonry of the cathedral builders, Accepted Freemasonry where the builders who had accepted into their lodge people who were not of their trade, the period which today we call that of Speculative Freemasonry began, a period when it is no longer building materials but ideas which are used for building...[39]

After 1717, London's Grand Lodge quickly spread throughout the British Empire. Beyond the British sphere it assumed exotic

39   Grand Orient de France, *ibid.*

forms, some at variance with the Grand Lodge's doctrines that still professed to be Christian and abjured 'stupid atheists'. This is an example of what Evola, described previously, called 'replacing infiltrations' where Counter–Tradition takes over an institution and completely converts it, until such time as the lower level initiates no longer know the true origins of the institution. In this instance the disaffected middle class and sections of nobility grafted themselves onto the Traditional associations of craftsmen's' guilds. Anti-Traditionalists infiltrated, subverted and usurped the institutions of Tradition: the venerable Medieval guilds that had been the foundation of the Traditional social order of Europe for centuries, became a subversive antithesis.

Grand Orient de France

The Grand Orient de France (GODF) is, like the subsequent Illuminati, a specifically revolutionary form of Masonry. It has played a major role in the revolutionary upheavals of Europe and Latin America. Despite the attempts of Grand Lodge Masons and others to discredit such claims as paranoid conspiracy theories, the present-day GODF is open about its revolutionary role. The GODF states that Masonry reached France from England via 'seafarers and traders [and the] first Masonic Lodges were set up in France between 1726 and 1730, particularly in ports such as Bordeaux and Dunkerque'. GODF maintains its revolutionary legacy and claims to be continuing the ideals of the French Revolution. The GODF also states the distinctions between the Grand Lodge and GODF:

> But in this period when the new ideas of Liberty, and Equality were to be born, which would lead to the French Revolution and the Republic, France entered the age of enlightenment. From being a sort of 'Club' as in England, the Masonic Lodges which very quickly spread in our country became a sounding board for these great new ideas and turned into places where debates about the emancipation of Man and Society took place. The Grand

Grand Orient de France, in Rue Cadet, Paris.

Orient de France which was set up in 1733 and was, until the end of the 19th century, the only Masonic Order in France, is still fighting for these ideals.[40]

However, where did the revolutionary doctrines originate? From English Masons and Rosicrucians. One of the major figures, the philosopher John Locke, a seminal founder of Liberalism, influenced Voltaire, Rousseau et al. He is reported by 'the famous Dr Oliver' in the *Freemasons' Quarterly Review* (1840) as having been initiated, with an allusion to letters by Locke dated March 30 to July 2, 1696.[41] UGL Masons are pleased to boast of their influence on politics when speaking among themselves, and lauding the 'progressive' and 'enlightened' ideas for which they claim credit, if not as originators then at least as carriers.

The motto of the GODF remains that of the French Revolution: 'Liberty, Equality, and Fraternity'. That is to say, the French

40   Grand Orient de France, '*History*'.
41   Ronald Paul Ng, '*The Age of Enlightenment and Freemasonry*'.

Revolutionaries adopted the motto from the Freemasons. The GODF adds:

> Thus Lafayette received a sword from George Washington in honour of the part played by French Freemasons in the American War of Independence. In this way, the preparation of the ideas of Liberty and Equality in the Masonic Lodges contributed to the great reforms of the French Revolution.[42]

The GODF boasts of its continuing influence in France and further afield, to the extent that its doctrines can permeate society, and become law and custom within months:

> These 950 Lodges throughout France and the world composed of people from different horizons - professionally, socially, culturally, philosophically, politically - enables us to have the most credible views possible and make suggestions for improvements which are often brought into force in the country within a few months.[43]

The GODF claims to be continuing the legacy of various revolutionary thinkers and activists including the most extreme anarchists Blanqui and Bakunin (Bakounine), who will be considered further:

> For the freemasons of the Grand Orient de France, the search for progress has always been the force behind their reflection and their activities, to such an extent that this principle is an integral part of the tradition of this form of Masonry. We are the heirs of men and women who all, in their own way, worked to improve Humankind: Voltaire, La Fayette, Garibaldi, Auguste Blanqui, Victor Schoelcher, Emir Abd-El-Kader, Louise Michel, Bakounine, Jean Zay, Félix Eboué, Pierre Brossolette and so many others.[44]

---

42   Grand Orient de France, *'History'*.

43   Grand Orient de France, *'History'*.

44   Grand Orient de France, *'History'*.

Strict Observance

We have already considered something of the Strict Observance in regard to Cagliostro. Karl Gotthelf von Hund formed the Strict Observance, claiming Templar origins, circa 1760, having studied Masonry in France. In what became a tradition among all manner of occult societies to the present day, he claimed that at the head of his Order were Unknown Superiors. For a time Hund dominated German Masonry, and was courted by princes who hoped to gain both wealth and political influence.[45] There was a close association between the Strict Observance, the Illuminati and Cagliostro's Egyptian Rite.

Antient & Accepted Scottish Rite

The Scottish Rite was formed in France in 1747 as Ecossais (Scots Masters Lodge) by Estienne Morin, on Saint-Domingue, conferring 25 extra degrees with the authority of the French Grand Lodge. It spread to Germany within several years. Like Freemasons in general, who had no genuine kinship with the guild stonemasons, the Scottish Rite no more kinship with the Scots, than Mizraim Masonry has with Egyptians. It is yet one more affectation.

The Scottish Rite was taken to America in 1761, the year that Morin had been conferred by the French Grand Lodge with the title: 'Grand Inspector for all parts of the New World'. The 33 degrees of the Scottish Rite were established by the Supreme Council for the Antient & Accepted Scottish Rite, convened in Charleston, South Carolina in 1801.[46] It is from this Supreme Council, now based in Washington, that all other Supreme Councils directly or indirectly derive their authority.[47] A Supreme Council of the Scottish Rite was established in England in 1801. The Scottish Rite has spread throughout the world from Europe to Latin America, and will be considered further, particularly in regard to its political role in Mexico.

---

45   Partner, pp. 117-120.

46   Jackson, p. 45.

47   Pick, p. 238.

The Scottish Rite succinctly expresses its creed, which is readily seen to be the communistic doctrine of the Grand Orient and of the Illuminati: 'Human progress is our cause, liberty of thought our supreme wish, freedom of conscience our mission, and the guarantee of equal rights to all people everywhere our ultimate goal'.[48]

How this creed of 'liberty' worked out can be seen in the events of early 20th century Mexico where, when the Scottish Rite established its political control, a bloody persecution of the Catholic peasantry ensued, reminiscent of the Jacobin genocide of the Vendées.

Martinism & the Rites of Memphis and Mizraim

Cagliostro established an 'Egyptian Rite' at The Hague in 1775, which recruited women, and can therefore be regarded as a precursor to Co-Masonry. We have previously encountered Cagliostro in reviewing Iain McCalman's generally useful biography. Cagliostro was feted throughout Europe by Freemasons and in Royal Courts as a miracle worker, physician and psychic. A laudatory biography by Lewis Spence states that Mizraim Masonry preached the communistic doctrines of the Illuminati including feminism and republicanism. Indeed, we have previously seen that Cagliostro was initiated into the Illuminati by adepts of the Strict Observance.

In 1785 Cagliostro was implicated in a scandal in the French Royal Court – the infamous necklace affair - and exiled himself to England where he wrote revolutionary propaganda against the monarchy and declared that the French Throne would be overthrown by Revolution. His 1786 Letter to the French People declared prophetically that the Bastille would be stormed and the governor killed. Spence states that Mizraim Masonry had been set up to subvert the traditional society of Europe, and received large financial backing:

48   Scottish Rite Creed.

There is a small question either that the various Masonic lodges which he founded and which were patronised by persons of ample means, provided him with extensive funds, and it is a known fact that he was subsidised by several extremely wealthy men, who, themselves dissatisfied with the state of affairs in Europe, did not hesitate to place their riches at his disposal for the purpose of undermining the tyrannic powers which then wielded sway.[49]

Despite his infamy as a charlatan Cagliostro was accorded great honours by Masonry. When he arrived at Lyons in 1784 hundreds of Masons left their previous Lodges to join his new 'Egyptian' lodge, La Sagesse Triomphante, in what he called the 'true and ancient order of the Higher Rituals of Egyptian Free Masonry', with himself as the Grand Copt.[50] In 1785 the Lodge of Philalèthes in Paris met to discuss the character and future of Masonry. Their number included French and Austrian princes, bankers, military men and diplomats, 'two professors of magic', and M de Langes, 'a royal banker who had been prominent in the old Illuminati'. Many of the Philalèthes adepts joined Cagliostro.[51]

Cagliostro was arrested by the Inquisition in 1789 in Rome whilst attempting to establish Mizraim there. He died in prison in 1795. However, despite McCalman's assessment, Cagliostro was no naïve adventurer who got into some wrong company. He 'prophesied' revolution against the French Royals. Upon his release from prison in France in 1785 he was greeted by a crowd of 8000 as a hero against Royal oppression.[52]

Martinism

Martinism originates with a Cabalistic mystic and Illuminatist, Martinez de Pasquales, who founded the Order of Elect Priests

---

49 Lewis Spence, p. 92.

50 Hancock and Bauval, p. 363.

51 Evans, 1927, cited by Hancock and Bauval, p. 403.

52 Hancock and Bauval, p. 377.

(Elus-Cohen) in Paris in 1754.[53] In discussing the allegations of Jewish involvement in Masonry as a motive for anti-Semitism, the prominent 19th century Jewish author Bernard Lazare alludes to M de Pasquales' role in the Illuminati: 'There were Jews in the circle around Weishaupt, and a Jew of Portuguese origin, Martinez de Pasquales, established numerous groups of Illuminati in France and gathered a large number of disciples'.[54]

Louis Claude de Saint-Martin was initiated into de Pasquales' Order of Elect Priests in 1765, and became his personal secretary in1771.[55] Louis Claude is described by his adherents as 'one of the most important personages of Illuminism'.[56] In 1772 de Pasquales left for Haiti, and the high adepts of the Order of Elect Priests joined the Strict Observance, Von Hund's Order based in Germany. Louis Claude however studied Rosicrucianism and a society of initiates arose around him.[57] He moved about revolutionary France undisturbed, and was asked to teach at the Ecole Normal, a school with the aim of shaping a new generation of teachers for Revolutionary France.

With his death in 1803, Louis Claude's legacy was not resumed until taken up by the French occultist Papus (Dr Gérard Encausse) and Augustin Chaboseau in 1888, who founded the Martinist Order.[58] The formal alliance with Rosicrucianism was established in 1939 when Ralph Maxwell Lewis, Imperator of the Ancient and Mystic Order of the Rose-Cross (AMORC) was initiated as a Martinist and, with war looming in Europe, Martinist documents necessary for the continuation of the Order were entrusted to Lewis, and the Imperator of AMORC in the USA assumed the role of Sovereign Grand Master of the

---

53   Traditional Martinist Order, p. 4.

54   Lazare, p. 153.

55   Traditional Martinist Order, p. 6.

56   *Ibid.*, p. 4.

57   *Ibid.*, p. 9.

58   *Ibid.*, p. 10.

Martinist Supreme Council,[59] although this was not the only continuation of Martinism.

Memphis

The Memphis-Rite was introduced to the USA in 1862, and to England in 1872 by John Yarker. Under Yarker's jurisdiction, Memphis and Misraim (or Mizraim) combined. This unification was called The Antient and Primitive Rite of Memphis and Misraim, or Memphis-Misraim. Memphis-Mizraim was attached to Martinism, as shown by a present-day paper from a Martinist Order, on the history of Martinism, stating of the period of the 1930s:

> It had an outer circle in the 'College d'Occultisme' in Paris, and an antechamber to the Order, the two lodges of Memphis-Mizraim, 'La Jerusalem Egytienne' and 'L'Age Nouveau', provided the Masonic qualifications required for Martinist membership who had to progressively take degrees in Memphis-Mizraim as successive prerequisites to admittance to the Martinist degrees of Initiate and then Superior Unknown.[60]

Martinism is described as 'being intimately intertwined with the teachings of Illuminism, whose influence is felt across Europe and clear into Russia', and as the 'continuation of the work of the Illuminist movement', based on the teachings of the 18th century alchemist St Germain, whose teachings included occultism and 'political philosophy', 'allied to the Illuminati'. The present Bulgarian branch of Memphis-Mizraim states of these teachings, 'These were cultivated in Rosicrucian, Masonic, and Illuminati Lodges', through 'Asiatic Brethren, the Fratres Lucis, the Illuminati and other 'LVX' brotherhoods, and the Philosophers of Light who preceded them. The Martinist Order was incorporated into the Oriental Rites of Memphis and

---

59   *Ibid.*, p. 12.

60   Rose Croix Martinist Order of Ontario.

Mizraim, which work 90° and 96° respectively.[61] Hence, these rites are all conjoined and claim a legacy from the Illuminati.

Rene Guénon was initiated into Martinism by Papus and into Memphis-Mizraim. Guénon founded a Masonic lodge, The Great Triad, in France, with the intention of setting up a genuine Traditionalist system in opposition to the Anti-Traditional and Counter-Traditional currents that control Masonry. When he intended founding a new 'Templar'[62] order Guénon came up against Papus, who proscribed Guénon's Order in 1909.

The 'Perfectibilists': Order of the Illuminati

Professor Adam Weishaupt founded the Order of the Illuminati as a revolutionary society within Masonry in Bavaria in 1776. The original name was the Order of Perfectibilists.[63] It is important to note this doctrine of 'perfectibilism' as it had its origins in 18th century Rationalism and the Enlightenment, and is based on the assumption of the 'perfectibility' of humanity by means of what is now called social engineering.

According to this doctrine, humanity is infinitely malleable, putty in the hands of self-appointed improvers. This perfectibility of humanity is the stated aim of Masonry, symbolised by the rough hewn 'ashlar' or stone block, representing humanity, chiselled into smoothness by Masons. This doctrine found its most excessive expression first in the Reign of Terror inaugurated by the French Revolution, then under Communism. In its 'softer' version it is the same doctrine now considered normal and 'democratic', based on the doctrine of environmentalism: change the environment and humanity is changed; perfect the environment and humanity is

---

61 Ancient & Primitive Rite of Memphis-Mizraim, Bulgaria, '*History*'.

62 There are many different types of mystic who claim the Templar legacy, including both Traditionalists like Guénon and Anti-Traditionalists grafting 'Templar' degrees onto Masonry. Franz von Liebenfels for example founded his Order of New Templars in Austria based on a racist theology antithetical to the liberal doctrines of others claiming to be 'Templars'.

63 Porter, p. 27.

perfected. It is the doctrine that shaped the Jacobin Declaration of the Rights of Man, the US Declaration of Independence, the United Nations Universal Declaration of Human Rights, and ongoing declarations from the UNO and the like; all based on the 18th century doctrine of human 'perfectibility' by chiselling away at the block of humanity. The problem is that when the block does not shape up to the desired result, the mason of 'perfectibility', whether calling himself a Communist or a Liberal, keeps chiselling away until there is nothing left. That is the doctrine behind both Communism and Liberal-democracy, and it is fallacious. The Jacobin and Bolshevik regimes soon resorted to mass terror because this doctrine, being a fraud, does not work in practise and can only be maintained by tyranny, under the banner of 'liberty'.

The doctrine of 'perfectibility' would, stated Weishaupt, free man from religion, rank and wealth, and establish a state of 'liberty and moral equality' to achieve 'universal happiness' and 'freedom'. This would be achieved by the 'Illumination' of 'reason'.[64] 'And what is the general objective? THE HAPPINESS OF THE HUMAN RACE'.[65] At the lower grade of 'Noviciate' the Illuminatus was told that the Order represented 'the perfection of Christianity', the doctrines of which would be imparted to him at the higher degrees, but for the moment he can know that the aim is 'establishing an universal equality of condition and religion, through the checking of the tyranny of princes, nobles and priests'.[66]

Weishaupt was initiated into the Strict Observance in 1777. By 1782 the Illuminati had approximately three hundred members in Germany, Austria, Italy, Grenoble, Lyon and Strasbourg, and later in Bohemia, Milan and Hungary.[67] Baron Von Knigge, a Mason, joined in Frankfurt in 1780. Knigge was more mystically

64   Robison, p. 64.

65   *Ibid.*, p. 65.

66   *Ibid.*, p. 75

67   Roberts, p. 125.

inclined than the rationalist Weishaupt. Under Von Knigge's influence new grades required that the higher levels were only achieved by Freemasons.[68]

In 1783 a Bavarian Court of enquiry began its investigation of the Order.[69] On 23 June 1784 the Bavarian Elector, Karl Theodor, published an edict prohibiting secret societies. On March 2, 1785 another edict was published condemning Freemasons and Illuminati explicitly. Weishaupt had already fled. In 1786 Illuminatist Franz Xavier von Zwack's lodgings were raided after he had left Bavaria, and hundreds of papers were seized and published the following year.

Weishaupt defended himself with his Apologie der Illuminaten in 1786 and two further volumes the following year. The Bavarian authorities published further papers in 1787. Knigge published an account of the Illuminati in 1788. Both Professor Robison and the Abbé Barruel extensively used these officially published papers when writing on the Illuminati and Freemasonry.

On August 16 1787 a Bavarian edict prescribed the death penalty for recruiting for the Illuminati. However Professor Robison viewed the end of the Illuminati after its prohibition as unlikely. He considered that the Illuminati continued through 'reading societies' and a new group called the German Union. Citing documents circulating at the time under the name of the German Union, Robison concluded that the doctrine was the same as that of the Illuminati. One primary aim was to recruit eminent writers. This was also a stated aim of Weishaupt.[70] Publicly the German Union would be known as a 'Literary Society'.[71]

Given that the Illuminati was perhaps the first to be structured on a cell system, where only a few members knew the identity

---

68   Roberts, p. 126.

69   Robison, v.

70   Robison, p. 168.

71   Robison, p. 169.

of their immediate superior, it seems naïve to believe that Royal edicts would eliminate the Illuminati, any more than State prohibitions against the similarly organised Communist parties of our own time are sufficient to eliminate Communism, of which the Illuminati was a precursor.

Bohemian Grove, Illuminati & The Owl

While the All Seeing Eye and Pyramid motif are continuously referred to in anti-Masonic literature as the symbol of the Illuminati, I have not seen any evidence for this. Rather the symbol seems to have been that of an Owl holding an opened book. This symbol is minted into two types of Illuminati seals for the Grade of Minerval. Across the pages of the open book are the initials PMCV : *Per Me Caeci Vident* ('Through Me the Blind Become Sighted'). A laurel leaf surrounds the image.[72]

While Lodge 322, The Order of the Skull & Bones, described below, is often regarded as an American successor to the Illuminati, another secretive conclave of American wire-pullers, the Bohemian Club, has as its emblem a brazen Owl, one version before which rituals are performed, being of giant stature,[73] which makes the common symbology between the Bohemians and the Illuminati a fascinating avenue for hypothesis. Considering the importance attached to symbolism in the esoteric societies, this common symbology is something that should at least be noted. The owl was also used as the symbol for the Illuminati 'church', Freising Minerval Church, in which it stands atop an open book, across which are the initials SEMT: *Sigil Ecclesiastic Minerva Thebes* ('Seal of the Freisling Minerval Church').[74]

Burnett dismisses the influence of the Bohemian Club, founded as a club for drunken revelry by journalists in San Francisco

---

72   Howard, p. 4.

73   Howard, p. 5

74   For illustrations of the Illuminati Minerval Seals and the Bohemian Club see: T Melanson.

Emblem above the entrance to the Bohemian Club in Taylor St, San Fransisco.

in 1872, with the same levity as that applied to Lodge 322 as just a 'Yale frat', and to the Illuminati as just a 'reading society'. While mentioning that the Bohemians are 'usually entertained by serious speakers', that their membership has included most U.S. presidents, and that deals are struck at the Bohemian Grove where 'politicians mix with industrialists, financiers and stars from the entertainment world in a relatively secure theme park', all this is just a harmless expression of nostalgia for one's Frat days at college, 'that pays homage to the college fraternities these powerful men obviously sorely miss'. Like Skull & Bones and the Illuminati, Burnett is assured that there is no sinister intent, in this instance because of the long tradition of drunken hi-jinx:

> Claims are made by conspiracy theorists that some of the major decisions concerning the military industrial complex have been made at Bohemian Grove, citing the case of Grover Edward Teller, the father of the H-bomb. Somehow the association of thermonuclear weapons systems and drunken urination in the woods of California seems too surreal. Theorists become too sidetracked on the bizarre aspects of the Owl ritual and its simulated human sacrifice, and seldom delve into the origins of the summer camp and who exactly controls the event.

Future U.S. presidents, Ronald Reagan and Richard Nixon, are pictured with Harvey Hancock (standing) at Bohemian Grove in the summer of 1967.

As an organization of powerful men who want to get drunk, dress up as prostitutes with fake breasts and fishnets and let off steam in crazy, fraternity-style antics, Bohemian Grove is without equal. As a source of secret control over the United States' domestic and foreign policy, it has to be consigned to its own funeral pyre.[75]

Another opinion on 'the Grove' has been provided in a Doctoral dissertation by Peter Phillips, and can be read online.[76]

---

75   Burnett, pp. 31-32.

76   Phillips, 1994. https://www.counterpunch.org/2003/08/13/inside-bohemian-grove/

Lodge 322 - Order of the Skull & Bones

Let me warn you that your enemies are numerous, industrious and daring, full of subtlety, and full of zeal, nay some of them are your own brethren, and endeared to you by ties of nature. The contest is therefore fraught with hazard and alarm. Were it a war of arms, we would have little to dread. It is a war of arts, of enchantments. A war against the magicians of Egypt in which no weapons avail but the rod of God. — Yale University President Timothy Dwight, 1801.[77]

What is one to make, however of the claims by Burnett that such societies cannot be taken seriously because of the juvenile antics of their members? Is there nothing more to such shenanigans among the rich and powerful than a discrete way of 'letting off steam'? Alternatively, could not such antics serve a more serious purpose of breaking down ego barriers as a means of recreating that individual as someone bonded to the group?

Antony Sutton, in citing a ground-breaking article on Lodge 322 by journalist Ron Rosenbaum for Esquire in 1977, states of the initiation of some of America's elite: 'Supreme Court Justice Potter Stewart... dressed up in a skeleton suit, howled wildly at an initiate in a red velvet room inside the tomb...' McGeorge Bundy, whose family has a long association with Lodge 322 as well as providing personnel for the top echelons of the U.S. Establishment[78] who served as Special Assistant on National Security Affairs (1961-1966) to Presidents Kennedy and Johnson, and as President of the Ford Foundation, 'wrestled naked in a pile of mud as part of his initiation'.[79] Rosenbaum, referring to a 1940 initiation notes:

New man placed in coffin – carried into central part of building. New man chanted over and reborn into society.

---

77   Quoted in Dunn, p. 32. Three decades later Lodge 322 was established at Yale.

78   Sutton, 1984, pp. 57-64.

79   Sutton, *Ibid.*, p. 7.

Removed from coffin and given robes with symbols on it (sic). A bone with his name on it is tossed into bone heap at start of evening. Initiates plunge naked into a mud pile.[80]

The basis of the Lodge 322 initiation rite is Masonic, with the predominance of skull and skeleton symbolism and the use of a coffin to symbolise the death and rebirth of the initiate.

Sutton wrote on the ramifications and history of Lodge 322 in a series of volumes after a disgruntled member had given him the complete membership rosters.[81]

During the closing years of the 18th century there emerged what has been called 'Illuminati scares'.[82] In 1798 Reverend Jedidiah Morse addressed his Boston congregation on the danger of the society that aimed 'to root out and abolish Christianity, and overthrow all civil government', to promote libertinage, abolish private property, condemn patriotism and justify suicide.[83] The preacher's warnings spread throughout New England and reached George Washington and President John Adams, both of whom concurred that concerns were justified.[84] Despite the ridicule that today's writers such as Porter give this 'scare', Washington, as a highly honoured Freemason was surely in a position to judge such concerns and expressed himself thus, alluding to the Democratic party that was founded by Thomas Jefferson in 1792:

It was not my intention to doubt that the doctrines of the Illuminati and the principles of Jacobinism had not spread in the United States. On the contrary, no one is more satisfied of this fact than I am. The idea I meant to convey, was, that I did not believe that the lodges of Freemasons

80   Sutton, *ibid.*
81   Sutton, 1983, p. 19.
82   Porter, p. 83.
83   Porter, *ibid.*
84   Porter, p. 84.

Lodge 322 members - standing 6th left is George H W Bush.

in this country had, as societies, endeavoured to propagate the diabolical tenets of the first, or pernicious principles of the latter. That individuals of them may have done it, or that the founder or instruments employed to have found the democratic societies in the United States may have had this object, and actually had a separation of the people from their government in view, is too evident to be questioned. [85]

Thomas Jefferson, in response to such concerns, expressed himself in sympathy with Weishaupt, whom he termed an 'enthusiastic philanthropist, believing in the 'infinite perfectibility of man'.[86] Drawing on the Illuminati documents released by the Bavarian authorities, Professor Robison had mentioned the presence of 'several' Illuminati lodges in America prior to 1786.[87] Sutton believed that Lodge 322, founded in 1832 by William Huntington Russell and Alphonso Taft as an American chapter of an unnamed German university society, raised the possibility that the Illuminati reached the USA directly from Germany.

---

85   Letter from Washington, dated October 24, 1798. Washington, Vol. 20, p. 518.

86   Jefferson to James Maddison, January 1800, quoted by Porter, p. 104.

87   Robison, p. 116.

Lodge 322 has attracted some attention occasionally, particularly during the 2004 presidential election when some wondered about both contenders, Bush and John Kerry, being 'Bonesmen'. Lodge 322 is at times the subject of lampooning, which could be considered to its advantage. To consider Lodge 322 as just another student 'Frat' at Yale full of youthful hi-jinx, as contended by Thom Burnett, is to misunderstand its history and influence. Actually, U.S. college fraternities, not just Lodge 322, often establish 'old boys' networks in business and politics and also often have crypto-Masonic symbolism.

Lodge 322 only 'taps' 15 candidates annually at their final year at Yale. At any one time it has about 600 living members. It is therefore organised with the view towards post-graduate membership, and members continue to meet on 'Deer Island'. Despite the occasional publicity, very little is known about the aims of Lodge 322, and nothing is known about their retreats on Deer Island.

In 2003 CBS '60 Minutes' ran a documentary on Lodge 322 based on the findings of Yale graduate and New Yorker staff member Alexandra Robbins, author of *Secrets of the Tomb*. Veteran interviewer Morley Safer stated by way of introduction: 'Skull & Bones is an elite secret society at Yale University that includes some of the most powerful men of the 20th century'. Robbins stated: 'Apart from presidents, Bones has included Cabinet officers, spies, Supreme Court justices, statesmen and captains of industry'. Robbins said she was able to talk to about 100 disgruntled members of Lodge 322, but about twice as many refused to comment, and she was subjected to harassment and threats.[88]

An historical address given by Timothy White (initiated 1849) had the theme: 'An Historical Discourse Pronounced before our Venerable Order on the Thirtieth Anniversary of the Foundation of our American Chapter in New Haven July 30th 1863'.[89] The description of Lodge 322 as the 'American Chapter' implies that

---

88   CBS 60 Minutes.

89   Although Lodge 322 was founded in 1832 the first meeting was 1833.

it is a branch of a parent body from outside the USA. Sutton cites an anonymous pamphlet distributed at Yale in 1876 called *Skull & Bones* relating a break-in of the Lodge Temple. He reproduced the pamphlet. It refers to Russell as having been in Germany where he was initiated into a society, which he brought back to Yale. According to the anonymous author, what he saw when breaking into the Lodge Temple, were rooms adorned with German phrases and slogans attesting to the German origins. The description of the Temple interior mentions a card reading: 'From the German chapter. Presented to Patriarch D C Gilman of D. 50'.[90]

The most compelling association between Lodge 322 and Weishaupt's Illuminati is the common motto of both from a phrase by eminent German dramatist, playwright and Freemason Gotthold Lessing[91]. Above the arched chamber of Lodge 322's initiation room a sign reads in German:

Wer war der Thor, wer Weiser, Bettler oder Kaiser? Ob Arm, ob Reich, in Tode gleich.[92]

Robison, drawing on the Illuminati documents released by the Bavarian authorities, gave the initiation ceremony of the Illuminati Degree of Regent, one of the highest degrees:

The candidate is presented for reception in the character of a slave; and it is demanded of him what has brought him into this most miserable of all conditions. He answers – Society – the State – Submissiveness – False Religion. A skeleton is pointed out to him at the feet of which are

---

90   Sutton, 1986, p. 58. Sutton had been a Research Fellow at the Hoover Institute, Stanford University, and had been a professor of economics at California State University. He was a specialist on Soviet technology and had written a three-volume study of Western technological transfers to the USSR, summarised in National Suicide.

91   Lessing became a Master Mason in the Hamburg Lodge, 1770. Mackey states: 'Lessing was initiated in a Lodge at Hamburg, and took great interest in the Institution'. (Mackey, *Encyclopaedia of Freemasonry,* entry: 'Gottfried Lessing')

92   'Who was the fool, who was the wise man, beggar or king? Whether poor or rich, all's the same in death'. (Sutton, 1986, p. 58).

laid a Crown and a Sword. He is asked whether that is the skeleton of a King, a Nobleman or a Beggar? As he cannot decide, the President of the meeting says to him, 'the character of being a Man is the only one that is of importance'.[93]

A description of the Lodge 322 initiation rite from 1940 includes the initiate emerging reborn from a coffin. Again, there is similarity here with both the Masonic and Illuminati initiations. The symbol of Lodge 322, as the informal name, Order of the Skull and Bones, suggests, is a skull-and-crossbones. Explaining the significance of the skull and bones in Masonry with an allusion to the initiation, as well as the symbolic rebirth from a grave (coffin) John Lord, Senior Lecturer in Art History at the University of Lincoln, states:

> A third associated strand comes with freemasonry, which uses the skull and crossbones as a symbol of mortality. In one layer of initiation the candidate is lowered into a representation of a grave, which has within it a skull and crossbones.[94]

When the running of two 'Bonesmen' for the 2004 presidential elections directed some public attention towards The Order, Don Oldenburg wrote in the Washington Post:

> It's no secret that Bush and Kerry are both Yalies. Bush graduated in 1968, Kerry in '66. It's no secret either that they both come from privileged preppy backgrounds. What remains shrouded in mystery is their membership in Skull and Bones, an elite, covert club for which involvement continues long past the last refrain of 'Pomp and Circumstance' on graduation day.
>
> 'What is so staggering about two Bonesmen running

93   Robison, p. 110.
94   John Lord, 'Skull and Crossbones'.

against each other for president is that it's a tiny club with 15 members a year and only 600-some living at any time. What are the odds?' says Alexandra Robbins, author of the 2002 book Secrets of the Tomb: Skull and Bones, the Ivy League, and the Hidden Paths of Power.[95]

Despite some public misgivings and questions by the news media, both Bush and Kerry regarded their oath of secrecy as of first importance. Oldenberg writes that when questioned on their Lodge membership, both refused to comment and referred to their oath:

Don't bother asking Bush and Kerry the odds. Both would rather advocate raising taxes. Neither talks publicly about Skull and Bones – except to say he can't talk about it.

Neither man responded to repeated requests for interviews for this article. But when Tim Russert asked Bush about Skull and Bones in February on 'Meet the Press,' the president said: 'It's so secret we can't talk about it.' When Russert asked Kerry last August what it meant that both he and Bush are Bonesmen, the Massachusetts senator replied: 'Not much because it's a secret.'[96]

Oldenberg gives some indication as to the prominence of 'Bonesmen':

A roster of Bones alumni, known as 'patriarchs,' surfaced in the mid-1980s. Included are names of the nation's oldest, wealthiest and most powerful dynasties – Whitney, Adams, Lord, Rockefeller, Payne, Pillsbury, Weyerhaeuser. Other famous names on the list: poet Archibald MacLeish; writer John Hersey; political commentator William F. Buckley; Time-Life founder Henry Luce; investment banker Dean Witter Jr. and Morgan Stanley founder Harold Stanley,

---

95   Don Oldenburg, 'Bush, Kerry Share Tippy-Top Secret'.

96   Don Oldenburg, ibid.

among others who built Wall Street; diplomat Averill Harriman and FedEx founder Frederick Smith.

Since Bush moved into the White House, he has nominated or appointed at least 10 Bonesmen to prestigious positions – among them the head of the Securities and Exchange Commission, Bill Donaldson, '53; Assistant Attorney General Robert McCallum, '68; General Counsel to the Office of Homeland Security Edward McNally, '79; and his close friend Ambassador to Trinidad and Tobago Roy Austin, '68.[97]

Lodge 322 has a matron goddess, which it calls Eulogia. The Lodge was originally called the Eulogian Club and has been known also as the Knights of Eulogia. In describing Lodge 322 the Canadian Grand Lodge Masons state:

Russell and a group of classmates decided to form the Eulogian Club as an American chapter of a German student organization. The club paid obeisance to Eulogia, the goddess of eloquence, who took her place in the pantheon upon the death of the orator Demosthenes, in 322 B.C., and who is said to have returned in a kind of Second Coming on the occasion of the society's inception. The Yale society fastened a picture of its symbol – a skull and crossbones – to the door of the chapel where it met. Today the number 322, recalling the date of Demosthenes' death, appears on society stationery.[98]

This reference to a 'Second Coming' of the Goddess with the founding of the Lodge, places it in the context of a 'Mystery Tradition'. The goddess of eloquence might have originally been seen as a fitting matron because of the importance that the Illuminati attached to propaganda, particularly through the recruiting of the literati and the formation of literary societies

---

97   Don Oldenburg, *ibid*.

98   Grand Lodge of British Columbia & the Yukon, 'Anti-Masonry'.

as fronts. Alexandra Robbins was able to obtain details of an initiation rite, during which the initiate has a hood placed over him, and 'marched throughout the Tomb on a pseudo-tour, during which the knights and patriarchs shriek in high-pitched voices jokes about the initiate's girlfriend or dog, akin to benign 'yo' mama' cracks".[99] 'Eulogia! Eulogia! Eulogia!' is shrieked as the initiate is escorted to the inner temple and signs an oath of secrecy. The initiate is brought before a picture of Judas Iscariot, whose name the group screams three times, and he is pushed to his knees before a human skull filled with blood, placed at the foot of a skeleton called Madame Pompadour. The Knights and Patriarchs shout 'Drink it! Drink it! Drink it!' and the initiate drinks the blood from the human skull. He is then whipped in the face by the tail of a Bonesman dressed as the Devil, and then brought before a Bonesman dressed as the Pope. The initiate bows down to kiss the Pope's slippered toe resting on the skull.[100] It appears from this rite that Lodge 322 is of a more esoteric nature than is generally supposed and the initiation has the elements characteristic of the revolutionist, anti-clerical doctrines of the Illuminati.

An additional curiosity is the presence in the rite of a skeleton named Madame Pompadour. Marquise de Pompadour (1721-1764) was the mistress of King Louis XV. What is significant here is that she founded her own salon that was frequented by Voltaire and many of the other philosophes who provided the intellectual fermentation that led to the French Revolution. She had long known Voltaire, who acted as her adviser, as she welded considerable influence in the Royal Court. Pompadour was a protagonist for the Encylcopédie of Diderot, et al which provided the intellectual foundation for the Revolution several decades later, and she persuaded Louis XV to allow the sale of the Encylcopédie.[101] Given the other features of the Bonesmen's initiation rite, reminiscent of the subversive versions of Masonry from the 18th century, it is plausible to suggest that the Madame

99   Robbins, p. 119.

100 Robbins, p.120.

101 Hackett, *The Enlightenment And The Age Of Reason In Philosophy*.

Pompadour represented by a human skeleton is in honour of a woman who provided influential patronage to the Masonic philosophers who paved the way for the Revolution.

Theosophy

The Theosophical Society was established by Helena Blavatsky, a Russian mystic, on authority she claimed from 'Hidden Masters' and 'Secret Chiefs' controlling the world from a subterranean centre in Tibet, which has been referred to as Shambhala. Theosophy emanated from several forms of Masonry, and in turn has spawned the current 'New Age' phenomenon. It is one of those 'counterfeits' that were remarked on by Evola and Guénon as seeming to be from the school of Perennial Tradition, yet its universalistic doctrine, under the guise of connecting with all Traditions, becomes a means of obliterating all Traditions and establishing a new syncretic religion. This syncretism is the means by which the Counter-Tradition is establishing a 'world religion' as the spiritual edifice for its 'new world order', and will be considered later. In Guénon's view, the name Theosophical Society is incidental and bears no relationship to theosophy as a study of arcane knowledge from the various Traditions of East and West.[102]

Blavatsky's two-volume work *The Secret Doctrine* claims to have been based on an immeasurably ancient manuscript called The Book of Dzyan, which was shown to her alone by The Hidden Masters. The Theosophical Society describes itself thus:

> The Theosophical Society may be said to have begun when H P Blavatsky (HPB), under instructions from her Adept-Teachers, returned from India in 1871 to found an organization through which the West and the world in general would benefit from the Wisdom Teachings known today as Theosophy.[103]

102 Guénon, *Theosophy: History of a Pseudo-Religion*, p. 4.
103 Theosophical Society, *'Early History'*.

The aim of the Theosophists in common with other Anti-Tradition currents is to create a Universal Republic. The first of its 'Objects' is: 'To form a nucleus of the Universal Brotherhood of Humanity, without distinction of race, creed, sex, caste or colour'.[104]

At Benares in December 1879, a General Council of The Society was held under the title of 'the Theosophical Society, or Universal Brotherhood'. At this meeting the Rules were revised, in the first of which appeared the words: 'The Theosophical Society was formed upon the basis of a Universal Brotherhood of Humanity'. Among the plans declared in Rule 8 appeared the following: (c) 'To promote a feeling of Brotherhood among nations'.[105]

Hence, Theosophy places itself in the current of the Anti-Tradition and in the service of what has been called the 'Black Adepts'. Should there be doubt as to Blavatksy's initiation into the Anti-Tradition, she wrote in 1878 to The Franklin Register of her Masonic initiations into what John Yarker referred to as a 'Branch of Adoptive Masonry' under the jurisdiction of the Grand Orient de France and the Rites of Memphis and Mizraim, recording that she received the 32° in the Ancient and Primitive Rite of England and Wales. The Ancient and Primitive Rite was originally chartered in America, on 9 November 1856, with David McClellan as Grand Master, and in 1862 submitted to the jurisdiction of the Grand Orient de France. Blavatsky was initiated on 24 November 1877 by John Yarker, 33° Sovereign Grand Master; M Caspari, 33° Grand Secretary; A D Loewenstark, 33° Grand Secretary, as Apprentice, Companion, Perfect Mistress, Sublime Elect Scotch Lady, Grand Elect, Chevaliere de Rose Croix, Adoniramite Mistress, Perfect Venerable Mistress, and a Crowned Princess of Rite of Adoption.[106] Blavatsky further writes of her initiation into the 33°, 'from the oldest Masonic body in the world', under the auspices of Yarker. Blavatksy

104 Theosophical Society, '*Objects*'.

105 Theosophical Society, '*Early history*', 'Founders Settle in India'.

106 Yarker, letter, 1929

emphasised that she was initiated into the Rites that are under the jurisdiction of the Grand Orient de France.[107]

Guénon was unequivocal in his opposition to Theosophy as a weapon of the Counter-Tradition, writing a book dedicated to the subject, tellingly called *Theosophy: History of a Pseudo-Religion*. Guénon shows that Theosophy is a façade for destructive purposes, one being, according to Blavatsky's own statement, under the guise of presenting Eastern wisdom to the West, to 'sweep Christianity from the surface of the earth'.[108] He states that according to Blavatsky's own account she was sent from Paris to contact a spiritualist group in the USA and especially to contact future Theosophical luminary Henry Olcott, a Freemason and 'spiritist'.[109] It was from this group of spiritualists that the Theosophical Society emerged.[110]

Guénon, in applying the doctrine of the Traditionalist to examining the doctrine of Theosophy pointed out that its embracing of 'progress' or 'evolution' is contrary to genuine Traditionalism in either East or West. Hence, Theosophists are 'not what they claim to be'; they are not drawing on the Perennial Tradition. Guénon called the Theosophical portrayal of cycles as 'an absurd caricature' of the Hindu – and in general, Perennial Traditionalist – doctrine of cycles.[111]

Drawing on the romantic image of Lucifer as the Light-Bringer to humanity, which became a popular notion among revolutionists and reformers during the 19th century, Blavatsky began the organ of the Theosophical Society in 1887 with the name Lucifer. This Luciferian doctrine is one that she would have found in the Scottish Rite doctrine of Albert Pike.

---

107 Blavatsky, 1878

108 Guénon, *Theosophy: History of a Pseudo-Religion*, p. 2.

109 Guénon, *Ibid.*, pp. 11-12.

110 Guénon, *Ibid.*, p. 20.

111 Guénon, *Ibid.*, pp 98-100.

Luciferianism in Theosophy

Synthesising esoteric, religious and mystical doctrines from a myriad of times and places, Blavatsky stated that according to Eastern occultism light can only manifest from darkness. This also accords with Rosicrucian doctrine, and Blavatsky quotes Robert Fludd: 'Darkness adopted illumination in order to make itself visible'.[112]

In this cosmology 'Light' equates with 'matter' and 'darkness' with pure spirit'. Blavatsky wrote that Lux (Lucifer) 'Luminous son of the Morning [was] transformed by the Church into Lucifer or Satan because he is higher and older than Jehovah and had to be sacrificed to the new dogma'.[113] In this doctrine can be seen the recurrent Masonic and Illuminatist theme of both anti-Catholicism and a Gnostic interpretation that portrays Satan as the 'serpent of wisdom' who liberates humanity from ignorance, and the Christian God, Jehovah, who is a 'lesser demiurge' that holds humanity in bondage.[114]

Drawing from Cabalistic Jewish mystical doctrine in citing the Zohar Blavatsky identifies the 'Black Fire' with 'Absolute Light, which Christianity identifies with the "rebel demons"'. However, 'esoteric philosophy admits neither good nor evil per se, as existing independently of nature'. Within the Kosmos good and evil represent the 'necessity of contraries or contrasts'. This moral relativity applies to devils, angels and humans:

> Thus Lucifer – the spirit of Intellectual Enlightenment and Freedom of Thought – is metaphorically the guiding beacon which helps man to find his way through the rocks and sandbanks of Life, for Lucifer is the Logos in his highest, and the 'Adversary' in his lowest aspect…[115]

---

112 Blavatsky, 1888, Vol. 1, pp. 70-71.

113 Blavatsky, *ibid*.

114 Pagels, pp. 56-57.

115 Blavatsky, 1888, Vol. 2, p. 162.

Hence, Blavatsky identities Satan as the 'lower aspect' of Lucifer, and here Blavatsky had taken on the 19th century romantic image of Satan as revolutionary leader, which will be considered further in regard to the views of Karl Marx and others. She writes of this doctrine:

> Evil is a necessity for progress and evolution, as Night is necessary for the production of Day, and Death for that of Life. Lucifer is divine and terrestrial light, the 'Holy Ghost' and 'Satan', at one and the same time. And now it stands proven that Satan... and Lucifer or 'Light-Bearer' is in us: it is our mind – our Tempter and Redeemer, our intelligent liberator and saviour from pure animalism.[116]

When Anti-Tradition, taking its doctrine from Counter-Tradition, refers to the 'Christ' within the individual, and to connexion with that 'Christ' as the means towards deifying Man, the 'Christ' or 'Redeemer' being referred to is Lucifer, the Light-Bearer and Satan the Adversary. Descriptions of such doctrines as 'true Christianity', 'esoteric Christianity', and the like are a façade that has been used as a trick since at least the time of the Illuminati. The doctrine is that of the so-called 'enlightenment of humanity', or Illuminism, Illuminati meaning the 'Enlightened Ones' who will guide humanity to a new order. Blavatsky is called by her adherents The Light-Bringer.[117] Whether by coincidence or deliberation, it is an acknowledgment of the Illuminatist current in which Theosophy works, and is an acknowledgment to the continuing luciferic current of Theosophy.

Annie Besant: 'New Beginning' for Theosophy

Annie Besant joined the Theosophical Society in 1889. Prior to that she had been a well-known socialist and atheist in England. In 1893 Besant settled in India and mixed Theosophy with agitation against British rule among the Indian bourgeoisie.

---

116 Blavatsky, *Ibid.,* Vol. 2, pp. 513.

117 Theosophical Society, *'Early History'*, 'Enter Annie Besant'.

The Society says of this:

> With Mrs Besant a new era began. She gave a great lead in making Theosophy practical, urging members to apply the light of Theosophy to the various fields of human activity: religious, social, economic, political, etc. For this purpose she instituted the Theosophical Order of Service, and the Sons of India, in 1908.[118]

Besant brought the Theosophical Society into the Anti-Traditionalist current of Illuminism, the Grand Orient and others, by synthesising mystical doctrines with 'social reform'. In 1902 she introduced International Co-Freemasonry into England as the Lodge Human Duty # 6, London, which was consecrated by officers of the Supreme Council Le Droit Humain in 1902. In 1912 she co-founded the Order of the Temple of the Rosy Cross in London.[119]

International Co-Freemasonry, Le Droit Humain, was founded in 1893 as a form of Masonry that includes women. La Droit Humain works the 33° system of the Scottish Rite. Its symbol includes the double headed eagle and reference to 33° that designates allegiance to the Scottish Rite. It embraces the Illuminatist doctrine of 'perfectibilism'. La Droit Humain maintains the revolutionist slogan of the Grand Orient de France: 'liberty, equality, fraternity'.[120] Besant's background was as a 'free thinker' and a Fabian-socialist who had joined the Secular Society and worked for the socialist paper, National Reformer, whose editor, Charles Bradlaugh, was a leader in the atheist movement. Together they wrote a book advocating birth control, and after a six-month jail sentence for 'obscene libel' was overturned Besant wrote a further book on *The Laws of Population.*

---

118 Theosophical Society, *'Early History'*.

119 Grand Lodge, British Columbia & Yukon, 'Annie Wood Besant'.

120 International Order of Co-Freemasonry.

Her partner, Bradlaugh, was an initiate of the Loge des Philadelphe[121] which had been founded as a revolutionary Lodge and included seminal revolutionists such as Louis Blanc,[122] Blanqui and Marx. Loge des Philadelphe operated under the jurisdiction of the Rite of Memphis-Mizraim.

In 1888 Besant was on the executive committee of the Fabian Society, the influential organisation that aimed to introduce socialism by stealth rather than by revolution. Members included Marx's eldest daughter Eleanor. Both Eleanor Marx and Besant were romantically involved with atheist lecturer Dr Edward Aveling, who became Eleanor Marx's common law husband and translator of Marx's magnum opus, *Das Kapital.* Besant was also involved with the Social Democratic Federation and co-founded the Law & Liberty League. This socialist connection was continued in Theosophy. With the politicisation of the movement under Besant there were Theosophists who formed an important element of socialist movements. Canadian Theosophist T G Davy wrote of this:

> It is known that in 1894 at least six of the Toronto Theosophist-Socialists were also officers of the Socialist League of Canada, including its President and Vice-President. Prominent among the names is Phillips Thompson (1843-1933) who served as a Director. In the 1890s Thompson was by far the best-known socialist in Canada.[123]

The 'World Teacher'

One of the doctrinal premises of not only the Theosophists but also the derivative New Age movement is that a World Teacher will ascend to rule a unified humanity under a world government. This World Teacher is also called Maitreya, and The Anointed

---

121 Wisdom Lodge # 202, 'Famous Masons: UK'.

122 Wisdom Lodge # 202, *Ibid.,* 'France'.

123 Davy, *'Early Canadian Theosophist & Social Reform'.*

One, misleadingly called 'Christ', and is a typical product of the syncretic religion that the Counter-Tradition seeks to impose upon humanity on the ruin of the Traditional faiths.

In 1926 Annie Besant and her deputy, Charles Leadbeater attempted to foist upon humanity a World Teacher in the person of J Krishnamurti, whom they had adopted as a child and attempted to rear in Theosophical doctrine. Despite Krishnamurti's own repudiation of the title three years later and admission that he had digested little of Theosophical doctrine, he continues to be celebrated by Theosophists. Krishnamurti nonetheless continued his life as a quite widely esteemed philosopher, one of his present-day adherents stating of the Theosophical effort in regard to Leabeater's claim that Krishnamurti had remarkable powers:

> The President of the Theosophical Society, Annie Besant, confirmed this observation and both agreed that K[rishnamurti] was to become not only a great teacher but the 'vehicle' or incarnation of the Lord Maitreya. Maitreya, in Hindu mythology, was a divine spirit that incarnated on earth every two thousand years or so to found a new, up-to-date religion. (In Buddhism, Maitreya is to be the next Buddha.) According to the Theosophical extenuation of this myth, both the Buddha and the Christ had been manifestations or avatars of Maitreya.[124]

Aleister Crowley was scathing in his condemnation of Krishnamurti and the Theosophical Society, calling the World Teacher an 'imbecile' and a 'retard'. Issuing a broadsheet ca. late 1925 called The Avenger to the Theosophical Society, Crowley called Besant a 'shameless and nauseating fraud' while Leadbeater had practiced 'obscene manustuprations on the wretched Krishnamurti, with a view to making him a docile imbecile.'[125] Crowley considered Besant to be an agent of the Black Adepts and the attempt to promote their World Teacher

124 Gullette.

125 Starr, p. 164.

as an example of the occult war that was taking place between the White and Black Schools of Magick. He wrote to an acolyte in 1943 that Besant had been:

> charged by her Black Masters with the mission of persuading the world to accept for its Teacher a Negroid Messiah. To make the humiliation more complete, a wretched creature was chosen who, to the most loathsome moral qualities, added the most fatuous imbecility. And then blew up![126]

The present head of the Theosophical Society, Radha Burnier, was closely associated with Krishnamurti until his death in 1986. Burnier is a Trustee of the Krishnamurti Foundation India. On 4 November 1980, at her invitation, Krishnamurti visited the world headquarters of the Theosophical Society in Adyar after an absence of 47 years. Burnier, like Besant, was an initiate of Le Droit Humain and is presently Head of the Eastern Order of International Co-Freemasonry. Crowley wrote of this association with Co-Masonry as part of Anti-Tradition, alluding to forms of Masonry as being of a subversive nature:

> Co-Masonry, under Mrs Besant, whose hysterical vanity compels her to claim any high-sounding title that she happens to hear, Le Droit Humain in France, and similar movements almost everywhere, were bringing masonry into contempt by their sheer silliness…. The meaning of masonry has either been completely forgotten or has never existed, except insofar as any particular rite might be a cloak for political or even worse intrigue.[127]

Besant proceeded in her position as head of both Theosophy and of Co-Masonry to transplant her socialistic beliefs to the Raj, where she was active in undermining British authority. This involvement started in 1913 when Besant organised the All-India Home Rule League that spread throughout India. Besant

---

126 Crowley, *Magick Without Tears*, p. 83
127 Crowley, *The Confessions of Aleister Crowley*, p. 696

also started the Young Men's Indian Association in 1914 to train a leadership cadre for post-imperial governance, and founded two journals influential in promoting Indian independence, The Commonweal and New India. Such was her prominence that she was elected president of the Indian National Congress. Her disagreement with Gandhi about tactics ended in her becoming an unpopular figure among Indian nationalists.[128]

Besant & the Luciferic Current

In 1880 Besant declared in her closing speech to the Congress of Free Thinkers in Brussels that the aim is 'above all to combat Rome and her priests, fight against Christianity all over the world, and chase God out of heaven'. To what extent does this express the sentiments of an 'atheist' who does not believe there is any god in heaven to 'chase out', and to what extent, rather, that of an illuminatus who recognises there is a God but rejects the Divinity? 'Chasing god from heaven' is a typically satanic notion. Did Besant see Theosophy and Masonry as a means by which God could be 'chased out of heaven' and the Church defeated via a syncretic alternative spirituality, masquerading as a type of crypto-Christianity or even esoteric Christianity? The Illuminati as we have seen, was presented in its lower degrees as 'true Christianity'. Blavatsky expounded a theme that has become the basis of New Age doctrine, that of the 'Christ' within, which is revealed by Besant as Lucifer. Besant states this view as follows:

> …The Theosophical view … regards man as essentially divine, but the divine in him crusted over with a thick veil of matter; this divine essence in man is the Buddha, the Christ, and it is the 'light that lighteth every man that cometh into the world'. Through the veil of matter the light shines dimly, but in the lowest and the vilest some gleams of light are seen from time to time. Every man is a potential Christ, and the work of evolution is to render

128   Theosophical Society, 'Annie Besant: Political Work for India'.

this potential Christ an active one; man's strength wells up from the divine within him, it is an essential property, not an external gift; the light is there – his work is to render his lower nature translucent, and to let it shine.[129]

God, Christ, and Satan-Lucifer are presented as being integral parts of a wider cosmic dialectic, in this instance as a direct repudiation of the Church, Besant writing:

The truth of the Hermetic maxim, 'Demon est Deus inversus'[130] is borne in upon us when the Church lifts before our eyes the figure of the great 'Angel of Darkness', and we see that his symbols are the same as those of the Christ. Satan has been painted as man's direst foe, as his adversary and accuser, his tempter and would-be destroyer; Christ is represented as the very antithesis of this; as man's most compassionate friend, as his helper and defender, his guide and would-be redeemer. How, then, comes it that two characters so diverse bear the same symbols, are presented under the same image? Lucifer is the Son of the Morning, the star falling from heaven; Christ is the bright and morning Star. Lucifer is the Dragon, the Serpent, twined round the Tree of Knowledge; Christ is the Serpent lifted on the Cross – the Tree of Life. The characteristic attribute of the Serpent – Wisdom – gives us the key of the allegory, for both are types of the human mind, of the double-faced entity, by which alike we fall and rise. For the Star that fell is our Divine Ego, that was the bearer to animal man of the heavenly light, Lucifer, light-bearer, in very truth. And entering into man, it became indeed his tempter, for the very powers it brought made such evil possible as the animal could never know and, united in man with animal desire, it brought memory and subtlety of enjoyment, and anticipation of renewal, and so became man's ever present tempter, plunging him into evil in its

---

129 Besant, 1932, p. 13.
130 'The Devil is the mirror image of God'.

search for sensation and for experience of material life. And then it became his accuser, when evil brought suffering, and sensation brought satiety, and ignorant desire worked out into pain; for it accused the body as its deluder when itself had guided the body, and the man of flesh had been but the instrument of the thinking man. Thus was the Ego the bringer of disharmony, for its own will ruled it and it was ignorant in matter, and blindly eager for experience, and its ignorance and eagerness wrought for pain and hence for its education. And then it began to turn its face upward instead of downward, and to aspire to the Divine instead of seeking for the brute, until striving ever towards the Spirit it lifted animal man from animality, and became his redeemer instead of his tempter, his purifier instead of his degrader. For as intellect materialised is Satan, so is intellect spiritualised the Christ, and therefore is it that both bear the same symbols, and the Fallen Angel becomes the Angel of Light.[131]

These doctrines are at odds with Christianity, as Besant asserts.

As these conceptions of man's real nature become clear and definite, it is manifest that our whole method of dealing with men will change, and the popular ideas of virtue and vice, with heaven as the reward of virtue, and hell as the penalty of vice, will appear to us to be at once puerile and inefficient. And here we come into conflict with popular Christianity. For if man's heart be naturally corrupt, if that which is deepest in him be evil and not righteous, if he turn naturally towards the bad and can only with difficulty be turned towards the good, then it seems reasonable to allure him to the distasteful good with promises of future happiness, and to scare him from the fascinating bad with threats of future pain. Whereas, if man's nature be essentially noble, and the Divine Ego, which is his very Self, be only blinded with matter, and even in its darkness seeks for light,

---

131   Besant, 1932, p. 14.

and in its bondage yearns for liberty, then all this coaxing with heaven and threatening with hell becomes an irrelevant impertinence, for man's innermost longing is then for purity and not for heavenly pleasure, his innermost shrinking is from foulness and not from hellish pain.[132]

Again there is the identification of satanic rebellion as the means of giving consciousness on humanity, thereby transcending animal instinct, the theme of revolutionaries and the Counter-Tradition alike: the remaking of man-as-god. These doctrines coalesced into a popular form that could be sold to the masses as well-meaning and humane; the so-called 'New Age' movement. Guénon presented the Traditionalist perception of Lucifer and of Satan as currents that are being purveyed by Counter-Tradition via such Anti-Tradition movements as Theosophy, pointing out the difference between the Traditionalist conception and that of the Counterfeit Tradition that sees humanity as ascending in a type of evolution: '...Every theory that notably disfigures the Divinity should in some measure be regarded as satanic; and conceptions of a limited God and of a God who evolves should here be placed in the front rank'. This evolving God, or what the Theosophists and New Agers call the 'Christ within' humanity that is the spark of evolution is 'satanic' because it 'openly submits the Divinity to becoming'.[133] What Guénon identified as 'spiritist evolutionism', and consequently an inversion of Tradition, is the same as the 'Perfectibilist' doctrines of Illuminism, Masonry, Theosophy and the 'New Age', which preach the 'perfectibility of man' in common with the atheistic creeds of socialism. We have today accepted this perfectibilist doctrine under the term 'progressive'.

There should therefore be no mistake among Traditionalists as to the character of Satanism, and Luciferianism; these doctrines are the inversion of Tradition, and one does not have to be a Christian to realise this. That is why Traditionalists who are non-Christian nonetheless refer to these currents as 'Black Magick' promoted

---

132 Besant, 1932, p. 15.

133 Guénon, *The Spiritist Fallacy*, p. 257

by 'Black Adepts'. The Traditionalist does not aspire to manifest himself as a 'god', in some supernaturalised version of evolution, progress, or 'perfectibility', but to follow his dharmic path, as far as it is possible in the Kali Yuga; or alternatively if this becomes impossible, to 'ride the tiger' and try to keep a spark burning to pass along to future generations in other eras.[134]

Lucis Trust

This Luciferic current has been brought to a wider audience via Alice and Foster Bailey, heirs to Blavatsky and Besant, who can be regarded as the founders of the now quite pervasive New Age movement. With husband Foster, Alice founded the Lucifer Trust in 1922, re-named the Lucis Trust the following year.

Foster was a 33° Mason, National Secretary of the Theosophical Society in the USA and Chairman of the Lucis Trust. He wrote a book, *The Spirit of Masonry*, exalting Masonry as having the potential to become the world religion of a New World Order. The book, published by Lucis Trust, is advertised by The American Mason thus:

> *The Spirit of Masonry. Masonry Explored* by Bro. Foster Bailey. This penetrating look into the spiritual foundations of Freemasonry proves a unique learning experience for both beginner and veteran seekers of light that will reveal the Craft and its teachings. Author is Bro. Foster Bailey of the United Grand Lodge of England and husband of the late Alice A. Bailey, founder of the international Arcane School which teaches the Ageless Wisdom. Lucis Publishing Company.

Hence, Foster Bailey is regarded with esteem by Masonry, and in this instance by United Grand Lodge Masonry. Foster Bailey's book The Spirit of Masonry claims to be the instructions to Masons from a Tibetan 'Hidden Master'. The 'Foreword' to the

---

134 Evola, *Ride the Tiger*.

book states: 'Another 33° Freemason, Foster Bailey, sponsored his wife, Alice A. Bailey, into Co-Masonry, where she became a key leader. Alice was also the top leader of the House of Theosophy from the 1920's to the early 1950's'. The connection between the New Age movement, Freemasonry, and Theosophy is thereby established.

Foster was clear in describing the aim of the New Age movement as being the creation of a syncretic world religion, explaining that from ancient times, 'Masonry was the first United World Religion. Then came the era of separation of many religions and sectarianism. Today we are working again towards a World Universal Religion'.[135] He states: 'Is it not possible from a contemplation of this side of Masonic teaching that it may provide all that is necessary for the formulation of a universal religion?'[136] He also identifies Masonry as part of an initiatory process involved with the Illuminati and as the 'light-bearers' to the world, in keeping with the Luciferic teachings of Blavatksy and Besant, and of his wife:

> They are therefore sometimes known as the Illuminati. They are the Rishis of the oriental philosophy, the builders of the occult tradition. Stage by stage they assist at the unfolding of the consciousness of the candidate until the time comes when he can 'enter into light' and, in his turn become a light-bearer, one of the Illuminati who can assist the Lodge on High in bringing humanity to light'.[137]

Foster Bailey was no fringe writer. He spoke at Masonic Lodges and his book continues to be distributed by Masons. He states that the Illuminati continue to exist, working through Masonry, and that the purpose of Masonry is to construct a universal religion. The Masonic Temple was to be the new universal church in the coming new world order, 'whose

135 Foster Bailey, 1996, p. 31

136 Bailey, *Ibid.*, p. 13

137 Bailey, *Ibid.*, pp. 22-23

doors will stand so wide open that all men can enter it, and the message which will send forth from its precincts will be one of liberty, fraternity and equality... based upon a oneness of origin, of endeavour and of goal'.[138] As any reader of the Perennial Tradition will immediately recognise, this doctrine is not that of Tradition but of the Counter-Tradition warned of by Guénon and Evola. Foster Bailey held out the prospect of Masonry unfurling its banners over the world, as it had over the barricades of the 1870 Revolution in Paris, to lead the way to a new world order, where 'the glory of Masonry of the ancient days is but a faded splendour when compared to that which is to come. The Masonic Fraternity itself is about to be raised'.[139] It is clear enough from Foster Bailey's pronouncements to his fellow Masons that the purpose of the New Age network that was developed by his wife and himself was to create a Masonically-based religion that would serve as the universal faith for all humanity in a world order. This is the meaning of the proliferation of the New Age movements today.

New Age

The Lucis Trust has spawned an array of New Age movements and projects. One of the primary functions of these organisations is to advocate the establishment of what Alice Bailey called a 'new world order', and to prepare the way for the emergence of a world ruler, Maitreya, the World Teacher, served by a world government.

World Goodwill, a branch of the Bailey network, has issued a list of organisations under the name 'Transition Activities', which are assisting through what they call the 'period of transition into the new world order' (sic).[140] Among the Bailey global network are:

---

138 Bailey, *Ibid.*, p. 103.

139 Bailey, *Ibid.*, p. 121.

140 Cumbey, pp. 243-6.

- Lucis Trust Publishers
- Arcane School
- World Goodwill
- Triangle Centres

If this phenomenon was merely a network of muddle headed dreamers that one sees buying and selling crystals and Tarot decks at the stalls of 'alternative lifestyle festivals' and authors of books on such subjects as dolphins from outer space and the channelling of Chief Black Hawk, the interest would be as a sociological curiosity. However, this movement is pervasive, and is well connected. We will examine the New Age movement later, in connection with the United Nations Organisation.

The Cult of the All-Seeing Eye

Symbols are oracular forms–mysterious patterns creating vortices in the substances of the invisible world. They are centres of a mighty force, figures pregnant with an awful power, which, when properly fashioned, loose fiery whirlwinds upon the earth.[1]

The presence of the All Seeing Eye with a pyramid or triangle is an indicator of occult influences working politically, but despite frequent claims to the contrary, the symbol does not seem to be that of the Illuminati which, as previously shown, used the image of an owl. However, there have recently been attempts at refutation, contending that the combination eye, triangle/pyramid motif is not a symbol of significance to Masonry, or at least is not widespread. The Grand Lodge of British Columbia & Yukon for example, in refuting anti-Masonic conspiracy theories, comments on the frequent claim that the sign on of the reverse Great Seal of the USA is a Masonic emblem:

Of the four men involved in designing the USA seal in 1776, only Benjamin Franklin was a freemason, and he contributed nothing of a Masonic nature to the committee's proposed design for a seal. ...

The single eye was a well-established artistic convention for an 'omniscient Ubiquitous Deity' in the medallic art of the Renaissance...

The first 'official' use and definition of the all-seeing eye as a Masonic symbol seems to have come in 1797 with The Freemasons Monitor of Thomas Smith Webb – 14 years

1   Manly P Hall, *Lectures on Ancient Philosophy*, p. 356

127

after Congress adopted the design for the Seal...

> Neither the eye nor the pyramid have ever been uniquely Masonic symbols, although a few Grand Lodge jurisdictions incorporate them into their seals. The combining of the eye of providence overlooking an unfinished pyramid is a uniquely American, not Masonic, icon. There are no available records showing the all-seeing eye, with or without a pyramid, associated with freemasonry prior to 1797 and none at all related to the Bavarian Illuminati...[2]

This Masonic refutation has widely appeared in both Masonic and non-Masonic sources including for example an entry in Wikipaedia.

Early Masonic Use of Eye & Pyramid/Triangle

The website Pietre-Stones Review of Freemasonry only accepts articles from Master Masons of the UGL (i.e. the same Masonry as that of the BC & Yukon Grand Lodge) and those recognised by the UGL. It is therefore an authoritative source from the perspective of UGL Masonry. In a section illustrating 'Masonic Tracing Boards'[3] there are a number that depict the All Seeing Eye, including the triangle and pyramid, as a primary symbol. The earliest shown is from Germany and dates to 1770; well before the designing of the Great Seal of the USA. Illustrations of early tracing boards incorporating the All Seeing Eye motif include:

- Ancient Tracing Board, Germany, 1770.
- Lodge Union no. 129 Kendal 1772.
- 1796 Union Lodge, Boston.

---

2   Grand Lodge of British Columbia & Yukon, 'Anti-Masonry Frequently Asked Questions'

3   Masonic Tracing Boards comprise symbols for the instruction of Masons as they are initiated into each degree. They are laid out on the chamber floor and form the basis for lectures on Masonic allegory, history, ritual and doctrine relevant to that degree. Any symbol on a TB is therefore of importance to Masonry.

George Washington's Masonic Apron, given to him as a gift from General LaFayette, a hero of the American Revolution who was also to become a primary figure in the French Revolution, embroidered by Lafayette's wife, includes the All Seeing Eye, and dates to 1784.

In 1796, a year prior to the supposed 'first use' of the symbol by American Masonry, it appears on the Tracing Board of the Union Lodge, Boston. Paradoxically, on the website of the above cited Canadian Masons there are several such signs included as examples of Masonic symbolism. That website includes a section headed 'Masonic Art'. One of the examples is a painting by the Florentine artist Jacopo Carucci, entitled 'Supper at Emmaus' (1525). The Masons involved with this website have gone to the effort of isolating an All Seeing Eye and triangle detail from the painting, reproducing it in three sizes, and state that it was probably added later by Jacopo da Empoli (1554-1640). For a symbol that is supposedly of no great significance to Masonry it is odd that the Canadian Masons have gone to these lengths to highlight the detail.

In an article entitled 'The Masonic Landmarks' by Athena Stafyla, written for Pietre-Stones *Review of Masonry*, she (or the editor) includes illustrations of both the Great Seal of the USA and a painting (presumably Masonic) of Egyptian masons working on an uncompleted pyramid. The pictures are carried without explanation. The pyramid without its capstone symbolises the work of Masonry to complete the perfection of humanity, as per the Enlightenment and humanistic doctrines that have been purveyed by Masonic philosophers. The Masonic doctrine is that the initiated Freemason is working to craft humanity towards perfection[4]. It should be recalled that the original name of the Illuminati was the Order of Perfectibilists.

---

4   The Masonic Ashlar, the symbolic rough and smooth hewn stone blocks represent the same allegory in Masonic symbolism. (See below, UN Meditation Room).

All Seeing Eye on the American Dollar Bill

Reporting on an exhibition of Rosicrucian MSS at the Rosicrucian Museum, San Jose, Gary Singh writing in Metro wrote of a conversation he had with the curator on the Great Seal of the USA and the All Seeing Eye:

> We then come back to Roerich's[5] volume and discuss the Great Seal of the United States and the all-seeing eye. I mention it's amazing that it took so long for the seal to make it onto the back of the dollar, and that I wonder why George Washington and crew didn't put it there from the beginning. 'Yeah', said Armstrong. 'Considering they were all Masons'.

Discussing a book by Nicholas Roerich:

> Roerich, a Rosicrucian, played an influential role in the administration of Franklin Delano Roosevelt, as he was the mover and shaker behind FDR putting the Great Seal of the United States and the all-seeing eye on the back of the $1 bill. The eye is a Masonic and Rosicrucian symbol dating back centuries.

The influence on the Roosevelt Administration to get the All Seeing Eye upon the Dollar Bill came via Roosevelt's pro-communist Secretary of Agriculture Henry Wallace, a devotee of Roerich and a 32° Mason. If the All Seeing Eye was not a Masonic symbol one must wonder why it was considered important by Wallace? In a eulogy to Wallace as a Mason, Masonic researcher Dr Robert L Uzzel 32°, writes:

> In 1934, while serving as Secretary of Agriculture, Wallace, for the first time, saw a picture of the reverse of the Great Seal of the United States and took it to the President. He reported: 'Roosevelt, as he looked at the colored reproduction of the Seal, was first struck with the representation of the

---

5   Nicholas Roerich, Russian mystic, author and painter, who will be considered later.

The Masonic 'All Seeing Eye' on the back of the US One Dollar Bill.

all-seeing eye – a Masonic representation of the Great Architect of the Universe. He was impressed with the idea that the foundation for the new order of the ages had been laid in 1776 but that it would be completed only under the eye of the Great Architect. Roosevelt, like myself, was a 32nd Degree Mason. He suggested that the Seal be put on the dollar bill.[6]

Manly P Hall was of the opinion that the US Great Seal represents a specific occult influence on the founding of the USA:

On the reverse of our nation's Great Seal is an unfinished pyramid to represent human society itself, imperfect and incomplete. Above floats the symbol of the esoteric orders, the radiant triangle with its all-seeing eye. There is only one possible origin for these symbols, and that is the secret societies which came to this country 150 years before the Revolutionary War. There can be no question that the great

---

6   Uzzel is a member of the Research Society of Scottish Rite Masonry.

seal was directly inspired by these orders of the human Quest, and that it set forth the purpose for this nation.[7]

Henry Wallace was imbued with occult doctrine, particularly that of Masonry. He regarded the USA as having a messianic destiny to lead humanity into a new world order. He saw that mission symbolised in the Great Seal. He wrote, alluding to the Masonic significance of the unfinished pyramid, the Masonic conception of God as the Great Architect of the Universe, and the motto on the Great Seal referring to a 'New Order of the Ages':

> It will take a more definite recognition of the Great Architect of the Universe before the apex stone is finally fitted into place and this nation in the full strength of its power is in position to assume leadership among the nations in inaugurating 'the New Order of the Ages'.[8]

Here is an indication of the esoteric meaning and origins of what is now being called a 'new world order', and the place of the USA in fulfilling this centuries' old aim.

Rosicrucian Connection

We have seen that Masonry had precursors prior to insinuating their bourgeois adherents into the craft guilds of stonemasons. The immediate precursor, as shown previously, was the mysterious fraternity of the Rose Cross that emerged in Europe during the 17th century. The Canadian Grand Lodge Masons state of this era:

> The single eye was a well-established artistic convention for an 'omniscient Ubiquitous Deity' in the medallic art of the Renaissance. In 1614 the frontispiece of *The History of the World* by Sir Walter Raleigh[9] showed an eye in a cloud

---

7   Hall, 1944, p. 174.

8   Wallace, pp. 78-79

9   The cover illustration can be seen at William L Clements Library, http://www.clements. umich.edu/exhibits/online/bannedbooks/entry3.html Raleigh's work was a forerunner

labelled 'Providential' overlooking a globe. Du Simitiere, who suggested using the symbol, collected art books and was familiar with the artistic and ornamental devices used in Renaissance art.[10]

Of note, it is precisely this 'omniscient Ubiquitous Deity' or God of 'Providence', derived from Rosicrucianism, that became the Great Architect of the Universe, the syncretic God of Freemasonry, which forms the basis for a syncretic universal religion, and the 'God of Providence' that was alluded to by the American Founding Fathers as the focus for the religion of Deism that had a major impact on both the American and the French revolutions.

Manly P Hall writes in reference to Sir Walter Raleigh and the cover of his book *The History of the World:* 'The engraving is a mass of Rosicrucian and Masonic symbols, and the figures on the columns in all probability conceal a cryptogram'.[11]

Robert Fludd is widely credited as being a Rosicrucian. At least he was a public apologist for the underground fraternity.[12] The title page of his book on occultism depicts the All Seeing Eye.[13] Other occult works from the period depicting an All Seeing Eye as a central motif on the cover art include:

- Jacob Boehme, *Theosophishe Wercken* (Theosophical Works), Amsterdam, 1682.

- Daniel Cramer, *The True Society of Jesu & the Rosy Cross, an apologia for the Rosicrucian Fraternity*, Frankfurt, 1617.

---

of the Encyclopedie of pre-Revolutionary France and was suppressed by James I for being of subversive intent.

10   Grand Lodge of BC & Yukon, FAQ: 2

11   Hall, 1951.

12   Fludd, 1617.

13   Fludd, 1621.

While the BC and Yukon Masons state that the designers of the Great Seal, Thomson et al, were not Masons, the symbolism did not come into existence in an ideological vacuum. The symbols express the doctrinal milieu in which Thomson and his associates were operating. The Federal Citizens Information Center homepage, under its section on the Great Seal alludes to this:

> On July 4, 1776, the Continental Congress passed a resolution authorizing a committee to devise a seal for the United States of America. This mission, designed to reflect the Founding Fathers' beliefs, values, and sovereignty of the new Nation, did not become a reality until June 20, 1782.

All Seeing Eye of Grand Orient Masonry

The All Seeing Eye is an important symbol in Grand Orient and associated forms of Masonry throughout the world. Among the items depicted on the Grand Orient website that show the All Seeing Eye as the central motif are:

- The Symbol of the Grand Orient de France. This shows a radiating All Seeing Eye above the Masonic Compass & Square.

- 1848 GODF medal commemorating the French Republic. This shows an All Seeing Eye within the centre of two triangles, around which are the words of the GODF motto: 'Liberty, Equality, Fraternity', which became the slogan of the French Revolution and subsequent revolutions.

Religious Foundations

'Enlightenment' & Atheism

Although the Revolution of the 'Enlightenment' first transpired in America, the doctrinal foundations were previously fermented in France. The 'Enlightenment' that prepared the way for the French Revolution and the mid-19th century revolutions, centred around mostly Masonic philosophers, the so-called *Encyclopédists*, who aimed to publish a compendium of all the sciences that would undermine the 'superstition' that they considered was the basis of both religious and state authority.

However, like other forms of politicised atheism, such as Communism, this Enlightenment atheism itself adopted religious forms such as Deism and the 'worship' of 'Nature' and of 'Reason'. Under the regime of the French Revolution this 'Reason' took excessively irrational forms. These will be considered further.

Conrad Goeringer, a notable American Atheist historian, writing approvingly of this humanistic ferment during the 18th century, provides some valuable background on the role of Freemasonry and derivative societies in the fermenting of atheism and rationalism leading to the French and American revolutions:

> In the history of Atheism, no period is as complex and exciting as that time we know today as the Enlightenment. Cultural historians and philosophers consider this era to have spanned the eighteenth century, cresting during the French Revolution of 1789. It was a phenomenon which swept the western world, drowning in its wake many of the sclerotic and despotic institutions of l'ancien regime or old

order, and helping to crystallize a new view of man and the roles of reason, nature, progress and religion.[1]

Goeringer explains that much of the agitation was motivated by a hatred of Catholicism, as the foundation of Traditional social remnants:

And too, the Enlightenment was a feverish period of Atheistic thought and propaganda. Many of the leading philosophers of the time were Atheists or deists, opposed to the cultural and political hegemony long exercised by the Vatican and its shock troops, the Jesuits. Much of the political, social and literary activity of the Enlightenment was characterized by a repudiation of Christianity, and the formulation of doctrines calling for separation, if not outright abolition, of state and church.[2]

Masonic lodges provided the vehicle by which this movement was created, fermented and organised, culminating in the revolutionary outbreak of 1789 in France and that of America in 1776. Goeringer alludes to the atheist current present in the American Revolution 'on the field of Lexington and Concord', as being the product of doctrinal ideas percolating in the secret societies, including the Illuminati. What is particularly perceptive is that Goerigner points out that these doctrines of humanism and rationalism formed the basis of what is today considered normative democratic thought. Goeringer continues:

While there are many currents to this period, one of the fascinating and little-explored backwater eddys of particular interest to Atheists and libertarians is the role of Masonic lodges and 'secret societies' during this time. Surprisingly little objective historical work exists on this area. The drama of social revolution and intellectual apostasy was taking place not only in the streets of Paris, or

1   Goeringer, 'The Enlightenment, Freemasonry'.
2   Goeringer, ibid.

the open fields of Lexington and Concord, but in countless lodges and sect gatherings and reading societies as well. These conclaves, with their metaphorical-hermetic secrets, symbolism and lore, were the crucibles of 'impiety and anarchy' so bemoaned by church dogmatists of the time like the Jesuit Abbe Barruel. Of all of the clubs, societies, libraries, salons and lodges of this stormy time, perhaps none has been so vilified, attacked and misunderstood as that group known as the Order of the Illuminati.

My purpose here is not to write a history of the French Revolution, or even attempt the herculean task of digesting the complex fabric of the Enlightenment. We do know, however, that much of the best in western civilization today rests on some of the ideas germinated or reformulated during that age of revolution, ideas formulated by Atheists, deists, rationalists and state-church separationists...[3]

Goeringer describes the purposes and importance of the *Encyclopédists*. Of interest is Goeringer's allusion to the 'atheism' of Diderot, et al, while the first edition of the *Encyclopédi* is adorned with Lucifer, striking heroic pose, crowned and holding a sceptre, illuminated by the sun, and standing upon a mountain of books and the Masonic symbols of square and compass. Could it be that this 'atheism' was a façade for Luciferianism practised in the higher degrees of some types of Masonry? Goeringer describes the *Encyclopédi* thus:

Atheism and militant anti-clericalism were both important elements in the Enlightenment. The French philosopher Voltaire saw priests and Christianity as a scourge on the human race, exclaiming 'E'crasez l'infame!' (Crush the infamous things!). The clergy were perceived as corrupt, the pope considered a tyrant, the king despised as a lackey and errand boy for the whoremaster in Rome. If the bible was the holy book of the Christian enlightenment, then the

Encyclopaedia was the inspiration of the Enlightenment. Here was a compendium of human knowledge dealing with arts, sciences mechanics and philosophy which swelled to some 36 volumes by 1780. Begun by the Atheist Diderot in 1751, the Encyclopedia bore the imprints of Voltaire, Montesque, Rousseau, Buffon, Turgot and others. Gracing the title page of Diderot's compendium in the first edition was a drawing of Lucifer, symbol of light and rebellion, standing beside the Masonic symbols of square and compass.[4]

Goeringer discerns that rationalism became a substitute religion, makes some insightful comments on Deism, which was particularly attractive to the American Founding Fathers, and provides an insight into the nature of the 'Great Architect of the Universe'. This Rationalism or 'Enlightenment' is described as the mirror image of Christianity, and hence of a satanic character, with its own substitute God, which was to manifest in France not only as a type of Gnostic remote Deity, but also in the wild cults of Reason and Nature, which rival French revolutionists attempted to impose upon the people on the ruin of their Church:

> The Enlightenment mirrored the Christian religion. Reason became its revelation, nature its god. If the Enlightenment did not abolish the myth of god, it reduced god to a sort of absentee deity, a caretaker to the universe who was nevertheless subject to the laws of nature. Deism arose from the same fertile soil of the Enlightenment as had Atheism, and no doubt many deists were actually Atheists. The deistic god was symbolized in the Masonic lodges as the 'Great Architect of the Universe', certainly not the god of the Christian superstition…[5]

Goeringer concludes by identifying the Masonic Lodge of Voltaire and Benjamin Franklin, the Lodge of the Nine Muses in Paris:

4   Goeringer, *ibid*.

5   Goeringer, *ibid*.

Voltaire had been initiated into the Lodge of the Nine Muses, and Frederick [ruler of Prussia] had long been a Freemason, serving as Grand Master and head of the Scottish Rite. To his credit, Frederick helped secularize many of the institutions of Prussia during his reign.

Benjamin Franklin (1706-1790) was a deist, signer of the Declaration of Independence, …he was a member of the Paris 'Lodge of the Nine Muses', one of the continental masonic groups where the 'revolution was hatching'.

To what extent can Goeringer's claims be verified from reputable Masonic sources? The Masons of the Grand Lodge of British Columbia and the Yukon, acknowledge Voltaire as:

The embodiment of eighteenth century Enlightenment. Author of Lettres philosophiques 1734, Candide 1759 and the Dictionnaire philosophique 1764, his ideas were an important influence on the intellectual climate leading to the French Revolution. Initiated: April 7, 1778, Loge des Neuf Soeurs.

Goeringer's statement that Lodges and 'secret societies' laid the intellectual groundwork for the revolutions in both France and America, is in agreement with the history of the Loge de Neuf Soeurs, written by Louis Amiable and cited by Masonic historian Mackey as given on the Canadian Masons' website. Mackeywrote:

The history of the Lodge of the Nine Sisters was written by Louis Amiable, lawyer, once Mayor of the Fifth District of Paris, Councillor of the Court of Appeals, Grand Orator of the Grand College and formerly Member of the Council of the Grand Orient of France.

Brother Amiable's book, Une Loge Maçonnique d'Avant 1789, has the charm and 'go' of an alluring novel full of remarkable incidents and striking people – better, indeed, than any novel could be, because the adventures are historical and the actors are real. The wonderful book sketches with almost breathless sweep the electrically charged zone of the French Revolution. For Freemasonry in France, like the progress of the Craft in American Colonial days, was a school of patriotism. Freemasonry of the French and American Revolution was neither watery nor apologetic. In truth it was a home and a laboratory for the cleansing fluid that acidly tried men's souls, that assayed the pure gold from the dross and sent the refined product out into the world to hang together or hang separately in the sacred cause of freedom.[6]

Mackey quotes Brother Amiable:

Freemasonry was incontestably one of the factors of the great changes which were produced in North America and in France, not by means of some kind of international conspiracy, as has been pretended so childishly, but in the elaboration of ideas, in rendering public opinion clearer, wiser and stronger, fashioning the men in the fray and whose action was decisive. Of all the Masonic Lodges who exerted that influence in our country (France) the best known, or perhaps I had better say, the least unknown today, is that which received Voltaire some weeks before his death.[7]

Here, as one might expect, the UGL Masons object that all of this Masonic ferment, this organisation, propaganda, and fashioning of men, is 'not a conspiracy', as any such notion would be 'childish'. The candid boasts are mitigated by lame denial.

---

6   Mackey, *An Encyclopaedia of Freemasonry.*
7   Mackey, *ibid.*

The Rebel in the Cosmos

Satan-Lucifer became a romantic figure among certain literati during the 19th century. Prior to that, as mentioned, the heroic figure of Lucifer as the Light-Bearer, had adorned the cover of the Encyclopédie, the bible of the French Revolution. This romanticisation of Satan by eminent literary figures is epitomised by Baudelaire's *Litanies of Satan*. A few verses will suffice to show the literary trend:

> Wisest of Angels, whom your fate betrays,
> And, fairest of them all, deprives of praise,
> Satan have pity on my long despair!
>
> O Prince of exiles, who have suffered wrong,
> Yet, vanquished, rise from every fall more strong,
> Satan have pity on my long despair!
>
> All-knowing lord of subterranean things,
> Who remedy our human sufferings,
> Satan have pity on my long despair![1]

Emily DeFur writes of this literary genre:

> Satan, the angel and devil, is present in all types of literature. He is a pregnant symbol of punishment, heroism and rebellion that poets frequently use. Satan is living out the punishment of the ultimate crime. He must learn to live in another world as another being and serve out his sentence on Earth and Hell. Heroism is not usually identified with Satan; however, in poetry, he takes on the heroics attributed to a rebel. The demon fits in the mold of a 'Byronic hero'. Satan is the ultimate literary masterpiece of a rebel. He defied and continues to defy the ultimate authority, the one being who is infallible, the one who can do no wrong,

---

1   Baudelaire, pp. 170-72

God. Who else but Satan represents the extreme free will of a mind that wants to experience the fruits of the world without the harsh parent figure lurking in the background? This rebellion emphasizes the heroics and punishment of the true demon. The French poet Charles Baudelaire takes advantage of this biblical rebellion to illustrate a tragic hero living out a sentence for a tragic crime of defiance. His demon is able to take on the heroic role because he has rebelled like others have rebelled.[2]

Luciferianism

'No Masonic authority has ever written praisingly of Lucifer'.[3]

While Guénon commented in *The Spiritist Fallacy* that there have been 'few conscious Satanists' (as distinct from there being many 'unconscious Satanists' who unwittingly promote the Anti-Tradition) there did arise as a manifestation of Anti-Tradition a current of 'conscious Satanists' within the Lodges and among the revolutionists of the 18th and 19th centuries, embracing Satan-Lucifer in one or both aspects as 'Light-Bearer' and 'adversary'. This has already been considered in regard to Theosophy. Here we will consider the matter further, and look at the contentious writings of Albert Pike, the primary authority on Scottish Rite Masonry.

No source has been cited, especially by Fundamentalist conspiracy theorists, as frequently as Albert Pike in his several statements on Lucifer, to prove a Luciferic conspiracy. As one would expect the reaction of Grand Lodge Masonry is disingenuous, and the simple expedient can always been used of denying that Pike is a 'true Mason', because he was Sovereign Grand Commander of the Scottish Rite, Southern Jurisdiction, rather than Grand Lodge. UGL Masons contend:

2   DeFur, *'Satan in Literature'*.

3   Grand Lodge of British Columbia & Yukon, 'Luciferianism'.

Neither the attributes nor personification of Lucifer or Satan play any role in the beliefs or rituals of Freemasonry. The topic is only of interest insofar as anti-Masonic attacks have accused Freemasonry of worshiping Lucifer. The confusion stems from such 19th century Masonic authors as Albert Pike and Albert G. Mackey who have used the term 'luciferian' in its classical or literary sense to refer to a search for knowledge. John Robinson notes 'the emphasis here should be on intent. When Albert Pike and other Masonic scholars spoke over a century ago about the 'Luciferian path' or the 'energies of Lucifer,' they were referring to the morning star, the light bearer, the search for light; the very antithesis of dark, satanic evil.[4]

If Pike did not write much of 'Lucifer' per se, he did write of the god of 'Light' whose position in the Masonic Temple is at the East. In discussing the 18°, that of the Rose Croix, Pike stated that the real god of Masonry is Lucifer, which in the 18° is called the 'God of Light':

The Supreme Being of the Egyptians was Amun, a secret and concealed God, the Unknown Father of the Gnostics, the Source of Divine Life, and of all force, the Plenitude of all, comprehending all things in Himself, the original Light. He creates nothing; but everything emanates from Him: and all other Gods are but his manifestations. From Him, by the utterance of a Word, emanated Neith, the Divine Mother of all things, the Primitive THOUGHT, the FORCE that puts everything in movement, the SPIRIT everywhere extended, the Deity of Light and Mother of the Sun.

You see, my brother, what is the meaning of Masonic 'Light'. You see why the EAST of the Lodge, where the initial letter of the Name of the Deity overhangs the Master, is the place of Light. Light, as contradistinguished from

---

4   Grand Lodge of British Columbia & Yukon, 'Lucifer & Satan'.

darkness, is Good, as contradistinguished from Evil: and it is that Light, the true knowledge of Deity, the Eternal Good, for which Masons in all ages have sought.[5]

Because Pike does not use the name 'Lucifer' specifically, Masons such as those of the UGL can indignantly repudiate such accusations. It is doubtful however that there is any other interpretation of a 'Deity of Light' represented ritually in the direction of the East other than that of Lucifer or the equivalent in other cultures.

Luciferic 'Inner Society' within Masonry

Manly P Hall writes of a secret Order within Freemasonry:

Freemasonry is a fraternity within a fraternity – an outer organization concealing an inner brotherhood of the elect. Before it is possible to intelligently discuss the origin of the Craft, it is necessary, therefore, to establish the existence of these two separate yet interdependent orders, the one visible and the other invisible. The visible society is a splendid camaraderie of 'free and accepted' men enjoined to devote themselves to ethical, educational, fraternal, patriotic, and humanitarian concerns. The invisible society is a secret and most august fraternity whose members are dedicated to the service of a mysterious arcanum arcanorum. Those Brethren who have essayed to write the history of their Craft have not included in their disquisitions the story of that truly secret inner society which is to the body Freemasonic what the heart is to the body human.[6]

Albert Pike states the same, with the Masonic initiate learning the secrets of the Craft by Degrees, literally, as is common with occult societies:

---

5   Pike, Chapter 18, p. 281.

6   Hall, *Lectures on Ancient Philosophy*, p. 397

The Blue Degrees are but the outer court or portico of the Temple. Part of the symbols are displayed there to the Initiate, but he is intentionally misled by false interpretations. It is not intended that he shall understand them; but it is intended that he shall imagine he understands them. Their true explication is reserved for the Adepts, the Princes of Masonry. The whole body of the Royal and Sacerdotal Art was hidden so carefully, centuries since, in the High Degrees, as that it is even yet impossible to solve many of the enigmas which they contain. It is well enough for the mass of those called Masons, to imagine that all is contained in the Blue Degrees;[7] and whoso attempts to undeceive them will labor in vain, and without any true reward violate his obligations as an Adept. Masonry is the veritable Sphinx, buried to the head in the sands heaped round it by the ages.[8]

Hall states that the driving power of this invisible society is that of Lucifer, and that the occult powers certain Masons aspire to are derived from Lucifer.

When a mason learns the key to the warrior on the block is the proper application of the dynamo of living power, he has learned the mystery of his craft. The seething energies of Lucifer are in his hands and before he may step upward, he must prove his ability to properly apply energy.[9]

Pike wrote as one of the most influential Freemasons of his day, and continues to be revered as the leading authority on Masonic doctrine. It is misleading to think of Pike as merely a chief of a localised form of Masonry, as the Grand Lodge would have it. The Scottish Rite has international ramifications, some of which have been alluded to previously. For example Pick, in writing of Masonry in Latin America, mentions Grand Lodge, Grand

---

7   First Three Degrees to Master Mason, which are all that are operated by Grand Lodge Masonry.

8   Pike, p. 819, Chapter 30: 30° Degree of Knight Kadosh.

9   Hall, 1923, p. 48.

Orient and Scottish Rite versions all being present, Scottish Rite being the dominant form in some countries.[10] The online Masonic magazine, California Freemason, states of Pike:

> It would be impossible to overestimate the importance of Grand Commander Albert Pike's more than 30 years of work for Scottish Rite. Of primary importance, he edited our Rituals of the Degrees and compiled Morals and Dogma. Indeed, his work laid a solid foundation for increased interest in all things Masonic and particularly in Scottish.

Pike was among those who enthused of Lucifer as the great liberator and Light-Bearer to mankind, as did Besant, Blavatsky, Foster Bailey, and sundry Masonic revolutionists:

> Lucifer, the Light-bearer! Strange and mysterious name to give to the Spirit of Darkness! Lucifer, the son of the morning! Is it he who bears the Light, and with it's splendours intolerable blinds feeble, sensual or selfish Souls? Doubt it not![11]

Satan Mounts the Barricades

The romanticised cosmic rebel adorning the cover of the seminal Encyclopdia of Diderot, et al., which laid the philosophical groundwork for France's Jacobin bloodlust, was taken up in the polemics of revolutionists the following century. Mikhail Bakunin, the leading anarchist organiser and rival to Marx for the leadership of the First International, was initiated into the same branch of Masonry as Marx.

Of the ill-fated Paris Commune revolt of 1871, which brought the Masons out onto the barricades with their banners and a clarion call to defend the Communards, Bakunin wrote: 'The modern Satan, the great rebellion, suppressed, but not pacified!',

10   Pick, pp. 303-304.
11   Pike, p. 321.

writing of Satan as the archetypal revolutionary:

> The Evil One is the satanic revolt against divine authority, revolt in which we see the fecund germ of all human emancipations, the revolution. Socialists recognise each other with the words 'In the name of the one to whom a great wrong has been done.' Satan is the eternal rebel, the first freethinker and the emancipator of worlds. He makes man ashamed of his bestial ignorance and obedience; he emancipates him, stamps upon his brow the ideal of liberty and humanity, in urging him to disobey and eat of the fruit of knowledge.[12]

It is of note that Bakunin refers to socialists as greeting each other with: 'In the name of the one to whom a great wrong has been done'. This is suggestive of a satanic fraternity operating within the socialist movement. The reference to Satan having been wronged is hardly suggestive of atheism. Among Bakunin's colleagues in France was Pierre Proudhon, the leading anarchist philosopher, of whom Bakunin wrote in 1870: 'Proudhon, when not obsessed with metaphysical doctrine, was a revolutionary by instinct; he adored Satan and proclaimed Anarchy'. In his Philosophy of Misery, Proudhon wrote of Satan in the same terms as that of Bakunin, Marx and others, and expressed himself not as an atheist but as a Satanist, not disbelieving God, but repudiating God:

> Come Satan, slandered by the small and by kings. God is stupidity and cowardice; God is hypocrisy and falsehood; God is tyranny and poverty; God is evil. I swear, God, with my hand stretched out towards the heavens, that you are nothing more than the executioner of my reason, the scepter of my conscience. God is essentially anticivilized, antiliberal and antihuman.[13]

---

12 Bakunin, p. 112.

13 Proudhon, pp. 199-200, cited by Wurmbrand, 1986, p. 23.

Karl Marx

Marx is considered the father of Communism. However he was the culmination of a revolutionary process starting among secret societies reaching back several centuries, as we have seen. Before becoming a communist and a dialectical materialist Marx, raised a Christian, expressed beliefs in his early poems that are easily seen to be part of a Satanic gnosis. He expresses not a disbelief in God, as one would expect from a materialist, but a repudiation of God's authority, portraying Satan as the heroic and wronged rebel and liberator.

Did Marx expound Communism as a façade for advancing a Satanic gnosis in a manner similar to the methods used by the Illuminati and Masonry to advance luciferianism by Degrees, even although in the noviate degrees of these Orders 'true Christianity' was professed? In a poem, *Invocation of One in Despair* Marx writes:

> So a god has snatched from me my all
> In the curse and rack of Destiny.
> All his worlds are gone beyond recall!
> Nothing but revenge is left to me!
>
> On myself revenge I'll proudly wreak,
> On that being, that enthroned Lord,
> Make my strength a patchwork of what's weak,
> Leave my better self without reward!
>
> I shall build my throne high overhead,
> Cold, tremendous shall its summit be.
> For its bulwark— superstitious dread,
> For its Marshall—blackest agony.
>
> Who looks on it with a healthy eye,
> Shall turn back, struck deathly pale and dumb;
> Clutched by blind and chill Mortality
> May his happiness prepare its tomb.

Karl Marx and Friedrich Engels published the *Communist Manifesto* in 1848.

> And the Almighty's lightning shall rebound
> From that massive iron giant.
> If he bring my walls and towers down,
> Eternity shall raise them up, defiant.[14]

In *The Fiddler* Marx portrays a musician as if possessed, wild and inflamed, playing his 'death march', and having 'struck his deal' with Satan:

> How so! I plunge, plunge wihout fail
> My blood-black sabre into your soul.
> That art God neither wants nor wists,
> It leaps to the brain from Hell's black mists.

> Till heart's bewitched, till senses reel:
> With Satan I have struck my deal.
> He chalks the signs, beats time for me,
> I play the death march fast and free.

---

14   Marx, 1837.

The Rebel in the Cosmos

In *The Last Judgement: A Jest* Marx lampoons heaven and God, declaring that when he meets Judgement he will sing ironic hallegjuahs until the raucous results in his ouster from heaven:

> But I ruin the proceedings
> As my hymns of praise I holler.
> And the Lord God hears my screamings,
> And gets hot under the collar;
>
> Calls the highest Angel out,
> Gabriel, the tall and skinny,
> Who expels the noisy lout
> Without further ceremony.

In *The Pale Maiden: A Ballad* a woman's love is lost and she rejects Christianity to turn to Satan and spurns heaven for hell:

> All peace of mind is flown,
> The Heavens have sunk.
> The heart, now sorrow's throne,
> Is yearning-drunk.
>
> And when the day is past,
> She kneels on the floor,
> Before the holy Christ
> A-praying once more.
>
> But then upon that form
> Another encroaches,
> To take her heart by storm,
> 'Gainst her self reproaches.
>
> 'To me your love is given
> For Time unending.
> To show your soul to Heaven
> Is merely pretending."

She trembles in her terror
Icy and stark,
She rushes out in horror,
Into the dark.

She wrings her lily-white hands,
The tear-drops start.
Thus fire the bosom brands
And longing, the heart.

Thus Heaven I've forfeited,
I know it full well.
My soul, once true to God,
Is chosen for Hell.

In *The Player*, published in 1841, first published in the Berlin literay magazine *Athenaeum*, Marx described what appears to be a Satanic initiation:

The hellish vapours rise and fill the brain,
Till I go mad and my heart is utterly changed.
See this sword?
The prince of darkness
Sold it to me.
For me he beats the time and gives the signs.
Ever more boldly I play the dance of death[15].

In an obscure, drama called *Oulanem*, first published by Payne (1971, p. 63) Marx elaborates on a theme that is Satanic rather than atheistic. The name Oulanem is an inversion of a Biblical name for Jesus, Emmanuel, 'God is with us'. Inversion is a Satanic device. A few quotes from the drama *Oulanem* suffice to indicate its nature.

And they are also Oulanem, Oulanem.
The name rings forth like death, rings forth

---

15   Maltsev, p. 77.

Until it dies away in a wretched crawl.
Stop, I've got it now! It rises from my soul
As clear as air, as strong as my own bones.
Yet I have power within my youthful arms
To clench and crush you [humanity] with tempestuous force,
While for us both the abyss yawns in darkness.
You will sink down and I will follow laughing.
Whispering in your ears, 'Descend, Come with me,
friend.'[16]

At the end of *Oulanem* the goal is that of obliteration:

If there is a something which devours,
I'll leap within it, though I bring the world to ruins –
The world which balks between me and the abyss
I will smash to pieces with my enduring curses.
I'll throw my arms around its harsh reality:
Embracing me, the world will dumbly pass away,
And sink down to utter nothingness,
Perished, with no existence – that would be really living.

It is the destructive urge upon humanity that finds expression in communistic doctrines that literally invert all remnants of Tradition, making ascendant what Guénon termed the 'reign of quantity'. In another poem cited by Wurmbrand Marx writes:

Then I will be able to walk triumphantly,
Like a god, through the ruins of their kingdom.
Every word of mine is fire and action
My breast is equal to that of the Creator.[17]

Marx's doctrine, which is an elaboration of Illuminism, made him a destroyer of worlds, 'equal to the creator' in the sense that legend states Lucifer sought to become 'equal to the Creator', and in his 'fallen' state manifests as Satan, an entirely destructive

16   Payne, 1971, p. 63.
17   Wurmbrand, p. 11.

principle. 'Every word of mine', wrote Marx in this poem, 'is fire and action'. That was indeed the role of *The Communist Manifesto*, which intended to carry forward the current of destruction unleashed within the secret societies during the previous century.

Carducci's Hymn to Satan

Giosue Carducci (1835 -1907), was one of two principal deputies to Adriano Lemmi, who assumed the world leadership of Scottish Rite Masonry in 1893, when a European committee took over leadership from the Charleston, South Carolina based directorate, previously under the leadership of Albert Pike.[18]

Carducci, a Nobel Laureate, poet and literary critic, had been elected as a Republican Senator and was widely recognised as an agitator against monarchy and the Church. His poem 'Hymn to Satan', *Inno a Satana*, casts Satan in the figure of the heroic rebel.

The Italy in which Carducci flourished had endured decades of revolution fostered by the Lodges of the Carbonari, and under the leadership of the Masons Garibaldi and Mazzini. Garibaldi had reorganised Italian Masonry in 1873 under one authority, the Grand Orient of Italy, which also assumed jurisdiction over the Scottish Rite.[19]

The Church still retained power over Rome and the surrounding Papal States, with military support from Austria. The Carbonari and Young Italy, the latter being part of an international movement organised by Mazinni, attempted to destroy the remaining influence of the Church and to establish a secular republic.

The nature of Italian Masonry is shown by a description of the Masonic conception of 'God', the 'Great Architect of the Universe' as 'Satan', in *Rivista*, the magazine of Italian Masonry:

18   Queenborough, p. 292.

19   Pick, p. 272.

The formula of the Grand Architect, which is reproached to Masonry as ambiguous and absurd, is the most large-minded and righteous affirmation of the immense principle of existence and may represent as well the (revolutionary) God of Mazzini as the Satan of Giosue Carducci (in his celebrated Hymn to Satan); God, as the fountain of love, not of hatred; Satan, as the genius of the good, not of the bad.[20]

The Catholic Encyclopedia remarked on the above Masonic interpretation of Satan: 'In both interpretations it is in reality the principle of Revolution that is adored by Italian Masonry'.

Carducci wrote *Inno a Satana* in September 1863, as a toast that he recited at a dinner party. It was published in 1865, and again in 1869 in a revolutionary newspaper, *Il Popolo*, as a provocation to coincide with the 20th Vatican Ecumenical Council, when the Masonic revolutionaries were still fighting the remnants of Church authority. The following year, the Austrian military presence collapsed and the republican forces marched into Rome.

The following extracts from Carducci's lengthy *Hymn to Satan*[21] will suffice to show its character:

> To you, creation's
> mighty principle,
> matter and spirit
> reason and sense
>
> Whilst the wine
> sparkles in cups
> like the soul
> in the eye

---

20 *Catholic Encyclopedia*, 'Masonry'.

21 Carducci, *Poetry Classics*.

Whilst earth and
sun exchange
their smiles and
words of love

And shudders
from their secret embrace run down
from the mountains, and
the plain throbs with new life

To you my daring
verses are unleashed,
you I invoke, O Satan
monarch of the feast.

Examining Carducci's *Hymn to Satan*, Brother Giovanni Malevolti, of the Grand Orient of Italy, explains from a present-day Masonic perspective:

On the Mason Carducci, much has been said on his life within the institution, and his free, rebellious spirit, his secular and rational thought, is imbued in all his works. It is an example of the *Hymn to Satan* in which the poet celebrates the development of science and technology... as opposed to clerical obscurantism that denies not only scientific progress but also of ideas...[22]

The spirit of revolt inspired the Italian lodges to establish the Italian secular state on the ruins of Papal authority, as the Church's political role was reduced to the Vatican enclave. Of course, this is presented as 'progressive' and as a victory for rationalism over superstition, for liberty over tyranny.

However, in the long-term the creation of the modern concept of the nation-state was erected on the ruins of the old principalities and provinces throughout Europe as a mere phase in a dialectical

22   Malevolti.

process towards a universal republic. The Right today mistakes the present nation-states as expressions of Traditional social order. However, the modernist conception of statehood is a part of the Counterfeit Tradition that was used to destroy the remnants of Tradition and pave the way towards a 'new world order'. The nation-state was intended as a secular and republican phase in the path towards One Worldism. We shall examine this further in regard to the Masonic origins of the European Union, which is another stage towards a universal republic, and a travesty against Europe in the name of 'Europe'.

Communism Fermented in the Lodges

France provided impetus for the 18th century revolutionary underground. Secret societies provided the organisational basis for revolutionary groups. The American scholar Billington, in his study on revolution as 'faith' states that 'so great was the impact of freemasonry in the revolutionary era that some understanding of the Masonic milieu seems the essential starting point for any serious enquiry into the occult roots of the revolutionary tradition'.[1]

Philippe Buonarroti, the Italian exponent of the French Revolution, was initiated into Masonry in 1786. In 1808 he formed Les Sublimes Maîtres Parfaits. Like the Illuminati, within this was an inner circle organised to realise his political aims. Dr J M Roberts states that Buonarroti might have joined an Illuminati-influenced lodge in 1786.[2] Buonarroti had a major influence on Auguste Blanqui, and through his book *Conspiration pour l'égalité dite de Babeuf: suivie du procès auquel elle donna lieu*, was a seminal influence on the 1848 revolutionaries. Roberts describes Buonarroti as having established a 'career as the Grand Old Man of secret societies, advising republican revolutionaries in Italy right down to a young Mazzini'[3] With Francois Babeuf, Buonarroti had co-founded the Society of the Pantheon, one of the first of the revolutionary secret societies to emerge from the French Revolution. In 1796 the plan for a second revolution was discovered and two hundred arrests were made. Babeuf and a colleague were executed. Buonarroti was imprisoned in 1797.[4]

---

1   Billington, p. 92.

2   Roberts, p. 230.

3   Roberts, *ibid*.

4   Roberts, p. 237.

Buonarroti organised a group of Philadelphe Masonry within the Lodge Amis Sincères. Roberts states:

> What may be termed the first international political secret society, the Sublimes Maîtres Parfaits, was founded by Buonarroti, perhaps in 1808. Only freemasons were admitted to it. The Elect were aware that they were to work for a republican form of government; only the Areopagites knew that the final aim of the society was social egalitarianism, and the means to it the abolition of private property.[5]

Regarding Napoleon as as having 'delivered the coup de grâce to the revolution',[6] Buonarroti went to Geneva where:

> The Masonic lodges provided the ambience in which Buonarroti formulated in 1811 his first full blueprint for a new society of revolutionary republicans: the Sublime Perfect Masters... Both the society's name and the three levels of membership proposed for it had been adopted by Masonry. Indeed, Buonarroti sought to work through existing Masonic lodges...[7]

Buonarroti's blueprint for the revolutionary conspiracy was 'rich in Masonic symbolism', and provided the 'prototype for revolutionary organisation'.[8]

Anarchism

From the Illuminism that worked through Masonry, Jacobinism and the societies of Buonarroti, several major doctrinal strands merged that were designed to provide a 'scientific' doctrine for revolution: Communism and Anarchism. Proudhon coined the

---

5   Roberts, p. 266.

6   Billington, p. 90.

7   Billington, p. 91.

8   Billington, pp. 91-93.

term 'anarchy'. He was initiated into Masonry in 1847 according to a biographer, Brogan. Goeringer states that both Proudhon and Bakunin were Freemasons, and that Masonry provided the basis for the cells that were to organise the revolutionary outbreaks that spread throughout Europe in 1848:

> Michael Bakunin (1814-1876) and Pierre Joseph Proudhon (1809-1865), both Freemasons. When revolution again swept Europe in the mid-nineteenth century, it was the Masonic model of organization which provided an organization blueprint for Bakunin's International Brotherhood and the Revolutionary Alliance.

Bakunin acknowledged the role of Masonry in the revolutionary events of the late 18th to mid 19th centuries:

> Today, having sadly become a jabbering old intriguer, it is useless and worthless, sometimes malevolent and always ridiculous, whereas before 1830 and especially before 1793 it was active, powerful, and genuinely beneficent, uniting through its organizations the choicest minds and the most ardent hearts, the most fiery wills and the boldest personalities, with but a very few exceptions. We know that nearly all the main actors of the first Revolution were Freemasons and that when that Revolution erupted it found, thanks to Freemasonry, friends and powerful allies in every other country. This certainly contributed to its triumph...[9]

According to Nicolaevsky, Bakunin was a member of the Philadelphian Lodge, (affiliated with the Order of Memphis) which was a seminal influence on the organisation of the First International.

---

9   Bakunin, 'Open Letter To Swiss Comrades Of The International', cited by Cutler.

Marxism & the Order of Memphis

Marx's Communist League and *The Communist Manifesto* did not emerge from a void. Communism was the culmination of several centuries of agitation, theorising and propaganda from secret societies.

Louis Blanqui, a follower of Buonarroti, organised the League of the Just. German émigrés in Paris formed their own branch called the League of Outlaws, which became the Communist League, and in 1847 asked Marx to write *The Communist Manifesto*. It is from Blanqui that the dictum now credited to Marx, the 'dictatorship of the proletariat', originated.[10]

In 1810 a revived Order of Memphis was established in France working 90 Degrees. It was recognised by the Grand Orient de France in 1826, and underwent a further revision in 1838 under Jacques Étienne Marconis, establishing lodges in Paris and Brussels and claiming adherents in England.

Professor Mark Lause, a labour historian, offers an overview of this association in a paper entitled '*Walking Like an Egyptian*'.[11] Lause states of the years following the French Revolution and the rise of revolutionary secret societies:

> Since the French Revolution, those eager to build political organization found freemasonry a ready model. Doubtlessly, some revolutionaries had always sought the protective appearance of freemasonry. An Italian participant in the French Revolution, Filippe Michele Buonarotti survived decades of repression, prison, and intense police scrutiny to launch a series of secret societies that remained viable well

---

10   Conway, p. 146.

11   Lause specialises in the history of the labour movement. An associate professor of history at McMicken College of Arts & Sciences, University of Cincinnati, his faculty biography states that he 'teaches specialized courses in American Labor History, Comparative Labor History, and the Age of Jackson... For years, he has presented his work or participated in panels at the Annual North American Labor History Conference at Detroit, and the centennial conferences on Eugene V Debs and Henry George'.

into the 1830s. Towards the close of this period, a student named Louis Auguste Blanqui entered this conspiratorial world, and remained influential within it as late as the 1870s. Blanqui's Société des Saisons urged an ongoing revolutionary overthrow of ruling classes until the process left the working class alone to exercise power.[12]

Some of the German émigrés in Paris, founding the League of Outlaws, adopted the doctrines of Blanqui. The League was brought to Germany under the influence of Johann Hoeckering, who had been a protégé of Buonarroti. From here the League of the Just, which became the Communist League, was formed.

Among these secret societies was The Order of Memphis, an important Masonic current in France that included Mizraim, Martinism, the Scottish Rite and Grand Orient. The association between the Order and the revolutionists was apparent to the authorities, which considered banning it along with the League of Just and the Blanquists. In 1839 the authorities decided not to ban the Order, but it was declared dormant in 1841 to avoid a future possibility. The Order maintained its existence under its Paris organisation, Loge des Philadelphes, which had a leadership that ranged from Republicans to Blanquists. After the February 1848 Paris riots, the Order resurfaced but was banned and moved its headquarters to London. We shall see below that this Order was influential in the formation of the First International.

The provisional revolutionary Government mobilised the Parisian workers into co-operative enterprises, the National Workshops. Fearing the empowerment of the workers, however, the Government shut down the workshop project. Lause states that Louis Blanc, spokesman for the National Workshops, was the 'most prominent member' of the Conseil Supreme de l'Ordre Maconnique de Memphis, which became the major revolutionary faction. Lause writes:

12 Lause, *Walking Like an Egyptian.*

These radical masons rode the crest of radicalism into 'the June Days', when the government force of 40,000 moved against an indeterminate numbers of workers, leaving between 4,000 and 5,000 dead with an unknown number of wounded. The state of siege continued in October, and the dictatorship that emerged banned the Order of Memphis, which moved its Supreme Council to London.[13]

This outgrowth led directly to the founding of the First International. Lause states:

> Over the next fourteen or fifteen years, the order eased the alliance with revolutionaries of other nations. It fostered what became the International Association in March 1855. The Order of Memphis provided almost all of the French members of the General Council of the later International Workingmen's Association.[14]

Marx's Lodge

James[15] draws similar conclusions to that of Lause regarding Freemasonry and the rise of socialism: 'It's neither accidental nor an aberration that reformers Garibaldi, Mazzini, Charles Bradlaugh and Karl Marx were all Freemasons, as were many "labour movement" people in Australia'. James identifies the associations between the First International and the Lodge of which Marx was an initiate, along with other influential revolutionists:

> What the author [Yorke, 1871] called the secret history of the (First Communist) International asserts:

---

13   Lause, *Walking Like an Egyptian*.

14   Lause, *Walking Like an Egyptian*.

15   Dr Bob James is the Convenor and Co-ordinator of the Australian Centre for Fraternal Studies. He states of himself: 'I make these claims on the basis of 25 years of research, of ten years or so as Secretary of the Hunter Labour History Society, and as organiser of a National Labour History Conference'.

The IWMA [Industrial Working Men's Association] in Geneva sought and found a temple worthy of their cult…a Masonic Temple…, which they [Marx, et al.] rented. They put the name of 'Temple' on their cards and bills.

Bradlaugh[16] acknowledges having been initiated into the Loge des Philadelphes which is believed to have been Marx's lodge, his 'brothers' including Blanc, Garibaldi and Mazzini. Founded in London in 1850, its initial members were émigrés from recognised foreign Orders, which perceived Freemasonry as:

'An institution essentially philanthrophical, philosophical and progressive. It has for its objects the amelioration of mankind without any distinction of class, colour or opinion, either philosophical, political or religious; for its unchangeable motto: Liberty, Equality, Fraternity'.[17]

The First International

While conspiracy theorists state that Marx was in the employ of the Illuminati through the League of the Just, which is referred to as an Illuminati front[18] this theory is usually conjectural. It is, however, justified, as the association of Marx with Illuminism can be established from reliable sources. We have already seen how Marx begun his philosophic musings not as an atheist or a materialist but with a preoccupation with hell, witchcraft, Satan and occult initiations. We have theorised that his Communist doctrine could have been formulated as a means of enacting the destructive mission and vengeance that had fermented in his young mind through 1837-1841. If this is the case, then the occult lodges provided a means of propagating his doctrine.

---

16   Charles Bradlaugh, English radical and atheist, and collaborator with future Theosophist Annie Besant.

17   James, *Secret Societies and the Labour Movement*.

18   Allen, 1972, p. 30, note.

Mizraim Masonry had a direct association with the formation of the First International and with the emergence of Marxism. Lause, pointing out that 'conspiracy theories' have been 'dismissively' treated by historians, states:

> Nevertheless, there was at least one kernel of truth in the shadows of suspicion. Certainly, the tangled history of freemasonry has largely mirrored the political and social views of those drawn to the craft, and some of those drawn to the more peculiar pseudo-Egyptian forms of the order reflected views that were accordingly distinctive.[19]

B I Nicolaevsky had been a member of the Social Democratic Party in Russia, and Director of the Marx-Engels Institute in Moscow after the Bolshevik Revolution, but was deported from Russia in 1922. He then served as Director of the International Institute of Social History in Amsterdam, and Curator of the Menshevik Collection at the Hoover Institute. He is therefore a source of rare authority. Nicolaevsky states of the Masonic role in forming the First International that there existed in France an 'underground, revolutionary Masonry' whose role in the forming of the First International was 'enormous'. Nicolaevsky identifies this revolutionary Masonry with the Memphis Rite, which he states is that of the Philadelphe Lodge founded by Buonarroti:

> The Lodge of the Philadelphians was formally part of an association that, at the beginning of the 1850's, bore the name of the Order of Memphis. The history of this order is obscure. Historians of masonry do not accord it much attention or sympathy, and as a matter of fact, much of its history is contradictory and incomprehensible. An odd mixture of pseudo-Eastern mysticism and obvious leftist political sympathies on the part of the leaders of the order leaves a strange impression. As a rule, the left wing of Freemasonry tried to lead the movement away from mysticism in the name of rationalism and free

19   Lause, *Walking Like an Egyptian*.

thought, and insisted on simplification of the statutes. The Philadelphians had a completely different outlook. Not only did they trace their forebears to ancient Egyptian priests and to the legendary Chaldean magi who went to Bethlehem to pay tribute to the Christ child, but they preserved the 96 grades of initiation and the post of Le Grand Hierophante at their head. At the same time, almost from the moment the Philadelphians appeared on the scene during the July Monarchy, they tended to draw support from left-wing, even extreme-left-wing, elements. The historian is faced with the paradox that whereas Jean-Etienne Marconi, founder and head of the order for many years, was utterly indifferent to politics, the Supreme Council of the order for 1855 was composed entirely of Republicans and Socialists who sat with the extreme left in the National Assembly of 1848-49.[20]

The Philadelphians in London were established by French émigrés who also established La Commune Revolutionnaire. The Philadelphians:

> did not openly engage in political activities, unless one regards the banquets it organized as such activities. For political occasions it created special organizations, which formally led an independent existence but in fact were under the complete control of the Lodge, which used them as political instruments.[21]

Hence, the Lodge portrayed itself as a harmless society, in the manner of English Grand Lodge Masonry, even assuming the name of 'Grand Lodge', but formed fronts for political purposes. Nicolaevsky refers to Young Europe, of which Young Italy, and Young Germany, Young Hungary, etc. were national chapters, which instigated the 1848 revolutions throughout Europe, as being products of this crypto-Masonic underground, which laid

---

20   Nicolaevsky, *'Secret Societies and the First International'*.
21   Nicolaevsky, *'Secret Societies and the First International'*.

the foundation for the Communist movement. The failure of the 1848 Revolution obliged a return to the previous cell structure of the secret societies.

> Similar combinations of old forms of organizational structures and political activity were widespread in France during the Restoration and the July Monarchy, when revolutionaries generally belonged either to the Carbonari, Young Europe, and similar groups, or to groups of latter-day Babouvists; all these organizations were, to a greater or lesser extent, essentially conspiratorial in nature. It was only during the years immediately preceding the Revolution of 1848, principally under the influence of the English Chartist movement, that new forms of organizational structures as well as social and political activities began to emerge. The new organizations shifted their attention to the open propagation of Socialist and Communist ideas and to the building of mass organizations of laborers in the city and on the land. Throughout Western Europe, the general trend was away from relatively small groups of active revolutionary conspirators who were isolated from their environment, and toward mass political parties, political clubs, and labor unions. On the eve of the revolution of 1848, the new-style organizations increasingly tended to supplant the old, conspiratorial groups, which were under the influence of masonic principles of organization. The new-style organizations were thrown back two or three decades by the defeat of the 1848-49 revolution, and the old type of organization came once again to the fore. This trend was particularly marked among the French refugees from the Second Empire.[22]

The influence of the Commune Revolutionnaire, founded in 1852 under Louis Blanc, came to the fore. Blanc was a member of the Supreme Council of the Order of Memphis, whose operations were headquartered in London, after having been

---

22   Nicolaevsky, '*Secret Societies and the First International*'.

banned by the Paris police in 1852. Nicolaevsky states that 'When the Supreme Council was transferred to London, Blanc, as the Council's chief speechmaker, was able to direct its policy, and, at the same time, to influence the policy of the Lodge of the Philadelphians without officially becoming a member'.

In 1855 the Philadelphian Lodge established the International Association to liase with revolutionary cells throughout the world. The Philadelphian focus was on both opposing Napoleon III, which included terrorist tactics, and of supporting Garibaldi's revolutionary forces in Italy. Among these conspirators in the Philadelphian Lodge at this time was Charles Bradlaugh, whom we have seen as the colleague of future Theosophical Society president Annie Besant. From out of these activities emerged an organisation to replace the International Association, which was created in the first instance under the auspices of Garibaldi, the founding Congress being held in Brussels in 1863. With new input from French socialist émigrés in alliance with English socialists the Philadelphian Lodge played 'a great role' in forming the First International. Lodge initiate Victor Le Lubez organised the inaugural congress in 1864 and selected the founding council in which there were many lodge members.

Revolution

Novus Ordo Seclorum:
The American Revolution

The Revolution in the American Colonies pre-empted the French, but was the product of the doctrines of the philosophers that had been percolating in the lodges of France for several decades. The presence of General Lafayette, an initiate of the Lodge Contrat Social, from France, at the forefront of the American Revolution[1] signifies the bond between the French and American revolutionists. Benjamin Franklin cultivated the intelligentsia in the salons of Paris and became Venerable Master of the Nine Sisters Lodge in 1779, having been given the singular honour of initiating the venerable philosopher Voltaire into the Lodge the previous year. Franklin was assisted in the latter task by de Gebelin, the inventor of the Tarot[2] who might have seemed an odd choice to accompany Voltaire, celebrated as the philosopher *par excellence* of the doctrine of 'Reason', and as an opponent of all superstiton. However, it is an example of the conjunction that existed between humanism and occultism under the auspices of the Counter-Tradition.

In 1777 Franklin's agent Sileas Deane, recruited the Marquis de Lafayette who was sent to America is assist General Washington in his revolutionary battles.[3] Of the Masonic preparations in France for the American revolution: 'All in all, therefore, there is ample evidence of Masonic activity – in France – focused on the care and nurture of the American revolution and centred round

---

1   Hancock, pp. 14, 453.

2   Hancock, p. 14.

3   Hancock, *ibid.*

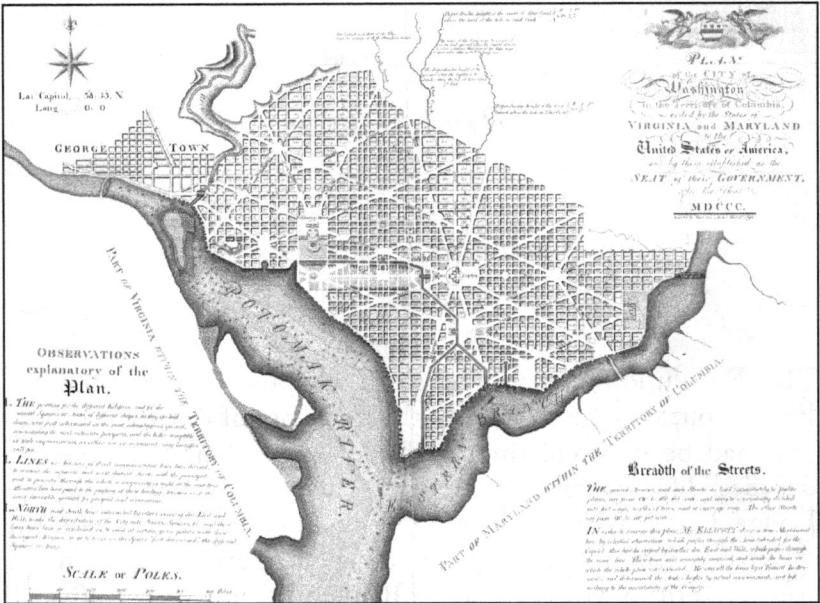

1792 Plan for the City of Washington by French freemason Pierre L'Enfant.

Franklin and the Nine Sisters Lodge'.[4] As one would expect from an esoteric current, the language of which is expressed in symbols, there are many symbols indicating the Masonic origins of the American Republic, as well as being incorporated into the architecture and design of monuments in the USA and particularly in Washington. These have been extensively written of in recent books such as that of Hancock and Bauval, and of Ovason. Washington is seen as a 'Masonic City' the plan of which was drawn up by the French freemason Pierre L'Enfant.[5] Thomas Jefferson regarded it as a 'Temple' dedicated to 'the sovereignty of the people'.[6] 'If a monument or building – or even, as we now can see, a whole city – can become like a living heart, a talisman charged with powerful ideologies and meaning, then the 'pacemaker' of such a talisman must be its cornerstone'[7]

4   Hancock, p. 15.

5   Hancock, p. 19.

6   Hancock, *ibid.*

7   Hancock, *ibid.*

The 'cornerstone ceremony', being one of the most important Masonic rituals, was performed for the consecration of the Capitol by George Washington in 1793, wearing the Masonic apron that had been presented to him by Lafayette, and 'in the presence of a congregation of high-ranking Freemasons'.[8]

While Grand Lodge Masons, depending on their mood, deny the significance of the Masonic symbolism on the Great Seal of the USA, the Scottish Rite sees it as a symbol of the Masonic foundations of the USA. The New Age, 'official organ' of the Scottish Rite Southern Jurisdiction, listed the Masonic symbols on the obverse side of the Great Seal in an article written by J Walker 32°:

- 13 leaves in the olive branches
- 13 bars and stripes in the shield
- 13 feathers in the tail
- 13 arrows
- 13 letters on the 'E Pluribus Unu' on the ribbon
- 13 stars in the green crest above
- 32 long feathers representing the 32°in Masonry
- 13 granite stones in the Pyramid with the All-Seeing Eye competing it.
- 13 letters in Annuit Copetis, 'God has prospered'.
- On the front of the dollar bill is the seal of the US made up of a key, square, and the Scales of Justice, as well as a compass which, of course, is an important symbol in Masonry.[9]

Whether the number 13 is merely a coincidental reference to the 13 colonies rather than actual Masonic design is questionable, however, this is how it was perceived by the highest degrees of the Scottish Rite.[10] Masonry, Grand Lodge or otherwise, generally seems agreed on the prominence of Masons in the American Revolution. George F Harrington, 32° Scottish Rite, states:

8   Bullock, p. 137.

9   J Walker, *'Masonic Symbols in a $1 Bill'*, Washington.

10   Walker.

It is particularly appropriate to honor and recall the exploits of so many of our Founding Fathers this month when we observe Independence Day, July 4. Many of these patriots were Masons, and their lives form illustrious examples of courage. Most Americans know, for example, the main outlines of the lives of such famous Masons as George Washington, Benjamin Franklin, Paul Revere, John Paul Jones, the Marquis de Lafayette, Henry Knox, Joseph Warren, Baron Von Steuben, and Richard Montgomery.[11]

Although it might be politically expedient for politicians to appeal to Christian bloc votes by referring to the USA as a 'Christian nation', the historical foundations of the USA are more indicative of the religious doctrines in vogue among the Enlightenment thinkers of the time. These doctrines were brought to excess in the French Revolution shortly after the American, while American revolutionary luminaries such as George Washington, despite his Masonic credentials, remained aware of the Illuminatist doctrines that could pose a danger to America.[12] Nonetheless, Washington had not been immune from the Illuminist current and remained a 'Deist'.

The founding documents of the USA are imbued with Illuminist and Enlightenment doctrines from the Continent and from England. The Declaration of Independence refers to 'Nature's God' who is the creator of life, giver of rights and 'supreme Judge of the world'. This conception of 'God' is thoroughly Masonic and Illuminatist. A faction of French Revolutionists attempted to impose a Cult of Nature while others attempted to enforce a Cult of Reason. 'Nature's God' is none other than Masonry's 'Great Architect of the Universe'. Weishaupt had stated his aim was to found a new religion based on 'Nature', when humanity would be 'redeemed' by 'Liberty and Equality', which is the 'proper STATE OF PURE NATURE'.[13] The US Constitution

---

11   Harrington, *'Masonic Heroes of the American Revolution'*.

12   Porter, p. 84.

13   Weishaupt's emphasis, Robison, p. 92

states '...no religious test shall ever be required as a qualification to any office or public trust under the United States'. The Treaty of Tripoli, 1796, intended to end the piracy of Barbary against American ships, states in Article 11 that, '.... the government of the United States of America is not in any sense founded on the Christian Religion...' These are secularist documents typical of the doctrines that continue to be promoted by the Grand Orient.

Deism or the belief in an impersonal God of Nature or of Reason was the religion of a number of the Founding Fathers. John Adams, second President, who proposed and signed the Treaty of Tripoli, wrote in 1814: 'Have you considered that system of holy lies and pious frauds that has raged and triumphed for 1500 years'.[14] After George Washington's death, a friend, Dr Abercrombie, wrote in reply to a question on Washington's religion, 'Sir, Washington was a Deist.' Farrell Till, editor of *The Skeptical Review*, and a member of the Council for Secular Humanism, describes the Founding Fathers principally as Deists:

> The primary leaders of the so-called founding fathers of our nation were not Bible-believing Christians; they were deists. Deism was a philosophical belief that was widely accepted by the colonial intelligentsia at the time of the American Revolution. Its major tenets included belief in human reason as a reliable means of solving social and political problems and belief in a supreme deity who created the universe to operate solely by natural laws. The supreme God of the Deists removed himself entirely from the universe after creating it. They believed that he assumed no control over it, exerted no influence on natural phenomena, and gave no supernatural revelation to man. A necessary consequence of these beliefs was a rejection of many doctrines central to the Christian religion.

These beliefs were forcefully articulated by Thomas Paine in Age of Reason, a book that so outraged his contemporaries

---

14   Cousins, pp. 106-7

that he died rejected and despised by the nation that had once revered him as 'the father of the American Revolution'. To this day, many mistakenly consider him an atheist, even though he was an out spoken defender of the Deistic view of God. Other important founding fathers that espoused Deism were George Washington, Thomas Jefferson, Benjamin Franklin, Ethan Allen, James Madison, and James Monroe.[15]

Note that the distinction is made between Deism and atheism. The Illuminists and Jacobins of the Revolutionary Terror in France were Deists. The socio-political application of their doctrine is 'secular humanism', insofar as they believe God has removed himself from human affairs, a doctrine shared with the Gnostics.

America's Masonic Goddess

Just as the 'secularism' of the French Revolution sought to install monuments to the Cults of Reason and of Nature on the ruins of Christianity, Masonry installed a 'Goddess of Liberty' in the USA. That its inspiration was a 'goddess' is attested to in a biography of its designer, Bartholdi, by Robert C Singer, Deputy Grand Master of the Grand Lodge, F. & A.M., New York:

> While standing on the deck of the ship Pereire steaming up Lower New York Bay, he caught a vision of a magnificent goddess holding aloft a torch in one hand and welcoming all visitors to the land of freedom and opportunity.[16]

The architect of the statue, Frederic-Auguste Bartholdi, and the designer of the structural framework, Gustave Eiffel, were both Masons. The principal architect of the pedestal was Bro. Richard M Hunt. The Ceremony of Consecration of the statue was organised by the New York State Grand Lodge. On 28 October

15   Till, 'The Christian Nation Myth'.

16   Singer, 'Masonry & the Statue of Liberty'.

1886, Edward M L Ehlers, Grand Secretary of Continental Lodge 287, read a list of items that was placed in a copper box in the cornerstone, among which was a parchment listing the Grand Lodge officers. A traditional Masonic ceremony was observed: The cornerstone being found square, level and plumb, the Grand Master applied the mortar and had the stone lowered into place. He then struck the stone three times, and declared it duly laid. The elements of 'consecration' were presented; corn, wine, and oil. The Most Worshipful Grand Master then spoke, and posed the question and answered:

> Why call upon the Masonic Fraternity to lay the cornerstone of such a structure as is here to be erected? No institution has done more to promote liberty and to free men from the trammels and chains of ignorance and tyranny than has Freemasonry.[17]

The principal address was given by the Deputy Grand Master, who stated:

> Massive as this statue is, its physical proportions sink into comparative obscurity when contrasted with the nobility of its concept. Liberty Enlightening the World! How lofty the thought! To be free, is the first, the noblest aspiration of the human breast. And it is now a universally admitted truth that only in proportion as men become possessed of liberty, do they become civilized, enlightened and useful.[18]

The Curse of De Molay
The French Revolution

There is a tradition among occultists that the curse uttered against the papacy and the throne of France by the last Grand Master of the Knights Templar, Jacques de Molay, as he was

---

17 Singer, *ibid*.

18 Singer, *ibid*.

being immolated for heresy, was taken up by secret societies and avenged through the French Revolution. Eliphas Levi wrote:

> Jacobinism had received its distinctive name before the old Church of the Jacobins was chosen as the headquarters of conspiracy; it was derived from the name Jacques – an ominous symbol and one which spelt revolution... while those who were prime movers in the French Revolution had sworn in secret the destruction of throne and altar over the tomb of Jacques de Molay. At the very moment when Louis XVI suffered under the axe of revolution, the man with a long beard.... ascended the scaffold and, confronting the appalled spectators, took the royal blood in both hands, casting it over the heads of the people, and crying with his terrible voice: 'People of France, I baptise you in the name of Jacques and of liberty'. So ended half of the work and it was henceforth against the Pope that the army of the Temple directed all its efforts.[19]

This imposing figure, 'the man with a long beard' – assuming mythic proportions - was talked of throughout France at the time of the Revolution. Levi states that the words he quotes from this figure were told to him by an old man who had been present. Levi states of this:

> Amidst the pressure of civil war, the National Assembly suspended the powers of the king and assigned him the Luxembourg as his residence; but another and more secret assembly had ruled otherwise. A prison was to be the residence of the fallen monarch, and that prison was none other than the old palace of the Templars, which had survived... to await the royal victim... There he was duly imprisoned, while the flower of the French clergy was either in exile or at the Abbey. Artillery thundered... unknown personages organised successive slaughters, while a hideous and gigantic being, covered with a long beard,

---

19   Levi, p. 310.

was to be seen wherever there were priests to murder.[20]

Levi states that as this devilish being was killing he would declare the victims to be in revenge for the Templars and other heretics:

> As one who was beside himself, he smote unceasingly, now with the sabre and now with axe or club. Arms broke and were replaced in his hands, from head to foot he was clothed in blood, swearing with frightful blasphemies that in blood only would he wash. It was this man who proposed the toast to the angelical Mlle. De Sombreuil.[21]

On the destruction of Christianity by the French Revolutionaries, Levi recounts events that were to be replayed with the 1917 Revolution in Russia:

> Spoliation of churches, profanation of sacred things, mock processions, inauguration of the cult of reason in the city of Paris – these were the chief signals of the war in its new phase. The Pope was burnt in effigy at the Palais Royal, and the armies of the Republic prepared to march on Rome.[22]

Grand Orient Masonry claims to have inspired the French Revolution. The slogan of the Revolution, 'Liberty, Equality, Fraternity', remains the motto of the Grand Orient in France and Italy. As previously quoted, the Grand Orient de France claims credit for incubating the doctrines that inspired the Revolution. One of the more obvious connections was the pivotal involvement (although Porter claims it is of little account[23]), of the Duc d'Orleans, the Grand Master of the Grand Orient in the events leading up to the Revolution. Philippe, Duc d'Orleans, cousin of King Louis XVI, was, according to Porter, 'a notorious libertine who scandalised French society long before he took up

---

20   Levi, *ibid.*

21   A heroine of the Revolution. Levi, *ibid.*

22   Levi, *ibid.*

23   Porter, p. 63.

the revolutionary mantle or liberty, equality and fraternity':

> As a young man his carriage was frequently seen careening through the streets of Paris, heedless of the welfare of any pedestrian unfortunate enough to fall beneath its wheels. Enjoying to the full extent all that his privileged life bestowed on him, the Duke quickly ran through the family fortune.[24]

It was to forestall financial ruin that Philippe created a 'perpetual carnival' or stalls and shops on his extensive estate[25] and it seems that it was here that he suddenly found new life as the exponent of the common people. He became a popular advocate of democracy, and when the Bastille symbolically fell to the mob they carried his bust through the streets, to wide acclaim.[26] With the triumph of the Revolution the Duke renounced his title and became known as 'Citizen Egalite', and he renamed his Palais-Royal 'le Jardin de la Révoluiton'.[27] He met his fate, like other revolutionists, at the guillotine in 1793, when the Revolution had begun to turn upon itself in contending factions and cults, one of the primary elements leading to his fate being his antagonism towards Lafayette.[28] Contrary to Porter, Hancock states that the Duc d'Orleans 'played a vital role in the events of the Revolution'.[29] He quotes from the documents of the lodge, La Parfaite Union in the city of Rennes:

> It is from our temples and from those elevated into the holy philosophy that emanated the first sparks of sacred fire which, spreading rapidly from east to west and from south to north of France, embraced the hearts of all citizens. None of us, my dear Brethren, can ignore that it was our

24 Porter, p. 62.
25 Porter, p. 63.
26 Porter, *ibid.*
27 Porter, p. 63.
28 Hancock, p. 383.
29 Hancock, p. 381.

Grand Master, the duc d'Orléans, who has participated more than anyone else in the happy Revolution that has just begun.[30]

D'Orléans was elected Grand Master of the Grand Orient in 1786. When he threw his lands open to commerce, the grounds also became a centre for mass political meetings where the crowds were orated by Count Mirabeau, a Mason who had contacted the Illuminati in Bavaria in 1776.[31] Hancock concludes that, 'there is evidence, somewhat downplayed by historians, that points to the existence of a sort of shadowy "government-in-waiting", led by the Duc d'Orléans and other agitators, which conducted subversive propaganda campaigns in many of the 600-plus Masonic lodges in France – of which sixty-five were in Paris'.[32]

The Mystical Symbolism of a Rationalist Revolution

The doctrines of Enlightenment and Reason, against papacy and 'superstition', were a façade for the destruction of the remnants of Traditional order and Faith, out of which could be constructed a new cult. Atheism, rationalism and the like hence were the means to an end. The Revolutionary France that emerged on the ruins of Throne and Altar was one of mass processions singing hymns to the Cult of the Supreme Being. All the symbolic accoutrements of a new religion were forthcoming in the wake of the Revolution.

Of sublime importance to Revolutionary France was the Declaration on the Rights of Man & the Citizen, which assumed the place of the Ten Commandments. The most common depiction is that of these rights inscribed on Moses-like tablets, above which is a radiating Eye in the Triangle, representing the 'Supreme Being' invoked in the preamble to the Declaration. (France Diplomatie). Another symbol that is odd for a seminal

---

30 Hancock, p. 382.

31 Hancock, *ibid*.

32 Hancock, p. 384.

"Declaration on the Rights of Man & the Citizen", with Masonic Eye.

document of the Age of Reason is the obscure presence of the self-devouring serpent, the Ouroboros, a Gnostic symbol regarded as 'the king of Magic' by alchemists and magicians.[33] Albert Pike, explaining the 25° of the Scottish Rite, the Knight of the Brazen Serpent, wrote, 'The serpent entwined around the [world] egg, ... referred to the creation of the Universe'.[34] Why is the seminal document of militant Rationalism adorned with mystical symbols? The answer lies in the origins of the Revolution as a manifestation of Counter-Tradition. Among the symbolism of the Grand Orient de France to the present day is the Ouroboros surrounding the Masonic Square & Compass, above which radiates an All Seeing Eye.

In 1983 Paul Goudot, the Grand Master of the Grand Orient de France stated that Freemasons 'like Condorcet, Saint-Juste, Danton ... applied the principles of the formation of the First Republic with its immortal Declaration of the Rights of Man which was formulated in our lodges'.[35]

33   Walker, p. 907.

34   Pike, p. 496

35   Hancock, p. 387

Contending Cults

Two factions competed to replace the Church: Robespierre advocated the Cult of the Supreme Being. Jacques Herbert and Pierre Gaspard Chaumette advocated the Cult of Reason.

Amongst the anti-Christian fervour babies were baptised not to the 'Father, Son and Holy Ghost', but to 'Liberty, Equality, Fraternity'. In 1793 the word Sunday (dimanche) was dropped, the Gregorian calendar was replaced by a French Revolutionary Calendar, it was prohibited to ring Church bells, display the crucifix, or hold religious processions. The Archbishop of Paris was obliged to resign his duties and was forced to wear the red Cap of Liberty instead of the Bishop's mitre. On 10 November 1979 a Feast of Liberty was held at Notre-Dame Cathedral, and an altar was erected to the Goddess of Reason, represented by an actress who had been paraded triumphantly through Paris. *The Catholic Encyclopedia* states of Christianity under the regime:

> The measures taken by the Convention to substitute the Revolutionary calendar for the old Christian calendar, and the decrees ordering the municipalities to seize and melt down the bells and treasures of the churches, proved that certain currents prevailed tending to the dechristianization of France. On the one hand the rest of décadi, every tenth day, replaced the Sunday rest; on the other the Convention commissioned Leonard Bourdon (19 September 1793) to compile a collection of the heroic actions of Republicans to replace the lives of the saints in the schools. The 'missionary representatives', sent to the provinces, closed churches, hunted down citizens suspected of religious practices, endeavoured to constrain priests to marry, and threatened with deportation for lack of citizenship priests who refused to abandon their posts. Persecution of all religious ideas began.[36]

After a year of revolutionary tumult and dechristianisation, Robespierre officially inaugurated the Cult of the Supreme

36 *Catholic Encyclopaedia*, 'Masonry'.

Being on 7 May 1794. Following a report by Robesepierre to the National Convention that governed France, an official declaration informed French citizens that 'the People of France recognise the existence of the Supreme Being and the Immortality of the Soul'.[37] Robespierre's cult celebrated 36 annual festivals of notable events of the Revolution, and of concepts such as the Supreme Being, Nature, Liberty and Equality.[38]

The first official ceremony of the Cult was held on 8 June 1794 in honour of the Supreme Being, in front of the Louvre Palace, where Robespierre gave a sermon, and a choir from the Paris Opera sung: 'Father of the Universe, Supreme Intelligence, Benefactor unknown to mortals. You will reveal your existence to those who alone raise altars in your name'.[39]

From out of a fire immolating a statue of atheism emerged a stone statue of Wisdom. Now that the Adepts had taken France they were empowered to reveal the religion that they would impose upon humanity in place of the Traditional faith.

In 1793 a statue (albeit hastily made of papier mache) of the Egyptian Goddess Isis was raised at the Place de la Bastille, and was known as the Isis of the Bastille and the Fountain of Regeneration. Reaching twenty feet high, the Goddess sat on a throne flanked by two lions, and at her feet was a large pool adorned with the ancient Egyptian sign of the winged solar disc. From her breasts gushed water into the pool at her foot, from which the populace imbibed the 'water of regeneration' while an orchestra played revolutionary anthems in a Festival of Reunion.[40] Egyptian iconography is fundamental to Freemasonry, and Mizraim Masonry claims, as the name suggests, to be practising an Egyptian system.

37 Décret de la Convention, 18 Floral an II, 7 May 1794; cited by Hancock, p. 180.
38 Hancock, p. 18.
39 Aston, p. 272.
40 Hancock, p. 389.

Voluptuous women dressed as 'Liberty', 'Reason' and 'Nature', covered with blue and white veils and wearing the red Phrygian cap paraded through the streets as representations of goddesses, followed by wild celebrations reminiscent of the ancient cults.

On 7 October 1793 ex-pastor Philippe Ruhl, a representative of the National Convention, under orders from Pierre Chaumette and Jacques-René Herbert, the primary instigators of the dechristianisation programme, had taken a glass chalice containing holy oil, the so-called Sainte-Amoule, used to consecrate the Kings and Queens of France since AD 496, from the Cathedral of Remes, and smashed it in the public square.

On 7 November the Bishop of Paris, Jean-Baptiste Gobel, was publicly defrocked at the National Convention, and then fearfully asked to be able to join Chaumette's Cult of Reason. On 10 November a mob entered the Cathedral of Notre-Dame de Paris, escorting Demoiselle Candeille of the Paris Opéra, who held a torch signifying Liberty as 'the light of the world'. Dubbed 'Liberty, goddess of Nature', Demoiselle Candeille was placed on the High Altar of Notre-Dame, and there followed a communion service for the 'new religion'. The Cathedral was deconsecrated by Gobel and Chaumette and renamed the Temple for the Goddess of Reason.[41] According to Revolutionary scholarship, the Cathedral had been erected on what was the temple of Cybele, who had been worshipped in France in ancient times, and was the same as Isis.

Vendée Revolt

1793 was a seminal year for the revolutionists. Louis XVI was executed. The regime started conscription for a revolutionary war against the rest of Europe, and as noted above, the creation of a new Cult on the ruin of the Church began in earnest. These events sparked the peasant revolt that began in the Vendée region, spreading to other parts of France. Sophie Masson, an Australian

41   Carlyle, Vol. 3, pp. 227-228.

novelist and playwright and descendent of Vendée folk, writes: 'The fact that the Vendée revolt was a popular one called into question the very nature of the Revolution, with its middle-class and aristocratic leaders'. More than that, it dared to oppose the 'despotism of liberty'. Republican armies led mainly by deviant ex-nobles and princes were sent into the rebellious province.

Despite brilliant Vendée guerrilla tactics and a peasant army of 150,000, the Jacobins mercilessly suppressed the revolt within the year, and 'in early 1794, the Convention decided to exterminate the Vendéens, to the last man, woman and child. And they found plenty who were happy to carry out these orders'. Masson describes what can only be regarded as a prelude to the Bolshevik terror over Russia around one and a quarter centuries later:

'Not one is to be left alive'. 'Women are reproductive furrows who must be ploughed under'. 'Only wolves must be left to roam that land'. 'Fire, blood, death are needed to preserve liberty'. 'Their instruments of fanaticism and superstition must be smashed'. These were some of the words the Convention used in speaking of Vendée. Their tame scientists dreamed up all kinds of new ideas – the poisoning of flour and alcohol and water supplies, the setting up of a tannery in Angers which would specialise in the treatment of human skins; the investigation of methods of burning large numbers of people in large ovens, so their fat could be rendered down efficiently.

One of the Republican generals, Carrier, was scornful of such research: these 'modern' methods would take too long. Better to use more time-honoured methods of massacre: the mass drownings of naked men, women, and children, often tied together in what he called 'republican marriages', off specially constructed boats towed out to the middle of the Loire and then sunk; the mass bayoneting of men, women and children; the smashing of babies' heads against walls; the slaughter of prisoners using cannons; the most grisly and disgusting tortures; the burning and pillaging of villages, towns and churches.[42]

Turreau de la Linières, who took command of the douze colonnes infernales ('twelve columns of hell') set about to exterminate the entirety of the Vendéens, including even Republican supporters, Turreau declaring: 'We can make no distinction. The entire province must be a cemetery'. Masson writes: 'In the streets of Cholet, emblematic Vendéen city, by the end of 1793, wolves were about the only living things left, roaming freely and feeding on the piles of decomposing corpses'.[43]

The extermination of Vendée did not end until the assumption of Napoleon I, who admired the courage and ability of the guerrilla fighters, and concluded a peace treaty. France had been reduced to an orgiastic, violent Black Mass, a hell maintained by the guillotine and massacre. Portuguese Masonic historian Goncalves poses the question in regard to the relationship between Masonry and the Jacobin Reign of Terror:

> Contacts and co-operation between French freemasonry and the Club of Jacobins are mostly accepted by historians. The club when transformed according with the revolutionary strategy defined by Robespierre or Mirabeau, acted according to freemasonry rites, rules of secrecy and organization, that helps to understand its expansion to all French territory. Does this co-operation which involved the most outrageous acts of the Terror, explain the slander of the Grand Master, Prince Égalité is something still to be answered?[44]

No people can long endure like this, despite being granted the 'happiness' to live in accord with 'Nature' and 'Reason' by the Black Adepts. Napoleon emerged from the tumult to restore order and hierarchy.

---

42   Masson, *'Remembering the Vendée'*.

43   Masson, *'Remembering the Vendée'*.

44   Goncalves, footnote 24.

Napoleon And After

Napoleon I, supposedly heir to the French Revolution, repudiated its doctrines, and sought to create a united Europe. In short, he 'ended the revolution' in a manner that has its historical analogue with Stalin, and it is notable that Trotsky, the Robespierre of his day, perceptively referred to his nemesis as a 'Bonapartist'. Napoleon sought an imperial Europe; not a Masonic 'universal republic'. He repudiated the free trade economics that the Revolution had inaugurated, ironically in the name of 'the people', and he sought to control commerce, fixed prices and started to re-establish the guilds that had been suppressed by Jacobinism, despite the objections of the moneyed interests that had assumed prominence as a result of the Revolution. In particular, Napoleon created a national bank, which, although being owned by private bankers, became subject to Napoleon's authority in 1806, with the government controlling dividends, and maintaining low interest rates.[45]

The manner by which Napoleon is regarded by Freemasonry is a paradox. While the Grand Orient is said to have 'flourished' under the Empire[46] imperial consent had to be obtained for regular meetings of more than twenty people, including those of the Lodges. An investigation of the Grand Orient by the interior ministry was undertaken to determine whether their loyalty could be assured.[47] The revolutions that convulsed Europe through the mid 19th century were under the direction of the secret societies, and when Napoleon's nephew assumed the rulership of France as Napoleon III he kept the Grand Orient under surveillance, imposing his own choice of Grand Master.

It might be recalled that Adolphe Cremieux, Grand Master of the combined Grand Orient, Scottish Rite and Memphis-Mizraim had begun as a supporter of Louis Napoleon, but was to become a bitter critic; his protégé Maurice Joly writing his

45   Holtman, pp. 104-106.
46   Holtman, p. 138.
47   Johnstone, p. 71.

satire against the Emperor. Napoleon III was deposed in 1870 with the French defeat during the Franco-Prussian War. The civil war that ensued saw Masons man the barricades of the Paris Commune in the fight against the French Government.[48] The Grand Lodge of British Columbia & Yukon, always at pains to repudiate any suggestion of nefarious activities on the part of Masonry, states of the Paris Commune that:

> Many, if not all, Parisian freemasons, members of lodges under the Grand Orient of France, were supporters of the Paris Commune of 1871. Minutes of a meeting of Loge LÕUnion de Belleville, held 28 April 1871, exemplify the sentiments that motivated a reported 10,000 freemasons to mount the barricades the following day.[49]

French Freemasonry mobilised to support the Communards after the issuing of a manifesto from the Loge L'Union de Belleville, which worked under the direction of the Grand Orient de France. The manifesto declares in part:

Considering that in the painful period of crisis through which we are passing, which is desolating our fatherland and afflicting humanity, it is the duty of all Masons to affirm the principles that appear to it to conform to universal morality, and those most apt to make the ideas of universal solidarity prevail. A solidarity that, the day it will exist, will prevent the renewal of all impious struggles among men and will cause the last seed of barbarism to disappear by reuniting all men in one family;

> Considering that the proclamation of the Paris Commune, addressed to the French people, contains nothing that is contrary to Masonic principles;
>
> Considering that it is thus the obligation of Freemasonry,

---

48 Johnstone, p. 71.

49 Grand Lodge of British Columbia & Yukon, *'Freemasonry & Nineteenth Century Revolution'*.

which has always been at the head of the march of progress, to employ all the moral force at its disposal to make those ideas in conformity with its principles prevail;

Considering that it is the duty of each lodge to indicate, not only to Freemasons, but to all citizens the path of the just and the true;

The Lodge 'The Union of Belleville' declares:

That it desires to stop the spilling of blood, while adhering to the program of the Paris Commune as contained in its proclamation to the French people...

By order: For the Lodge 'The Union of Belleville'

The Tit :.Sec:. The Ven:. Or :.

Voisin H. Fernoux[50]

On the deposing of Napoleon III, the subsequent regime was headed by Leon Gambetta, and included Gambetta's mentor, Cremieux, as Minister of Justice. It was from the time of the Third Republic established by Gambetta until the Republic's defeat by Germany in 1940, after which there was a brief return to Tradition under the Vichy regime of Marshall Petain, that international finance held sway. Professor Benjamin Ginsberg of Johns Hopkins University writes of this era that Paris became 'a major international banking and financial sector'. Professor Ginsberg described Cremiuex as 'Gambetta's first political mentor'. In a replay of the French Revolution, the Radical Party of Gambetta made socialist noises, but once empowered inaugurated a 'pro-business position' while also being identified as 'the chief proponents of anti-clerical legislation'.[51] Gambetta had been initiated into a Masonic Lodge at Bordeaux, and in

---

50   Grand Lodge of British Columbia & Yukon, *'Freemasonry & Nineteenth Century Revolution'*.

51   Ginsberg, *The Fatal Embrace: Jews and the State*.

1875 into the Lodge La Clemente Amitie .[52]

The anti-clerical legislation was continued by Jules Ferry, who served as President, 1880-1881 and 1883-1885. He was an initiate of the Alsace-Lorraine Lodge in Paris. (Denslow and Truman, p. 44), and, with Gambetta, was affiliated also with the Lodge La Clemente Amitie at Paris.[53]

Apart from the interregnum of Napoleon I, Napoleon III and the Vichy regime, the very foundations of the modern French State are maintained on the legacy of the Masonic Revolution, as are those of the USA and many other states in Europe and the Americas, and in the present era the entire edifice of the European Union. The present-day Grand Orient de France continues to be the vanguard of secular, modernist France, and to uphold the slogan of Liberté, Egalité, Fraternité. The GODF claims 47,000 initiates in over 1,150 lodges, committed to 'a humanist path'. Its creed continues to be universalism, stating 'the whole world is a great republic'. The Grand Orient is upheld as the guardian of the republican and universalistic creed it has promulgated since before the Revolution, and indeed it boasts of being the 'main architects' of France's state ideology:

> The Freemasons of the Grand Orient were among the main architects of the rise and the roots in our country of the Republic now part of French identity. They consider themselves a bit like the guarantors and the vanguard of the republican regime which alone can ensure the development of everyone in Liberty, Equality and Fraternity. The history of the Grand Orient de France is a series of commitments of its members designed to embody these values. Today the work of the Masons include on how to live these humanistic principles in a world changing and looking for new benchmarks.[54]

---

52 Ginsberg, *The Fatal Embrace: Jews and the State.*

53 Mackey, 1912, Entry: 'G'.

54 Grand Orient de France, 'A commitment to Humanism'.

Italy

As in France, the secret societies played a particularly influential role in establishing the modern state. Again, the predominant influence was the Grand Orient, around which were spun a network of revolutionary, crypto-Masonic societies that were to embrace the Continent under the name Young Europe, and extended, as we have seen previously, into Turkey to create what has been termed a 'Masonic state'.

The Supreme Council of the Grand Orient of Italy was established in Turin in 1859. When Guiseppe Garibaldi who, next to Mazzini, is the father of the modern Italian state, accepted the position of Grand Master of the Grand Orient, he acknowledged that Masonry was the method of revolt in Italy, and that its form of Italian 'nationalism' really aims to established a universal republic, nationhood being but a transitory step. Garibaldi wrote:

> I willingly take on the supreme office of head of the Italian Masonry constituted according to the Reformed and Accepted Scottish Rite. I take it on because it was conferred on me by the free votes of free men, to whom I owe my gratitude not only for the trust shown me in elevating me to such a high position but also for the help they gave me from Marsala to Volturno, in the great task of freeing the southern provinces. My nomination as Grand Master is the most solemn interpretation of the tendencies of my very soul, of my votes, of the aims towards which I have worked all my life. I assure you that with your mercy and with the cooperation of all our brothers, the Italian flag, which is that of humanity, will be the beacon from which the light of true progress will be shed all over the world.[55]

The identification of Masonry with the Italian modern state on the ruin of the former provinces and Papal states is acknowledged with pride by the Scottish Rite, Jack Buta 32°, writing:

---

55 Grand Lodge of British Columbia and Yukon, Giuseppe Garibaldi Massone - Gran Maestro Gustavo Raffi

Garibaldi, accepting the role offered to him by the Sicilian Scottish obedience, demonstrated that, in that phase, he identified Freemasonry with the national program and intended to use it as a means of organization and meeting point of the various democratic movements. It was not by chance that once arrived in Sicily, he attended the initiation of his son Menotti (1 July) and he, in person signed (3 July) the proposal of affiliation of the whole of his general staff (Pietro Ripari, Giacinto Bruzzesi, Francesco Nullo, Giuseppe Guerzoni, Enrico Guastalla and others). In the long term, once the fight for national independence was completed, the political plan of Freemasonry was to identify itself with a wider and more ambitious aim, that of liberation and the emancipation of the whole of humanity.[56]

Note that Bro. Buta, former Grand Master of Paradise Valley Silver Trowel Lodge #29, Arizona Grand Lodge, states:

- That the entirety of Garibaldi's General staff was initiated into the Grand Orient,
- That the Masonic doctrine was identical to that of the Italian revolution,
- That in particular 'the political plan of Freemasonry' was ultimately that of a world revolution.

Italian nationalism, as defined by Counter-Tradition, became a focus for the destruction of the Church, as it had in France. The failure of the 1864 expedition against Rome resulted in Garibaldi adopting the anti-Catholic programme of the Grand Orient, and he took up 'an intransigent anticlerical stand':

From that moment the General was more and more convinced of his identification with the position of Freemasonry, which was the main supporter in the peninsula of an inflexible secularism opposing the Vatican as the Catholic Church fought to retain control over Rome and the Vatican States.[57]

56   Buta, '*The Politics of Grand Lodge Foreign Relations*'.

57   Buta, '*The Politics of Grand Lodge Foreign Relations*'.

Garibaldi saw in Masonry the microcosm of future Italian statehood, and urged Masonic unity as the prelude to Italian unity, predicated on the destruction of Papal authority over Rome. In May 1867 on the eve of the Masonic Constituent Assembly in Naples, he declared:

> As we do not yet have a country because we do not have Rome, so we do not have masonry because it is divided. I am of the opinion that Masonic unity will lead to the political unity of Italy. Let, in Freemasonry, that Roman fasces[58] be made that notwithstanding great effort has not yet been obtained in politics. I believe the freemasons to be an elect part of the Italian people. Let them put aside their profane passions and with the awareness of the high mission that the noble Masonic institution has entrusted to them create the moral unity of the country. We still do not have moral unity; let Freemasonry achieve this and the other (unity of the nation) will immediately be achieved.... Abstention is inertness, it is death. I urge understanding, and in the unity of understanding we will have unity of action.[59]

The Masonic dream of marching into Rome did not eventuate until the Franco-Prussian war, when the French troops had to withdraw their protection and the Masonic forces occupied the Eternal City and the remaining Papal States succumbed.

As with France under Napoleon I, Napoleon III and Marshal Petain, Italy achieved a respite from Masonic intrigue with the triumph of Mussolini. One of the most significance achievements of the Fascist regime was to establish accord between the Church and the State as the foundation for a genuinely unitary nation.

---

58   Fasces, the bound bundle of sticks representing unity, from ancient Roman times, adopted in the aftermath of World War I as the name and symbol of the Fascist movement, ironically the first modern movement to rebel against the Masonic creed in Europe.

59   Buta, 'The Politics of Grand Lodge Foreign Relations'.

An early biographer of Mussolini, Giorgio Pini, writes of this:

> One point of exceptional importance completes the picture of the achievements of this period – conciliation between Church and State. This was effected on February 11, 1929, with the unexpected conclusion of the Lateran Pacts, nearly sixty years after the beginning of the grave conflict which had divided Roman society into two hostile factions and had been embittered by the ceaseless intrigues of Freemasonry, often acting in the interests of foreign Power and for over half a century had tormented the conscience of so many Italian.[60]

Pini wrote that this 'astounding achievement',

> closed a phase of history and secured from the Holy See the recognition of Rome as the capital of the kingdom of Italian under the Savoy monarchy, and created the new State of the Church by the delimitation of a territory known as the Vatican City. It realized the dreams of many laymen and ecclesiastics and conferred on Rome the functions which it had had only in the days of the Empire.[61]

Under Fascism, the malevolent spirit of Masonry that had established the Italian state had been overcome and the foundations had been laid for a new state based on tradition and genuine unity; albeit a nation that could not survive the combined forces of the Counter-Tradition.

Portugal

The Portuguese revolutionary regime of 1910 repeated the methods of destruction and fanaticism – in the name of 'Reason' - that had been enacted by the French Revolutionaries. This was again a clash between Masonry and its traditional enemy,

---

60   Pini, p. 166
61   Pini, p. 166

Catholicism, to the extent of making martyrs of three little peasant children as the foremost threat to the Masonic State.

In 1848, the year of revolutionary tumult throughout Europe, a subversive propaganda network, the Revolutionary Commission of Lisbon, was established as a prelude to the creation of the Republican Party. The Commission was headed by António de Oliveira Marreca, António Rodrigues Sampaio, and José Estevão de Magalhães, the latter two being Grand Masters of Grand Lodges. The organisation was mostly a Masonic undertaking. Other Masons assumed more revolutionary roles in the Carbonária, a branch of the Italian secret society, which was the primary organisation of the 5 October 1910 revolution. The Carbonária had been established in Portugal in 1822, and received impetus from the student organisation Maçonaria Académica, founded in 1896 by Luz Almeida. Portuguese Masonic historian, A M Goncalves, describes this period:

> This revolutionary and anti-clerical association became an important instrument for the diffusion of republican propaganda in cafés, schools, workshops, seminaries and in popular places of academic lampoonery. Gradually Carbonária established its connections within freemasonry through the lodge Montanha founded by the aforementioned Luz Almeida and participated in the political indoctrination of freemasons. Borges Grainha stresses that this contributed directly to the election of Sebastião Magalhães de Lima as Grand Master of the Grande Oriente Lusitano. This relationship was responsible for the expansion of Portuguese Carbonária. In October 1910, the time of the Portuguese Republican revolution, the Carbonária had about 40,000 members across the country.[62]

Goncalves states of the role of Masonry in fomenting the revolt in Portugal against the monarchy and the Church:

62   Goncalves, *'Breve historical da Maconaria em Portugal'*.

'The revolution of 1910 was the epilogue of several attempts to depose the monarchy that had existed at least from 1891'. He writes that the assassination of King Don Carlos I in 1908, and Prince Regent Don Luis Filipe, was perpetrated by the Republican Party 'with the support of Freemasonry'. The uprising of Republican army officers against the monarchy was 'the work of the Portuguese revolution due to freemasonry, uniquely and exclusively'. The head of the Republican provisional government, Teofila Braga, was a Mason, as were the Interior Minister and Minister of Justice. Goncalves writes: 'In the Parliament more than half the MPs were Masons. In the Government of 1910-1911 50% of the ministers were Masons, and this percentage was sustained until 1926. Three presidents of the Republic were Masons'.[63]

Fatima

A major setback for Counter-Tradition in Portugal was the cult that developed around the alleged visions of Mary by three peasant children at Fatima in 1917 and the witnessing of strange phenomena by 70,000 pilgrims and sceptics alike. The visions culminated in a series of statements to one of the children, Lucia, that came to be known as the 'Secrets of Fatima'. These included predictions of war, revolution, and world peace if the Pope would perform a consecration of Russia to Mary, the real nature of this consecration being a major source of contention among Catholic Traditionalists and the hierarchy within the Church.

The Portuguese authorities tried to suppress the growing cult of Fatima in vain, and this included blowing up the Fatima sanctuary. The result was a great revival of Catholicism in Portugal. In 1926 the Army overthrew the Leftist regime. Ever since Catholic Traditionalists have held Masonry accountable for not only the original attempts to silence the children, but for present attempts to undermine the doctrine and sanctuary of Fatima through ecumenicalism.

---

63   Goncalves, *'Breve historical da Maconaria em Portugal'*.

The Virgin Mary allegedly appeared to three Portuguese children (Lúcia Santos and her cousins Jacinta and Francisco Marto), six times in 1917.

Setting the Fatima apparitions in historical context, Father Nicholas Gruner, when head of the Fatima Network, wrote of the role of Masonry and the laws of the provisional government enacted against the Church:

> For over a century Portugal had been steadily declining due to Freemasonry, which dominated government and society. The Portuguese Revolution of 1910 had deposed the ruling monarchy and proclaimed the Republic, which was primarily composed of high-ranking Freemasons. The Church was the prime target during the revolution: Churches were pillaged, convents attacked and the religious harassed. The fiercest and most targeted attack, however, came through the anticlerical legislation the Republic passed. Immediately after the proclamation of the Republic, all convents, monasteries and religious orders were suppressed, the religious themselves were personally expelled and their goods confiscated. The Jesuits were forced to forfeit their Portuguese citizenship.

Then laws and decrees that aimed to destroy the country's morality were passed, one after another: a divorce law was passed; then a law on cremation, on the secularization of cemeteries, abolition of the religious oath, suppression of religious teaching in the schools, and the prohibition of the wearing of the priestly cassock. The ringing of Church bells and times of worship were subjected to certain restraints, and the public celebration of religious feasts was suppressed. The Government even interfered with the seminaries, reserving the right to name professors and determine the programs. In 1911 the persecutions culminated with the law of Separation of Church and State. The author of these ferocious laws, Alfonso Costa, declared: 'Thanks to this law of separation, in two generations Catholicism will be completely eliminated in Portugal'. It seemed that this prediction would prove true. But the Freemasons underrated the fervor of the Portuguese faithful and the strength of Pope Saint Pius X.[64]

The Fatima mayor holds a special role of infamy in the Fatima mythos. He is described as a prominent Freemason, who kidnapped the three children, and threatened them with torture and death in an effort to abort their pilgrimage to receive the final message of the apparition. Gruner wrote of this:

Fatima's local authority, Artur de Oliveira Santos, who was the Administrator of the district of Vila Nova de Ourem, was an anticlerical fanatic. Also known as 'The Tinsmith', he was a Freemason who enjoyed much power through his position, and ruled his district in a tyrannical fashion, imposing restrictions on Churches and religious services on his slightest whim. The Tinsmith decided to end the popular piety resulting from the apparitions at Fatima, through whatever means necessary.[65]

---

64 Gruner, *Historical Context of Portugal.*

65 Gruner, Fr. N. *Historical Context of Portugal.*

On 16 September 2005 'The History Channel' aired 'Fatima Secrets Unveiled'. Sister Lucia, the only survivor of the three children (the others dying soon after the apparitions) and the only one of the children to have allegedly heard the messages (as distinct from only seeing the apparitions), was interviewed shortly before her death. A nun served as interpreter. During the interview Sister Lucia remarked that Freemasonry had been involved in the attempted suppression of Fatima. Although the interviewer asked incredulously for an explanation, the interpreter cut in and the subject changed. It was Fatima that the Masonic regime rightly feared. The resurgence of Faith paved the way for the inauguration of Salazar's 'New State' following the 1926 *coup d'être*, and all the secularist laws of Masonry were reversed, the family upheld and labour honoured.[66]

In February 1927 Masons were involved in an attempt to overthrow the New State. Following moves by the authorities against the lodges the Grand Orient went underground in 1929, and the Masons were advised by Grand Master Norton de Matos to continue working against the State. In 1935 a Bill was passed outlawing the secret societies.[67]

With the Army coup of 25 April 1974, the so-called Carnation Revolution, the ban on the secret societies was lifted, and all documents and accoutrements of the Grand Orient returned. Although factionalised, Masonry has assumed its dominant form in Portugal under the Regular Grand Lodge, and is said to have greatly extended its influence throughout Portuguese society: 'The Regular Grand Lodge of Portugal has established an increasing influence within Portuguese society among the liberal professions, intellectuals, public servants, entrepreneurs and academics'.[68]

---

66 Egerton, inter alia.

67 Goncalves.

68 Goncalves.

Russia, Bolshevism & 'Red Shambhalla'

Two great dynasties stood in the way of the Black Adepts, the Romanov and the Hapsburg, and both were pitted against each other, to their mutual destruction, during the Great War. While Czar Nicholas II and his family were shot by the Bolsheviks towards the end of the intra-European conflagration, the spark that lit the powder keg of Europe had been the assassination of Archduke Franz-Ferdinand, heir apparent to the throne of the Austro-Hungarian Empire.

Austro-Hungary: The Preliminary Scene for Destruction

The Hapsburg Empire had been the subject of intrigue and terrorism by secret societies with the focus on fomenting Slavic and Serbian dissent. The Court proceedings against twenty conspirators produced evidence that the secret societies had been behind the assassination of Franz-Ferdinand, and the Archduchess, Sophie. The assassinations had been undertaken by the Serbian secret society Narodna Obrana. Cabrinovic, who threw the bomb at the Archduke's motorcade to enable Princip to shoot the Royal couple, stated during the Court proceedings that he had been told that Casimirovic, leader of Narodna, and a highly initiated Mason, had travelled to France, Russia and Budapest in planning the assassination. Cabrinovic told the Court that his colleague, Ciganovic, had told him 'that the freemasons had already condemned to death the heir of the throne two years ago'. The President of the Court was incredulous, but Cabrinovic insisted on the facts. However, when Cabrinovic was asked by the defending counsel whether he was a Mason he loudly replied that he could not answer. When asked whether another of the defendants, Tankosic, was a Mason, he replied affirmatively, as he did on the same question regarding Cignaovic.

When Princip, who fired the fatal shots, was asked about Masonry he replied that Ciganovic had stated he was a Mason, and had stated that the heir to the Throne had been condemned 'in a Masonic lodge'. The proceedings of the trial had been unreported and forgotten amidst the turmoil of the Great War.[69] The War brought down the monarchies of Russia, Germany and Austro-Hungary.

Masonic intrigue had for several centuries insinuated its way into the Royal Court of Russia, as it had prior to the Revolution in France. Cagliostro, the Illuminatus and founder of Mizraim, was involved in intrigue in both states.

Cagliostro arrived in Saint Petersburg in 1779.[70] He aimed to introduce Czarina Catherine II to 'the great light' of true Freemasonry, stating that he was 'the chief of princes of the Rosy Cross'.[71] Cagliostro was confident of his mission because of the popularity Masonry had assumed among the Russian nobility. Although this Masonry was mainly of a mystical and social orientation and was not of a subversive nature, there were also lodges of the Strict Observance and of the Rosy Cross. With Cagliostro's Mizraim Rite open to women, he hoped to attract the support of the Czarina. Catherine was antagonistic toward Masonry, and she discerned the potential of Masonry as a means of subversion.[72] Cagliostro attempted to establish his reputation as a spiritist, miracle worker and healer, and especially tried to win over the Empress with his skill as a physician. He failed. He was increasingly suspected of acting for foreign interests and of spying for Prussia and found it advisable to leave Russia before being imprisoned, travelling to Warsaw, where he had wide support.[73]

It was French Martinism that impressed itself upon Russia when Philippe de Lyon, under the direction of Papus (Dr Gerard Encausse), head of the combined Memphis-Mizraim and

69   DePoncins, pp. 80-83.
70   McCalman, p. 76.
71   McCalman, p. 77.
72   McCalman, p. 81.
73   McCalman, pp. 94-95.

Martinist Rites, arrived at the Royal Court and even initiated Nicholas II into Martinism. Philippe de Lyon reached Russia in 1899 to establish a Martinist Lodge at the Imperial Court. Papus went to Saint Petersburg on several occasions over the years 1900-1906. It was also during these years that the Russian mystic Sergei Nilus, an opponent of Martinism, published *The Protocols of Zion*. It was first suggested by the celebrated Jewish writer Israel Zangwill in a letter to the London Times that this was done to try and discredit the inroads of Masonry.

While it is claimed that Martinism was founded as a Traditionalist order, this is difficult to reconcile with the Illuminatist origins under de Pasquales. Martinists provided a cadre of revolutionaries in Russia, who were to continue in the echelons of the Bolshevik regime despite its supposed materialism and detestation of anything mystical. However, Masonic subversion was centred on the Social Revolutionaries, and was particularly evident in the regime arising from the March 1917 Revolution that overthrew the Czar.

A Masonic historian, Richard L Rhoda,[74] in tracing the history of Masonry in Russia draws a distinction between political and revolutionary Masonry and the non-political form that had long been in Russia and which did little, under the matronage of Catherine II, to welcome the advances of Cagliostro during the 18th century. Rhoda states that the centre of revolutionary doctrine remained in France, and affirms the role of the Grand Orient in the 1905 and 1917 Revolutions in Russia. Rhoda, writing from the perspective of a Grand Lodge Mason, states that the authorities in Russia discovered the Grand Orient in 1909, writing:

> The existence of Masonic Lodges was discovered by the Russian Government in 1909; it also became known to the authorities that they were of French origin. It was then decided by the Russian Lodges to suspend work,

---

74   Snr. Warden, Monument Lodge #96, Lodge of Research, Maine, USA.

and this was accordingly done till 1911, when some of their members decided to renew with due prudence their activities. One would not call these activities Masonic in any sense, as their chief aim was purely political—the abolishment of autocracy, and a democratic regime in Russia; they acknowledged allegiance to the Grand Orient of France.[75]

During the early 20th century Russian Masonry mainly existed among émigrés in France, and in particular involved the Scottish Rite. In 1908 the Polar Star Lodge was opened in Saint Petersburg by M M Kovalevsky. This operated under the jurisdiction of the Grand Orient de France, and was consequently of a subversive nature. The Lodge was established with the assistance of V Maklakov of the Constitutional Democrats (Cadets) Party; hence it had a political character. It was received into the Grand Orient of Russia's Peoples in 1911. These origins are also related by Wor. Bro. Dennis Stocks of the Barron Barnett Lodge,[76] in his essay on 'Russian Freemasonry', who writes of the Polar Star Lodge that:

> For a period of time prior to the first Russian Revolution (1917), the Grand Orient of France (considered irregular since 1877) attempted to recreate its own style of political Freemasonry in the last days of the Russian Empire. As early as 1908, Polar Star Lodge in St Petersburg and two other lodges (in Moscow and Warsaw respectively) followed the Grand Orient's political agenda.[77]

What is of particular interest about Kovalevsky is that he opened the L'Ecole de Hautes Etudes in Paris in 1901 under the auspices of the Cosmos Lodge # 288. The latter was formed in Paris in 1887 as part of the Scottish Rite, around which Russian

75 Rhoda, *'Freemasonry in Russia'*.

76 Barron Barnett [Research] Lodge, Queensland, Australia. http://barronbarnett.org.au/ Membership is only open to Master Masons.

77 Stocks, D. *'Russian Freemasonry'*.

émigrés gathered. Among the students at the L'Ecole de Hautes Etudes were G V Plekhanov, founder of the first Communist organisation in Russia and Lenin's early ideological mentor; V I Lenin; and A V Lunacharsky, who became first Bolshevik Commissar of Education, and was a 'member of a French Lodge'.[78] Hence, while claims that Lenin, Lunarchsky and other Bolsheviks were initiates of the Grand Orient of Russia's Peoples and other Lodges, are difficult to verify, what can be established is that they were in association, and indeed, under the instruction, of a college established under the jurisdiction of the Grand Orient de France and working within the Scottish Rite. Stocks comments additionally that the Bolshevik luminary Maxim Gorky was 'widely known to have been a Freemason'.

Priahin, who has researched Russian Masonry in the archives of Yale University, and elsewhere, states that the Grand Orient encouraged its initiates to undertake a subversive political agenda with the purpose of overthrowing the Czar. This movement against the Russian Monarchy ranged from Cadets (Constitutional Democrats) to Marxists. Priahin writes:

> Emissaries of the Grand Orient of Russia inspired Russian brothers to try and take high places in state bodies and diplomatic and military circles. They had their people in the French Embassy, State Council, Progressist block of the State Duma, Cadet, Oktyabrist, Trudovik (Labourist) Parties and factions, Working group of the Military Industrial Council, General Staff (after 1915), Moscow State Duma, Commerce and Industry Alliance, the Bar, professorship of St. Petersburg and Moscow Universities. Masons were especially active in IV State Duma where they formed the Progressists block (summer 1915) and tried to form the block comprising all opposition parties to eliminate the monarchy in Russia under the control of left liberals and democrats.[79]

---

78   Priahin, 'Noteworthy members Of the Grand Orient of France in Russi'.

79   Priahin, *Noteworthy members Of the Grand Orient of France in Russia*

Priahin states that Russian Masonry adopted a specifically subversive character when control was assumed 'by the left wing Constitutional Democrat (Cadets) Party led by N V. Nekrasov, later a minister of the Provisional government (March - November 1917)'. The Grand Orient of Russia became the Grand Orient of Russia's Peoples in 1913. From then the history of the revolutionary movement became synonymous with the history of Masonry in Russia. Priahin states that these Masons operated through a variety of parties, but their solidarity as Masons was maintained: 'Participation in a variety of parties gave Russian Masonry an excellent opportunity to act in many directions and in many fields at once. As A F Kerensky wrote, 'We never allowed anybody to erode our solidarity'".[80]

The Cabinet list for the future Revolutionary Provisional Government inaugurated after the March 1917 Revolution, was chosen by the Supreme Council of the Grand Orient, two years prior to the event. The first Cabinet of the Provisional Government comprised ten members, of whom nine were Masons. Some of these were also able to maintain positions in the Bolshevik regime. After the Bolshevik Revolution, the Grand Orient of Russia's People re-organised as the 'Free Russia' Lodge.

Just prior to the 1917 Revolution there was political division among these Masons, between the Constitutional Democrats and the socialist elements. Masons were particularly heavily represented in the leadership of the Cadets and the Social Revolutionaries. Their role in the Bolshevik party is less clear. Rhoda states that the Masons were a factor in the March Revolution and the Provisional Government. The dominant personality in this Government was Kerensky, a particularly active Mason of high initiation:

This political organisation comprised in 1913-1914 about forty 'Lodges'. In 1915-1916 disagreements arose between their members who belonged to two political parties (the

80   Priahin, *Noteworthy members Of the Grand Orient of France in Russia*

Constitutional Democrats and the Progressives) and could not agree on a common policy; ten Lodges became dormant. The remaining thirty Lodges continued to work, and took part in the organisation of the 1917 March revolution and in the establishment of the Provisional Government.[81]

Kerensky had been Chairman of the Trudovik (Labour Party) faction in State Duma; Chairman of the IV State Duma; Deputy to the Chairman of the Executive Committee of the Petrograd (St. Petersburg) Council of the Socialist-Revolutionary Party (from 1917); and a member of the Provisional Committee of the State Duma. After the March 1917 Revolution he became Minister of Justice in the Provisional Government (March - May 1917); Minister of the Military and Marine (May - September 1917); Premier-Minister of the Provisional Government (July-November 1917); head of the Directory (September), Chairman of the 3rd Coalition Government (October), and Commander-in-Chief of the Russian Army since September-November 1917.

As for Masonry, Kerensky was initiated in 1912 in La Petite Ourse (Ursa Minor) Lodge in St Petersburg. He became General Secretary of the Supreme Council of the Grand Orient of Russia's Peoples, 1915 – 1916 and was an initiate in the Rose Lodge ('Masons' Grouping' in the IV State Duma) and the Rosicrucian Order.[82]

Bolshevik Mahatmas

As noted, Martinism had been established in the Royal Court of Russia. Dr Richard Spence, Professor of History at the University of Idaho, and an authority on secret societies, cites an associate of Papus who claimed that Martinism 'was the germ of Sovietism.'[83]

---

81   Rhoda.

82   Priahin.

83   Spence, 2008, p. 54.

Martinists maintained positions under the Bolshevik regime and were particularly present in the secret police, the Cheka. This cabal centred around Aleksandr Vasil'evich Barchenko, the so-called 'Bolshevik professor of the occult', who had belonged to Masonic and Theosophist circles while a student in Paris 1901-1905, and joined the Martinist Order and the Kabbalistic Order of the Rose & Cross. It was at Paris that Barchenko heard of the mythical land of Shambhala, said to be the abode of the Hidden Masters of the World existing in Tibet.[84] This is an issue with which many occult orders are preoccupied, including those of Theosophy and the 'New Age' movements that claim their mandates from these 'Hidden Masters'.

Returning to Russia after World War I, Barchenko entered the service of the Bolshevik regime, and gave lectures on the occult to the revolutionary sailors of the Baltic Fleet.[85] Why he would be enabled to do this by a dictatorship based on atheism and materialism is a question that is probably best answered by the thesis of this book; namely that Bolshevism serves as a front for the Black Adepts – or Hidden Masters – of Counter-Tradition, who are of course not 'atheists', 'rationalists' or 'materialists' but comprise what Crowley called the Black School of Magick. These are the Hidden Masters that Theosophists and others wish to see 'walk among humanity', once they are able to take their place in the open after the ascent of a 'new world order'. That at least is the mythos around which several centuries of subversion and intrigue have been woven, whether as reality or fantasy.

Shambhala in Barchenko's doctrine was a 'primeval communist society', which had been part of a 'great universal federation of peoples'.[86] However, Barchenko was suspected of being involved with counter-revolutionaries and was summoned to the Petrograd-Cheka in 1918. Here, within the darkest bowels of the Soviet regime, were a cabal of Martinists, led by Konstantin

84   Spence, *ibid*
85   Spence, *ibid.*
86   Spence, *ibid.*

Konstantinovich Vladimirov. Another of the cabal was Yakov Blumkin. Hence, Barchenko, rather than being tortured and shot, like so many others, was promoted by powerful friends in the Soviet bureaucracy who were Martinists. Barchenko established a Masonic lodge, Edino Trudovoe Bratstvo (ETB), the United Labour Brotherhood, which included Vladimirov, and other Chekists, and an undefined association by Blumkin. Another member was Chekist Gleb Ivanonich Bokii, who combined life as a veteran Bolshevik with involvement in the occult. Prior to the Revolution he had, like Barchenko, been a member of the Kabbalistic Order of the Rose & Cross. With the assassination of Uritsky in 1918 Bokii assumed leadership of the Petrograd Cheka, and by 1924 headed the elite Special Department of the OGPU, the re-named secret police. One of the interests of this Special Department was to investigate the paranormal. Bokii put his fellow Rosicrucian, Barchenko, in charge of a 'neuroenergetics' laboratory within the All-Union Institute for Experimental Medicine, the purpose of which was to explore mind control and hypnotism.[87]

However, the primary purpose of Barchenko and the ETB was to establish contact with the Hidden Masters at Shambhala. Barchenko was in contact with a Tibetan lama who claimed to be a representative of the mythical land; and with a Mongolian official, Khayan Khirva, who became head of the Mongolian Soviet secret police, when that land was brought under Bolshevik rule.

In 1925 Blumkin, disguised as a Muslim pilgrim, crossed into British controlled Kashmir on his way to Ladakh to meet the Rosicrucian Adept Nicholas Roerich (Spence, *ibid.*), who had high-placed Masonic contacts among the political Establishment in the USA, reaching up to President Roosevelt 32°. Roerich aimed to enter Tibet and find Shambhala. Spence calls Roerich 'definitely a Theosophist and probably a Martinist', as well as being a Soviet agent.[88]

87   Spence, p. 55.

88   Spence, *ibid.*

Roerich seems to have reached a pro-Soviet sentiment while in the Theosophical milieu of Annie Besant in England, where the predominant view was in opposition to British imperial rule over the Eastern peoples. Roerich's wife here claimed to have started receiving mediumistic messages from one of the Hidden Masters in Tibet, Master Morya (Blavatsky's old Master), who stated that Roerich must create a state encompassing Tibet, Mongolia, parts of Siberia and parts of China. This would be the 'New Russia' or the 'New Country', with Roerich as the titular head, but under the leadership of Morya.[89] The first stage would be a 'Shambhala War', which would lead to the world dominance of Shambhala, with the Bolsheviks as the means of enabling this.

Roerich was joined in this plan by Vladimir Anatol'evich Shibaev, an agent of the Communist International (Comintern), who was working among Indian nationalists[90] Hence the anti-imperialist agenda of Annie Besant and Theosophy in India converged with Soviet activities.

The Roerichs moved to New York in 1920 and secured the patronage of Wall Street foreign exchange broker Louis Levy Horch, who was a secret operative for the Cheka/OGPU.[91] Roerich's 'Master School' was funded by Horch as a place where acolytes would go to hear the messages from the Master Morya channelled through Helena.[92] The couple told their devotees that they had actually met the Master.[93]

With Horch's funding, the Roerichs returned to India in 1925, and mounted an expedition with the intention of entering Tibet. The real purpose was to find Shambhala.[94] Roerich was joined by Blumkin. Skirting the peripheries of Tibet they entered Sinkiang

89   Drayer, 2005, p. 65.
90   Spence, p. 55.
91   Spence, *ibid.*
92   Drayer, 2005, p. 61.
93   Drayer, *Ibid.,* p. 64.
94   Drayer, *Ibid.,* p. 65.

and Mongolia, after having conferred with Soviet officials in Moscow.[95] There were Buddhists, 'Masons and Rosicrucians in the top echelons' of the Soviet Government when the Roerichs arrived in Soviet Russia in 1925.[96] The Roerichs had also been sent by the Master Morya as emissaries to the Bolsheviks.[97] Coincidentally, when Roerich and his son George were sitting in the waiting room of the offices of Felix Dzherhinsky, chief of the secret police, the bloody Commissar dropped dead.[98] Perhaps this was an omen from the White Adepts in the occult war against the Black?

However, Roerich proceeded and reached Mount Belukah in the Altai Mountains, the place that was chosen by the Masters to be the centre of 'New Russia' or Zvenigorod, as it was to be known. Roerich, to be the temporal authority sitting beside Master Morya, would guide the 'New Russia' with the code of the esteemed Genghis Khan.[99] Hence we have an insight into the planned future of humanity behind the façade of universal brotherhood, and the seemingly benevolent banner of a 'Red Buddhism'. There is another Buddhism that Roerich sought out – one that goes to primal sources, with the drinking of blood from human skulls and the celebration of cosmic violence, which has a legacy as vicious as that of Genghis Khan and of the Cheka. Under the rulership of Lord Maitreya, the world would be brought to heel, and Roerich was told of a prophesy by a learned lama, that:

> Verily, the time of the great advent is nearing. According to our prophecies, the era of Shambhala has already begun. Rigden Jyepo, the Ruler of Shambhala, is already preparing his unconquerable army for the last fight. All his assistants and officers are already incarnating.[100]

---

95   Spence, p. 57.

96   Drayer, 2005, p. 200.

97   Drayer, *Ibid.*, p. 203.

98   Drayer, *ibid.*

99   Drayer, *Ibid.*, p. 210.

100   Roerich, Heart of Asia, II.

The lamas told Roerich that they saw their prophecies being fulfilled in the revolutions and Great War that had been enacted in Europe.

There is much about what Roerich says that identified him as a Traditionalist, yet we should be mindful that, as Guénon and Evola had stated, the Counter-Tradition works through a Counterfeit-Tradition to beguile the well-meaning, and it is therefore often difficult to discern the motives of such individuals as Roerich. Here again we must look for what his goals for humanity were, and we find the same universalistic doctrine of the Grand Orient, and the Illuminati, continued by Theosophy, and the New Age movement: a World State ruled over by self-chosen 'Masters'. It depends on one's perspectives whether these Masters are regarded as Black or White Adepts. Crowley, for example, clearly identified them as Masters of the Black School of Magick, as did Evola and Guénon. Roerich, seeing in Soviet Bolshevism a transitional system on the path to a world state, under his own lordship, next to an incarnated Lord Maitreya, elevated his own 'Banner of Peace', gaining influential political support, and commended the internationalist creed of the League of Nations as the harbinger of a new era: 'The League of Nations, which has progressed toward international harmony, will not be opposed to this flag, for it expresses their aims of a world unity'.[101]

The nature of the Counter-Tradition behind the Roerichs, et al can be discerned from the messages Roerich passed along to the Soviet Education Commissar Lunacharsky and Tchitcherin, Commissar for Foreign Affairs, from the Hidden Masters, expressing support for the Bolsheviks:

> In the Himalayas, we know what you are accomplishing. You abolished the church, which was a breeding ground of lies and superstition. You destroyed the bourgeoisie who had become agents of prejudice. You demolished the

---

101 Roerich, 1930.

educational prisons. You destroyed the hypocritical family. You did away with the army, which had ruled as over slaves. You crushed the spiders of greed. You closed the night dens of cutthroats. You freed the land of wealthy traitors. You recognized that religion is the teaching of universal matter. You recognized the insignificance of private ownership. You foresaw the evolution of community. You pointed out the importance of knowledge. You bowed down before beauty. You brought the entire power of the Cosmos to the children. You opened the windows of the palaces. You saw the urgency of building homes for the Common Good. We stopped the revolt in India because it was premature, but we recognized the timeliness of your movement, and we send you all our help, affirming the Unity of Asia.[102]

There are many salient points here that expose the character of the Hidden Masters and their Illuminist doctrines. The Hidden Masters stated they had approvingly observed in the Bolshevik regime:

1. Destruction of Christianity
2. Extermination of class enemies
3. The destruction of the traditional family
4. Materialistic doctrines as the new religion
5. Elimination of private property
6. Destruction of nobility ('You opened the windows of the palaces')

All of this was accomplished with great bloodshed by the Cheka in their hellish torture chambers, where blood literally ran down drains. Roerich delivered a second letter, written in Tibetan, from the Hidden Masters, personally addressed to Commissar Tchitcherin, reading:

---

102 Drayer, 2004. Drayer, a follower of Roerich, states that she found the letter in: S Zarnitsky and L Trofimova, 'The Way to the Native Country', *International Life*, 1965, No.1, pp. 104-105.

Only deep comprehension of communism will give full well being to peoples. We know that some layers of peasantry cannot contain idea of communism. It is necessary of the new circumstance, which will enter them into a channel of a true Community. Such world circumstance will be acceptance of communism by Buddhist consciousness.

If the Union of Advice recognizes Buddhism as the doctrine of communism than our Communities can submit the active help, and hundred millions of Buddhists which scattered on the world, will give necessary power of unexpectedness.

We trust ours Messenger Akdorddze[103] to pass details of our offer - we can insist that the measures are urgently necessary for introduction of world communism as a step of urgent evolution. We send dirt for the tomb of our brother Mahatma Lenin. Accept advice and our greetings. (Rosov).[104]

The letters were signed by Gulab Lal Singh and 'D M'. Gulal Lal Singh was a pseudonym for Mahatma Morya. The letters accompanied a container of dirt with a Tibetan text reading: 'Mahatmas - to the tomb of Russian Mahatma', the latter being a reference to Lenin.

The Hidden Masters had declared themselves against the Russian peasantry, which was being slaughtered as a class enemy. Lenin was recognised as a fellow Mahatma, and an esoteric token was sent to his tomb which, it is interesting to note, was a stepped pyramid, his corpse having been mummified.

Aleister Crowley had a different view on the search for Shambhala and Roerich's association with the Bolsheviks that indicates Crowley was, despite certain idiosyncrasies such as

---

103 Akdorddze is a pseudonym for Roerich.

104 Roerich, Heart of Asia.

listing Weishaupt as a 'Saint' for his religion of Thelema, indeed in conflict with the Black Adepts. An oil painting by Crowley entitled 'Four Red Monks Carrying a Black Goat Across the Snow to Nowhere', expresses Crowley's contempt for the efforts of Roerich and the Soviet Commissars to reach Shambhala, the black goat that they are carrying symbolising that Black School of Magick to which these Bolshevik occultists adhered.[105]

The Hidden Masters sought the overthrow of European authority in Asia in alliance with the Soviet Union. They had been using Theosophy for that purpose in India. Behind Roerich's 'Banner of Peace', praised by luminaries such as Henry Wallace and the President of France, stood the aim of establishing a new order after a bloody conflict, and inspired by the example of Genghis Khan. The Hidden Masters of Roerich and Blavatksy, currently said to be guiding the New Age movement, had declared themselves to be behind Bolshevism, and saw Lenin as one of their own. Their bloody plans were stopped by Stalin, who suppressed the esoteric cabals in Russia, and shot the likes of Bokii, and Barchenko. It is no wonder that Trotsky damned Stalin as a 'Bonapartist'.[106]

Mexico: Battle Ground of the Scottish Rite

The revolt of the Cristeros peasant militia against the dechristianisation policies of the Mexican regime of Plutarco Elias Calles (President 1924-28) is reminiscent of the Jacobin extermination of the Vendée peasantry that rebelled for the same reasons in France. Mexico was dominated by the Scottish Rite, which pursued a revolutionary agenda with violence, like the associated Masonry in Spain and Portugal. Oscar J Salinas, Senior Grand Warden of the York Rite and head of the Royal Arch of Mexico, stated that 'I don't think it is a secret that Mexican Freemasonry has long had a reputation for being involved with political and religious issues and with the initiation of women'.[107]

105 Churton, p. 302

106 Trotsky, 1935, etc.

107 Salinas, *Mexican Masonry*.

The Scottish Rite had been introduced to the Americas first in the West Indies by Stephen Morin in 1761. The first recorded founding of a Lodge in Mexico was in 1791, when the meeting was broken up by authorities at the behest of the Inquisition. Consequently, identification of Mexicans who were Masons is not generally recorded, however it can be assumed that those who fought for independence from Spain included a large proportion of Masons. What emerged was a civil war between the York Rite and the Scottish Rite for the control of Mexico, a feature of Mexican history that is well-known and taught in schools. Both fought themselves to exhaustion while there arose a Mexican National Rite, around 1830. However Salinas states that, 'As the 19th century went on, Mexican Masonry embraced the degree system authored by Albert Pike and grew ever more anticlerical', which is to say, the 33 Scottish Rite degrees were worked.[108]

During the mid 19th century most Masons supported the Liberal party under Benito Juárez, and the 1857 Constitution 'curtailed the power of the Roman Catholic Church', which prompted a rebellion by the Conservatives known as the Reform War. This ended with the victory of the Liberals, who enacted the Reform Law, which instituted a secular regime. Another war erupted, when Napoleon III installed Austrian Archduke Maximilian in 1862, but Juárez again prevailed. Salinas states that most of the leaders involved in this revolt against Napoleon III and Maximilian were Masons.

In his history of Mexico published in 1935, The Most Reverend Francis Clement Kelley, Bishop of Oklahoma City and Tulsa, writes of Freemasonry as the 'hidden hand', 'which plays a part, in the Mexican tregedy'. Rev. Kelley stated that from the arrival of Spanish officers during and after the Napoleonic wars in Spain to the time of Juárez, 'Freemasonry kept the unfortunate country in a turmoil of troubles, including revolution, skirmishes and

---

108   Salinas, *Mexican Masonry*.

riots'.[109]   Kelley stated that Dr Joel Poinsett, later U.S. Secretary of War, was sent to Mexico by the U.S. government to counter influence from Europe. With a charter from the York Rite, he established this to counter the Scottish Rite. Rev. Kelley's comments concur with those of the Mason Salinas. However, both forms of Masonry wanted revolution and the destruction of religion.[110] In 1827 the York Rite, with the support of Poinsett, adopted a resolution to 'redouble its efforts' to take control of the education of the people away from the Church and control the education, culture and morality of the people.[111]

On the death of Juárez, another Mason ascended to the presidency, Porfirio Díaz, who established a Liberal dictatorship that imposed secularism and repressed political freedom. He sought to unite both Scottish and York Rites into a Grand Diet.

Salinas states that after the overthrow of Díaz in 1910 'a succession of Presidents who were Masons and strongly anticlerical ruled the country under the 1917 Constitution'. In the late 1920s the Church rebelled against State attempts to dechristianise Mexico, which Salinas describes as the State attempting to 'fully enforce the anticlerical measures of the Constitution'. The peasant folk organised into a resistance movement, which Salinas calls 'bands of Catholic sympathisers, often led by gun-toting priests'.

Former President Vincente Fox has been explicit about the nature of the Masonic role in his country:

After 1917, Mexico was led by anti-Catholic Freemasons who tried to evoke the anticlerical spirit of popular indigenous President Benito Juarez of the 1880s. But the military dictators of the 1920s were a lot more savage than Juarez.[112]

109 Francis Clement Kelley, p. 161.
110 Francis Clement Kelley, p. 169.
111 Francis Clement Kelley, p. 170
112 Fox, p. 17.

Members of the 'Cristeros', who sought to defend their Christian faith against the Mexican regime's persecution of Catholicism in the 'Cristeros War' 1926-1929.

Rev. Kelley ascribed Masonic subversion in Mexico to the Scottish Rite, calling it the advancecd guard of Juárez and Calles. He stated that the Scottish Rite spread rapidly in Meixco for the same reason that it did so in Spain. 'It offered the opportunity to plot unseen and unheard... For the French and Spanish the Scottish Rite was anti-royal and anti-Church. With many of its members the Scottish Rite was anti-God; perhaps with almost all of them. Thus it was presented to the radicals of Mexico... It captured the Mexican white collar class and some of the "literati", while accepting recruits also from the ranks of the lax and politically minded clergy'.[113]

During what is known as the 'Calles Persecution' priests were killed for performing the sacrament and altars were desecrated by soldiers. As in Vendeée, the people reacted and formed guerrilla bands called the Cristeros. The result was the 'Cristeros War' of 1926-1929, after enduring two years of persecution by

113 Kelley, pp. 164-165.

Calles, who had assumed the Presidency in 1924. Calles had been initiated into the Helios Lodge at Guaymas, and served as the lodge's secretary.[114]

The provisions of the 1917 Constitution were described as crippling. Priests were barred from teaching in schools. The State had sole prerogative over religious matters and did not recognise any church as a legal entity. All real and personal property belonging to the Church, clergy and religious orders could be expropriated by the State. Priests were denied civic rights and the right to hold public office. Church publications were prohibited from commenting on political matters. Anyone infringing these clauses would not be entitled to trial by jury.[115]

To these provisions Calles enacted the State licensing of priests, and the numbers were regulated by bureaucrats to ensure that the proportion of priests diminished. Because many Churches were now left without priests, the State used this as justification to turn them into museums and other public buildings. Crucifixes, Catholic statues and pictures were prohibited even in private homes. Expressions mentioning God, such as 'If God wills', or 'God forbid', were subject to a fine. Msgr Carvana, the Papal Nuncio, was expelled in 1926 after protesting against these actions. A present-day Catholic source states of the situation: 'Throughout the country, Catholic public figures were assassinated, girls coming out of church were kidnapped, imprisoned, raped'.[116]

On May 28, Calles received the Masonic medal of merit from the hands of the Great Commander of the Scottish Rite in Mexico. On July 12, the following communiqué appeared in the press: 'International Masonry accepts responsibility for everything that is happening in Mexico, and is preparing to mobilize all its forces for the methodical,

---

114 Denslow, p. 171..

115 Ehler, p. 579.

116 Lelibre.

integral application of the agreed upon program for this country.[117]

Following the programme of the French Revolution, Calles sought to establish a State cult, and Father Perez was proclaimed by the Calles regime as Patriarch of the Mexican Catholic Church. In the new rites, wine was replaced by the Mexican narcotic mescal.

Under such conditions, the Bishops, all in hiding or exile, suspended religious activities completely and called on the faithful to resist the State.[118] The Cristeros militia emerged, named in honour of an elderly shopkeeper who had been struck down by two policemen for having displayed a sign reading Viva Cristo Rey!, 'Long live Christ the King!' In response Catholics boycotted state-owned industries, and organised mass processions throughout Mexico. They were met by machine gun fire, and fell singing hymns and praying. As confrontations with the State increased the cry of the fallen shopkeeper went up and the Cristeros movement emerged. (Lelibre). While the Pope supported the Cristeros resistance the U.S. Scottish Rite responded in the magazine of the 33° Supreme Council Southern Jurisdiction, *The New Age*, December 1926:

> The Catholic Church has perverted the Mexicans for 400 years. Calles's merit is to have delivered them from ignorance and superstition. That is why he can count on our understanding and on North America's support.[119]

Despite the superior military equipment of the State, the Federales acted as drunken and doped-up pillagers, and they succumbed by their lack of discipline to defeat at San Julian in March 1927. In scenarios reminiscent of the Bolshevik revolution

---

117 Lelibre, citing *La Tribuna*, 12 July 1926, F M Algoud, 1600 Young Saints, Young Martyrs, 1994.

118 Elher, p. 579.

119 Lelibre.

in Russia, the Calles regime resorted to torture in attempts to make priests and Cristeros troops apostatise.

> Valencia Gallardo, a Cristeros leader, was tied to a stake and tortured but only cried out throughout: 'Long live Christ the King!' They tore out his tongue; he freed one of his hands from the bonds and pointed to heaven. They cut it off, and then split open his skull with their rifle butts.[120]

By 1929 rural Mexico had become ungovernable and the Calles regime had to withdraw to the cities. However, that year, with victory likely, the Vatican reached an accord with Calles through the mediation of U.S. Ambassador Dwight Morrow. The Cristeros were bewildered and disappointed but had no choice other than to follow Papal authority (Lelibre). The Cristeros laid down their arms and 5,000, including 500 leaders, were immediately massacred, many in their homes in front of their families, and their properties seized, leaving their families destitute. Their casualties in the rebellion had only reached 4,000. What remained of the clergy were excommunicated by the new Mexican episcopate. The threat of excommunication by the episcopate assured that attempts at further rebellion through the years 1934-1937 were abortive.[121]

When General Cardenas eliminated Calles' role from politics in 1936[122] he was given refuge in the USA in 1936, under the Presidency of Franklin D Roosevelt. However, the Church remained suppressed, particularly in the field of education. This secularisation of education drew support from U.S. officialdom, Ambassador Josephus Daniels praising the State during a talk at the American Embassy in Mexico City in July 1934, favourably quoting Calles who had said: 'We must enter and take possession of the mind of childhood, the mind of youth'.[123] The speech

---

120 Lelibre.

121 Lelibre.

122 Ehler, p. 580.

123 Kelley, p. 261.

caused an outcry from American Catholics who demanded that Daniels be withdrawn.[124] The Church was not recognised as a legal entity in Mexico until 1992.

Spain

Spain followed the same manner of fanaticism under the slogan of 'liberty', as France, Portugal, and Mexico.

Grand Lodge Masonry was brought to Spain in 1728 by the Duke of Wharton, who formed The Lodge of the Lilies. This immediately aroused the suspicion of the Church. During the mid 18th century the Spanish authorities, fulfilling Church edicts, took vigorous action to suppress the lodges, on the authority of the Papal Bull In eminenti issued by Pope Clement XII. This was reinforced by Pope Benedict XIV's Providas of 1751. Nonetheless in 1767 the Gran Logia Espanola was formed, independently from the jurisdiction of the English Grand Lodge. The first Grand Master was the Count d'Aranda, Prime Minister under Charles III. Most significantly, in 1780 the Gran Logia Espanola became the Grande Oriente Espanola under the jurisdiction of the Grand Orient de France. As we have seen, the Grand Orient was the harbinger of subversion and illuminist doctrines. The liberalistic, anti-clerical character of Charles III can explain the emergence of Grand Orient Masonry in Spain. Under Charles other Masons were placed in Government positions, although the anti-Masonic laws remained in theory.

V W Bro Martin I McGregor,[125]despite being under United Grand Lodge jurisdiction, expresses the same liberalistic doctrines as that of the Grand Orient, in stating that the philosophy of Masonry is Liberalism. Especially interesting is that,

> Freemasonry was the very embodiment of the Liberal spirit and in its organization a model of the Liberal ideal

124 *New York Times*, 1934.

125 Grand Lecturer and Grand Steward, Freemasons New Zealand.

of government. Freemasonry was, and is, in effect a parallel society to that of everyday society.[126]

McGregor acknowledges that Masonry is a state-within-a-state and the harbinger of what Traditionalists see as subversive doctrines, whether in Grand Lodge or Grand Orient form. McGregor notes the seminal revolutions in America and France that undermined the traditional order, and alludes to the 'individual Freemasons [who] featured prominently in both revolutions'. He alludes to 'individual Freemasons' because anything else is suggestive of Masonic plots.

Masons attempted a revolt in Spain in 1795, arms having been collected by the 'Respectable Lodge of Spain'. Rather than being executed the plotters were jailed in Panama, but escaped to Venezuela where they attempted a revolt in Caracas in 1797. This too failed and most of the leaders were executed; however two leaders, Picornell and Cortes escaped 'to link up with fellow Freemason, Francisco de Miranda, to raise the flag of rebellion in South America'.[127] These two were prolific producers of Jacobin propaganda and Picornell produced a Spanish translation of the Declaration of the Rights of Man and Citizen.

In 1808 a revolt led by the Count of Montijo, the Grand Master of the Grande Oriente, resulted in the dismissal of Prime Minister De Godoy and the abdication of the King. Although Joseph Bonaparte, who was installed by Napoleon as ruler of Spain, was Grand Master of the Grand Orient de France, as we have seen, Napoleon was neither a catspaw of Masonry nor an adherent of its doctrines, and Spanish Grand Orient Masonry helped in establishing a resistance Government in Cadiz and in formulating the 1812 Constitution. However, with the overthrow of the French in 1813 Fernando VII assumed the Throne and resumed the traditional Church policy against Masonry.

---

126   McGregor, *'The History and the Persecutions of Spanish Freemasonry'*
127   McGregor, *ibid.*

Nonetheless, in 1818 the Scottish Rite under Colonel Rafael de Riego instigated a rebellion among troops and forced Fernando VII to accept the 1812 Constitution, expel the Jesuits, and free all jailed Masons. In 1823, with the help of French troops, Fernando VII was able to resume his authority and in 1824 outlawed Masonry on pain of hanging, aware of the Masonic role in revolutionary intrigue. There was also acute awareness of the Masonic role in fomenting revolution in the Americas and of the activities of Masons such as Simon Bolivar who had detached Spain's American colonies from the motherland. The Lodge of Rational Knights of Lautoro had been formed in Spain for the purpose of assisting with the dismemberment of the Spanish Empire.

In 1868 a revolt toppled Queen Isabella after a military uprising in Cadiz led by Generals Pierrad, Moriones and Contreras, and supported by the political leaders Malcampo, Sagasta, Dulce, Prim, Ruiz Zorilla and Mendez Nunez, 'all of whom were prominent Freemasons'.[128] After a three-year reign with a Mason, Amadeus of Savoy, as President, and with Zorilla, Grand Master of Grande Oriente Espanol, as Prime Minister, a Republic was proclaimed, and laws against Masonry were revoked. Masonry became more overt and increasingly influential in Government. For example, Praxedes Mateo Sagasta, Grand Master of the Grande Oriente Espanol, served seven times as Prime Minister. 'Spanish Freemasonry went from strength to strength and was successful in attracting numerous members from the ranks of the armed forces, the civil service, politics and academia'.[129]

The dictatorship of General Miguel Primo de Rivera, 1923-1930, sought to bring order to Spain, but his regime fell in 1931, and King Alfonso XIII went into exile, with the declaration of the Second Republic. The Republic's first Prime Minster was a Freemason, Manuel Azana Diaz, and included 17 Ministers who were Masons, 5 Deputy Secretaries, 15 Directors General, 183 out of 470

---

128 McGregor, M. I. *'The History and the Persecutions of Spanish Freemasonry'*.

129 McGregor.

Parliamentary Deputies, 5 Ambassadors, 9 Divisional Generals and 12 Brigade Generals. These influential Masons included: Alejandro Lerroux y Gracia, Minister of State; Diego Martinez Barrio, Minister of War; Jose Giral, Minister of the Navy; Jose Salmeron, Director General of Public Works and Mountains; the Mayor of Madrid, Pedro Rico Lopez and Jaime Ayguade, Mayor of Barcelona. The former Grand Master of the Grande Oriente Espanol, Demofilo de Buen, was Counselor of State. 'Indeed, a sizeable proportion of the membership of Spanish Freemasonry were in a position of power and influence during the Second Republic'.[130]

The Grand Lodge called for 'Masonic nuclei' to be formed locally throughout Spain to support the Republic.[131] It was presumably as a revolutionary cadre to resist any attempt to overthrow the Republic that this 'nuclei' was formed, and one might ask whether it provided the basis for the formation of the Bolshevistic and anarchistic 'workers' militias' that were to become the fighting force of the Republic during the Civil War? As in other states where Masonry had become the dominant political influence, a dechristianisation programme was undertaken, which included expropriation of property belonging to religious orders. Although the 1933 General Election saw a move to the Right under Catholic political leader Gil Robles, it was Alejandro Lerroux, a Freemason and leader of the Radical Republican Party, who was asked to form the Government. This included 'Diego Martinez Barrio, former Grand Master of the Spanish Grand Orient, and huge numbers of other Freemasons'.[132]

The Republic was seeing increasing chaos and insurgence from the extreme Left. The 1936 elections resulted in a narrow victory for the Leftist Popular Front with the Radical Republican Party holding the balance of power. Azana again formed a Government, by which time the Communists were becoming increasingly volatile.

---

130 McGregor.

131 McGregor.

132 McGregor.

In June 1936, after just four months of the Azana administration, Robles informed Parliament of the outrages that were being committed against the Church, including the burning of 160 churches, along with 269 mostly politically-inspired murders and 1287 assaults, 113 general strikes and 228 regular strikes.

The Monarchist leader, Jose Calvo Sotelo, called for a State based on Catholic social justice where there would be 'no more strikes, no more lock-outs, no more usury, no more capitalist abuses, no more starvation wages, no more political salaries gained by happy accident, no more anarchic liberty, no more criminal conspiracies against full production'. As a consequence of his call for a just and orderly regime he was assassinated by those linked to the Socialist party. The murder was the last straw, and on the day of Sotelo's death General Emilio Mola Vidal issued an order for the army to mobilize against the Government, starting in Spanish Morocco. The Civil War had begun. Masonic army officers were quickly obliged to move aside, as Masonry had long been associated with communists and anarchists in the subversion of Spain. Those officers who resisted the Rightist insurgency were Masons such as General Gonzalo Queipo de Llano at Seville.

With the collapse of the Government of Prime Minister Santiago Casares Quiroga, a Freemason, President Azana asked Diego Martinez Barrio, a former Grand Master of the Grand Orient, to form a Government. The Barrio Government did not last a day. Azana next asked Jose Giral y Periera, another Freemason. Giral responded to the crisis by forming armed workers' militias, thereby empowering the Bolsheviks.

The Republican army was under the command of General Jose Miaja Menant, and with help from anarchist and communist militias, the International Brigades of foreign volunteers and tanks and planes from the USSR, the Republicans were able to postpone the capture of Madrid.

The territory controlled by the Republic saw an unleashing of the bestial forces against the Church in the manner of what had taken place in France, Mexico and Russia: thirteen Bishops were murdered, 4,184 priests, 2,365 members of religious orders and 283 nuns, 'some burned to death in their churches with reports of crucifixions, rapes, castrations and disembowelment'.[133] The Republicans shot approximately 2,000 prisoners as General Franco's forces approached Madrid.

In acknowledging the role of Freemasonry in the ruination of Spain, the Nationalist reaction was decisive, and many Masons were executed, although Franco imposed a moderated policy in 1938 when victory was in sight. The Right had seen the results of Masonic subversion since the 18th century, and in the present struggle identified Masonry as being in alliance with Communist and Jewish elements in attacks on the Church and Monarchy, in a Contubernio (secret alliance). In 1937 General Franco stated to the press that most of the leaders of the Republic had been Masons and that 'before their duty to their country came their obligations to the Grand Orient'. From the Masonic sources that have been considered here, his observations were justified, and it was a frequent theme of Church and Rightist propaganda. In 1940 the Franquist regime enacted a law prohibiting both Communism and Freemasonry as being responsible for the Civil War and Masons were purged from the public service. In 1945 Franco stated in an address to the Women's Section of the Falangist movement that he had thwarted a 'Masonic super-state' and that the foreign press hostility towards Nationalist Spain emanated from the influence of Freemasonry. The Caudillo exposed Masonry in a series of 49 articles for the Falangist journal *Arriba*, and these were published as a book in1952.

In his farewell address to the Spanish nation on 1 October 1975, Franco reminded Spaniards that Communism and Masonry remained their enemies and that the European Economic Community was a Masonic creation. As we shall now consider, Franco was again correct.

---

133 McGregor.

With the death of Franco in 1975 the way was cleared for Masonry to be re-established, and the Gran Oriente Espanol was back in 1977. In response to the conciliatory approach of the Gran Oriente Espanol towards the Church and Monarchy, the Grand Symbolic Spanish Lodge was formed in 1979, under the jurisdiction of the Grand Orient de France.

Counterfeit Europe

Stepping-Stone to the Universal Republic

As alluded to above, Franco was perceptive in identifying the EEC as of Masonic instigation. This, having been transformed into the European Union, Europe is a Counterfeit Europe, a Europe of commerce and secularist anti-culture; rootless, cosmopolitan, universalistic, devoid of the faith and spirit that is the basis of the real Europe. Its foundation in legalism and commercial treaties is typical of 18th century Liberalism. Europe had been emerging as a cultural unit since the 8th century.[1] It is the concept that Hillaire Belloc described in the term: 'The Faith is Europe and Europe is the Faith'.

Thus, when in 2009 the European Court of Human Rights ruled against the display of crucifixes in classrooms in Italy, stating that the presence of the crucifix ran counter to the 'right of children to believe or not to believe'[2] it was following the secularist doctrine that had been pursued by the Grand Orient and Illuminism for two centuries, under the now universal slogan of *le droit humain.*

The Grand Orient continues to avidly promote a secularist Europe, as seen in a meeting between European Union bureaucrats and Freemasons that occurred shortly prior to the European Court ruling against the crucifix, in June 2009. Present at the meeting were the President of the European Commission, José Manuel Barroso; the President of the European Parliament, Hans-Gert Pöttering; Louis Michel, Commissioner for Development and Humanitarian Aid, and Ján Figel', Commissioner for Education, Training, Culture and Youth, who met with a variety of 'secular'

---

1   de Rougemont, p. 45.

2   BBC News, 2009.

organisations. However, most of the delegates were from Masonic orders. In addition to five secular, humanist and 'human rights' groups being represented, there were seven Orders of Masonry: Grand Orient de Belgique, Grande Loge Symbolique Espagnole, Grand Orient de France, Grande Loge Feminine de France, Ordre Maçonnique International Delphi (Greece), Grande Loge d'Italie, and Grande Oriente Lusitano (Portugal). With these secularists and humanists represented in the majority by the Masonic Orders, European Commission president Barroso declared 'Europe's values' to be based on the humanist and secularist ideology of the Enlightenment. European Parliament President Pöttering referred to what can only be Masonry as the foundation of these pseudo-European values in ascribing them to the 'non-confessional humanist organisations, which emerged in the Enlightenment'.[3]

It is this secularist Counterfeit Europe that emerged from the Jacobins and Illuminism during the 18th century. Jean-Baptiste du Val-de-Grace, Baron de *Clootz*, who changed his Christian name to Anarchasis, declared to the French National Assembly on 13 June 13, 1790 that the Declaration of the Rights of Man and the Citizen must be adopted by all humanity, and that there must no longer be any sovereign nations. On 2 April 2, 1792 at the Convention he called for the creation of 'La Republique Universelle'.[4] These doctrines, applied first to Europe by the Revolutionaries, were – and are – intended as a universal creed for a New World Order, of which the Counterfeit Europe is not intended as the rebirth of the great impulse of European Unity, but as a stepping stone towards a Universal Republic.

Masonry acknowledges its seminal role in the creation of the bogus Europe of secularism and universalism.

Dr Corneliu Zeana, speaking as both a Masonic adept and as the president of the Romanian section of the European Movement,

3   Europa Press Releases Rapid.
4   de Rougemont, p. 180.

stated that it is a self-appointed 'Freemasonic elite' 'shaping events'. If any non-Mason alludes to such matters he is ridiculed as a 'conspiracy theorist', not least by Masons. Zeana writes:

> Freemasonic elite devotes praiseworthy efforts in order to shape out events and evolutions that become history due to their consummation through the irreversible passing of time. Freemasonic elite had many visionaries who were considered dreamers until their ideas became reality. They set out the blueprint of a better world according to the ideals of liberty, fraternity, dignity, justice, equity of justice and chances, moral status, prosperity and peace. It is a continuous fight against oppression, corruption, injustice, poltroonery, ignorance and lie; a perpetual searching for truth. Masons became history makers through this seeking of the ways towards a better and more righteous world.[5]

This 'Freemasonic elite' that 'shapes history', while building a bogus Europe, also pushed for the creation of the abortive League of Nations as the instrument for a Universal Republic. Gustavo Raffi, Grand Master of the Grand Orient of Italy, acknowledged the Masonic role in the foundations of the League of Nations and the United Nations Organisation:

> Our being outside of the parties and their dialectics, our being 'religious', but, at the same time, latitudinarian respect to the single theologies, allows the creation of a cultural web of peace education and dialogue - a task that our Institution has always tried to carry out also through the promotion of great worldwide operations that have given birth to Organisms like firstly the League of Nations and then U.N.O. [6]

Zeana likewise refers to the covert Masonic influences that emanate out into the world from the Lodges, reshaping humanity

---

5   Zeana, *'The European Union – a Masonic Accomplishment'*.

6   Raffi, Grande Oriente d'Italia.

according to their concept of the Supreme Being. It is the same doctrine of 'perfectibilism', 'Illuminism' or 'Luciferianism' that guided the Illuminati and is the aim of the New Age movement, and of Communism:

> Masonry is a way of perfection. The man, as an individual, ascends on the path of wisdom and selflessness; he comes near the Supreme Being. A Mason discovers inside the Lodge the atmosphere of fraternal harmony. It is herein that the Masonic demeanour is outlined and the moral values, which are to be followed in his profane life as well, are favoured. Yet Freemasonry is not limited to the individual and the group he establishes contact with. It is involved in scale projects hinting at the future of nations, their continents and the whole world as an ensemble, searching for the adequate ways and means to ensure an ascending evolution towards light, more and more light.[7]

Zeana is unequivocal in describing the European Union as 'a Masonic accomplishment'.

Dr Marian Mihaila, Assistant Grand Master of Romanian Masonry, which was founded under the jurisdiction of the Italian Grand Orient, credits Freemasonry with the birth of the contemporary concept of a Federal Europe. Having previously alluded to a magazine founded at the end of the 19th century by Victor Hugo and Garibaldi, called The United States of Europe, Mihaila writes in a section of an article which he calls 'The Masonic European Community', that it was 'important European Masons' who took up the concept of a federated Europe from the 19th century and brought it into the 20th century:

> Aristide Briand, the French Foreign Affairs Minister, delegate to the League of Nations, proposes, on 8 August 1929, for the first time in the name of a government, the creation of a federal European structure. The Briand plan is

---

7   Zeana, 'The European Union – a Masonic Accomplishment'.

elaborated until 1 May 1930 and after 17 days it is brought to the League of Nations for examination.

The father of this Counterfeit Europe is Count Richard Coundenhove-Kalergi. The Masonic affiliation of Kalergi and the Masonic foundation of his Pan-European Movement are confirmed by Mihaila:

> The adepts of the idea of a united Europe are grouped in the Pan-European Movement whose supporter was also a mason, Count Richard N.C. Kalergi (the son of an Austro-Hungarian diplomat and of a Japanese woman). He was encouraged and financed by a series of American masons who wanted to create thus, according to the American model (the first Masonic state in history) the United States of Europe.[8]

Mihaila states much in this paragraph:

1. The 'adepts' were grouped around the Pan-European movement
2. Kalergi was a Mason
3. American Masons financed Kalergi
4. The USA was founded as the first 'Masonic state' in history
5. The concept of United Europe is not that of the European Spirit but that of Masonic conceptions as established in the USA, which in turn was doctrinally inspired by the Masonic Enlightenment.

Kalergi confirmed the funding he received from international bankers, having stated in his book *Pan Europe*:

> Early in 1924 Baron Louis Rothschild telephoned to say that a friend of his, Max Warburg, had read my book and wanted to meet me. To my great astonishment Warburg

---

8 Mihaila, Paragraph 1.6.

immediately offered a donation of 60,000 gold marks to see the movement through its first three years. Max Warburg was a staunch supporter of Pan-Europe all his life and we remained close friends until his death in 1946. His readiness to support it (the movement) at the outset contributed decisively to its subsequent success.[9]

When Kalergi toured the USA he did so by the arrangement of Max Warburg's brothers Felix and Paul, the latter the architect of the Federal Reserve banking system in the USA.

Kalergi also wrote of receiving support from Masonic politicians such as deposed Masonic head of the Russian Provisional Government, Alexander Kerensky, and Aristide Briand, French Foreign Affairs Minister, who is cited by Mihaila as being the first to propose a federated Europe to the League of Nations.

Kalergi is today esteemed by the European Union as the father of their 'Europe' and, celebrating the 100th Jubilee of Kalergi, a 10 Euro coin was minted in his honour in 1972, and a stamp printed in Austria.

With the interruption of the Second World War to the Masonic schemes, the movement was resumed in 1946. Mihaila details those movements and people, again of Masonic origin: 'Being stopped during WWII, in August 1946 the Masons take up again their secular dream: they create the European Union of Federalists.' Note that Mihaila definitively calls the European Union a Masonic 'secular dream'. Likewise Zeana describes a federal Europe as being a manifestation of the 'Masonic spirit':

> The blueprint of a new Europe was created on the basis of the great values promoted by Masonry: peace, liberty, equity, and fraternity. Europe was tired because of the two World Wars during a single generation. The desire for long-lasting peace was great and justified, to say the

---

9   Kalergi, pp. 59-66

least, by the precepts of all the great religions. (One of the conditions of joining Masonry was the faith in God. The Christian religion, predominant throughout Europe, would not become exclusive).[10]

Here Zeana is more specific in his use of the Grand Orient slogan: 'liberty, equity [equality], fraternity'. The Grand Orient is precisely noted for its inclusion of atheism as well as the type of syncretic universal religion that Zeana avers to in the above passage, stating that, 'the Christian religion [despite being] predominate throughout Europe, would not become exclusive'.[11] Syncretic religion, as a basis for the Universal Republic, will be considered below.

According to Constantin Iancu, Sovereign Grand Commander of the Supreme Council of the 33° and Last Degree of A.A.S.R. (Scottish Rite) for Romania, 'As is well known, Modern Romania owes its existence to these Masons'. (Iancu, interview). The influence of Romanian Masonry on the politics of the country attests to the very real role Masonry plays as a political force today. To a question on this, Iancu frankly asserts:

> Today, as in the past, the Romanian elite gathered around Romanian Masonry. These include the most important politicians in all parties, leading bankers, businessmen, doctors, artists, professors and lawyers almost all of the Romanian elite.[12]

Mihaila in alluding to the Masonic affiliations of Winston Churchill et al, and the role of a Freemasonic pan-European group in the creation of the European Union, states of the resumption of the movement after World War II:

> On 19 September, in the same year, the Mason Churchill

---

10   Zeana, 'The European Union – a Masonic Accomplishment'.

11   Zeana, *ibid*.

12   Iancu, Masonic Forum.

holds a speech in which he declares himself in favour of the creation of the United States of Europe, saying it was urgent that France and Germany get together. Further on was Robert Schuman's plan, (skilfully conceived by Jean Monnet), Deputy Secretary General of the League of Nations, and by his close associates Étienne Hirsch, Paul Reuter and Pierre Uri.

Many of them are members in the European Union Chain (Chaîne d'union Européenne - C.U.E.), a Freemasons' group with representatives especially in Belgium, Germany, the Netherlands, Switzerland and France. CUE wants to reunite the European Freemasons irrespective of nationality, obedience, religious and philosophic ideas, race and language. In order to achieve its objective it organizes meetings of the Freemasons, when the problems of future Europe are discussed.[13]

Kalergi having laid the philosophical and organisational foundations for a counterfeit Europe since 1922 with the backing of the Warburg and Rothschild banking dynasties and his Masonic brethren over the entire Continent as well as in the USA, the concept was implemented in the aftermath of World War II via another secret coterie, the Bilderberg Group, fronted by Prince Bernhardt of The Netherlands. The Polish diplomat Joseph Retinger, the motivating force behind the European League for Economic Cooperation, the European Movement and the Council of Europe, had formed the Bilderbergers.[14] He was involved in secret political conspiracies in Mexico (as we have seen, a state dominated by Masonry) after having been asked to leave France in 1918. After a shadowy existence, Retinger emerged in 1924 promoting the concept of European Union, and with British Member of Parliament, E D Morel, established a secret organisation for the purpose. Following World War II Retinger became a leading advocate of European union, his

13   Mihaila, 'European Union and Freemasonry'.

14   Eringer, p. 16.

Richard von Coudenhove-Kalergi pioneer of the "European Union", and proponent of the destruction of the "White" European race, replacing it with a "Jewish, Negroid, Eurasian race similar to the ancient Egyptians"

speech on the subject to the Royal Institute of International Affairs on 8 May 1946 giving birth to the idea of a European Movement, formed in 1949 after a tour the previous year with Belgian Prime Minister Paul-Henri Spaak and Winston Churchill.[15] From this emerged the American Committee on a United Europe. Ex-CIA luminaries such as William Donovan and Allen Dulles led this committee.[16]

The Bilderberg Group was created from this background in September 1952 out of a small meeting where it was agreed that it was imperative to get the USA involved, and it was 'preferable to keep it all as discreet as possible'. With Prince Bernhard, Retinger went to the USA to gain the support of General Bedell

---

15   Zeana believes that Churchill's Masonic initiation and his role in the creation of a
      federal Europe are of significance, Zeana describing Churchill as a 33° Mason, initiated
      on the 24th of May 1901.

16   Eringer, pp. 19-20.

Smith, director of the CIA. An American committee was formed which comprised Rockefeller-connected luminaries, along with David Rockefeller himself. The first conference was held at the Hotel de Bilderberg in Holland, May 29-31, 1952.[17]

The initial post-war moves from limited economic agreements between European nations, to the EEC and finally to the European Union were part of a gradual process that Zeana describes. He states that the Constitution of the European Union was the work of Valéry Giscard d'Estaing whom he states was a Mason. Zeana concludes by stating that the contemporary moves for complete integration will continue under the watchful, all-seeing eye of Masonry:

> In the actual period, the European Union needs a Constitution. The Laeken Convention (also called Convent, an adequate Masonic term for the reality of this reunion led by Valéry Giscard d'Estaing, who needs no presentation for the illuminated and aware Masons) succeeded in editing it. Despite the difficulties we are sure that the endorsement of the European Constitution is not far. The realization of a United Europe cannot be done at once. It needs the successive periods of an uprising evolution, far from perfection. We are the contemporaries, apprentices, fellowcrafts, masters and architects of this great edifice. We cannot pass through without pointing out the evolution of the terminology. From the European Economical Community (preceded by the European communities, ECCS and the EURATOM), the European Community to the European Union and maybe this is not it. These changes point to the fact that starting with the economic, there is a tendency to unite the politics, the spirit, the concept, the moral. And maybe the United Europe must represent, above everything, a moral space. Regarding this transformation, the vigilance of Freemasonry is a mission.[18]

---

17   Eringer, pp. 21-22.

18   Zeana, *'The European Union – a Masonic Accomplishment'*.

Zeana describes the process in Masonic terms as being 'guided by apprentices, fellowcrafts, masters and architects of this great edifice'. Most unequivocally of all, Iancu, Sovereign Grand Commander of the Supreme Council of Scottish Rite Masonry, describes the role of Masonry today in his message celebrating the 200th anniversary of Romanian Masonry:

> As we are taught in the 32° as Princes of the Royal Secret the Supreme Council of the 33° and last degree of the A.A.S.R. [Scottish Rite] in Romania, will continue to fight for the Unity of Europe, so that, together with the other Brotherhoods American, Asiatic, African, to work for the Universal Brotherhood, for the restoration and instalment of the Temple of Solomon. For this creed Romanian Freemasonry has worked and suffered, has fought and is still fighting.[19]

Iancu states that the 'Unity of Europe' is just a prelude to the Masonic ideal of a 'Universal Brotherhood', with allusions to the rebuilding of the Temple of Solomon, the significance of which will be considered below.

Charlie Hebdo

When the small satirical magazine *Charlie Hebdo* was attacked by Jihaidists in France, killing key staff, a medium that had gloried in the ridicule of religious beliefs, particularly the Catholic and the Islamic, in the most puerile manner, became a *cause celebre* for the political, financial, and cultural ruling strata of Europe and the USA.

Charlie Hebdo came from the New Left milieu of the 1960s, as a product of the 1968 student revolt against President Charles de Gaulle. It happens that this revolt occurred at a time when (1) the CIA was sponsoring anti-Soviet New Left student organisations and other non-Soviet Left-wing endeavours throughout the

---

19   Iancu, Masonic Forum.

Charlie Hebdo anniversary edition depicts God as a terrorist. Note the eye and triangle symbol of Freemasonry prominently shown.

world;[20] (2) President de Gaulle was pursuing a course independent of U.S. foreign policy. The question remains as to whether the CIA were using the New Left in France to destabilise the de Gaulle regime? The reaction to the Jihadist attack on *Charlie Hebdo* exposed its backing by a combination of Zionism, Communism and Freemasonry. *Charlie Hebdo* advocates the 'Liberalism' and libertinage of the Jacobins. They epitomise the 'values of the French Republic'. An illustration of Jesus sodomising God,[21] and other such puerilities was long purveyed on a weekly basis.

The magazine was established in 1969 as the successor to *Hara-*

20   Bolton 2011, pp. 138-143

21   The cover illustration can be found at: http://www.australiamatters.com/cms/
       wp-content/uploads/hebdo_jesus_slander.jpg

Kiri magazine, founded in 1960. The first editor of *Charlie Hebdo* was François Cavanna. He was succeeded in 1992 by Philippe Val who had relaunched *Charlie Hebdo* in 1991 with Cavanna, Delfeil de Ton, and Georges Wolinski. Wolinski, one of those killed on 7 January 2015, was a Tunisian-born Jew, who had co-founded the satirical magazine L'Enragé during the 1968 revolt. He wrote for the Leftist newspaper *Libération*. His cartoons were in particular use by the Communist newspaper *L'Humanite*. Another *Libération* colleague on *Charlie Hebdo* was Dutch cartoonist Bernard Willem Holtrop. Renaud Pierre Manuel Séchan who became known as a singer and songwriter with 'Crève salope!' due to its popularity among the '68 revolters, was a founding shareholder of *Charlie Hebdo*.

Olivier Cyran, a former *Charlie Hebdo* staffer who was purged from the magazine, commented about the *Charlie Hebdo* editor's conception of 'liberty', referring to an 'Enlightenment despotism' that aptly describes the Jacobin legacy of *Charlie Hebdo*: 'The trouble is that this right so abundantly spread by the director of *Charlie Hebdo* is only for himself and those who think like him. His former employees of Charlie know something: in case of divergence, the Enlightenment suddenly turns to despotism'.[22]

Cyran gave the example of Philippe Corcuff who was pushed out of *Charlie Hebdo* for not supporting Islamophobia with sufficient zeal. In 2000 Mona Chollet was fired for objecting to Val's reference to Palestinians as 'uncivilised'. In 2013 Cyran wrote to the editor Charbonnaire ('Charb') and to Fabrice Nicolino[23] that *Charlie Hebdo* had made France 'a nastier place to live'. It was Val who sacked Siné for supposed 'anti-Semitism', although a case for wrongful dismissal was won against *Charlie Hebdo* in 2010. For services rendered Val was appointed in 2005 as director of France Inter, part of Radio France.

---

22   Cyran, 2006.

23   Injured during the 7 January attack on the *Charlie Hebdo* offices.

In 2006 Val co-signed a statement with Bernard Henri-Levy,[24] and ten others, published in *L'Express*, stating:

> After having overcome Fascism, Nazism and Stalinism, the world now faces a new global threat of a totalitarian nature: Islamism. We – writers, journalists, and intellectuals - call for resistance against religious totalitarianism to promote freedom, equal opportunities and secular values for all.[25]

The manifesto was a call to oppose the Islamic reaction to the cartoons of Muhammad appearing in Jyllands-Posten, Denmark, in 2005, as a calculated provocation by the newspaper's cultural editor, Fleming Rose. Cyran (2006) wrote that the re-publication of the Danish cartoons in a special issue of *Charlie Hebdo* entitled 'freedom of expression' was a 'masterstroke' as a 'publicity stunt'. On February 8 sales records had been broken with 400,000 copies of *Charlie Hebdo* sold. *Charlie Hebdo* was an important mouthpiece for U.S. and Israeli-Zionist policies.

Grand Orient de France

Among the dead on 7 January were two members of the Grand Orient de France. The Grand Orient wrote:

> Two of the journalists assassinated in the cowardly and barbarous attack on *Charlie Hebdo* were Freemasons. Bro Bernard Maris, economic columnist at *Charlie Hebdo*, and Bro Michel Renaud, formerly of *Europe 1* and *Le Figaro*, were both active Freemasons in the Grand Orient, Bernard in Roger Leray Lodge in Paris and Michel in Lux Perpetue Lodge in Clermont Ferrand. They died representing the values we stand for …[26]

---

24 An eminent Jewish philosopher, with a Leftist background that converges with U.S. globalism, Henri-Levy called for U.S. intervention in Serbia, and in 2011 against Syria. In 2010, at a conference in Tel Aviv he said of the Israeli Defence Force, 'I have never seen such a democratic army. There is something unusually vital about Israeli democracy'. He is a columnist and a Board member for *Libération*, owned by Eduard de Rothschild.

25 Val, et al, 2006

26 Grand Orient de France, Masoneria 357.

The Grand Orient officially identified the *Charlie Hebdo* doctrine as their creed, and joined with the mass demonstration of solidarity organised by Hollande, President of France. Daniel Keller, GODF Grand Master, wrote:

> The Grand Orient of France was present yesterday evening in the Republic Square to share the emotion of thousands of anonymous who came to express their support for the silent struggle of *Charlie Hebdo*. All were not Charlie readers but all were aware that Charlie is one of the standard bearers of democracy to which we are attached and for which Charlie journalists fought every day without ever escaping the risks that for that they had agreed to incur. Yes, they were all resistant to a faceless war on terror claims to impose abject and cowardly. In these circumstances, I would first like to emphasize the powerful outpouring of compassion expressed by members of our Obedience of all backgrounds who have expressed support but also their willingness to mobilize so that we, the living, may be worthy of those who were the victims of this blind barbarism.[27]

A special meeting for 12 January at the Arthur Groussier Temple, was called by the GODF Grand Master, Daniel Keller, to unify 'the thinking that must be ours on the values that we must promote in the light of the tragedy that has befallen our country'. The GODF Foundation funded *Charlie Hebdo* to ensure its continuation beyond its hitherto fringe existence. Keller's declaration reads:

1. The Grand Orient will participate in a spirit of Masonic unity alongside all liberal and non-dogmatic Obediences, at the Republican event taking place Sunday. The place and time of the meeting will be provided as it becomes available.

2. The Council invites the brothers and sisters of the

---

27   Keller, Circular 2015.

Obedience to take part in a special event Monday, January 12th at 19h at Arthur Groussier temple to federate the thinking that must be ours on the values that we must promote in the light of the tragedy that has befallen our country.

3. The Foundation will appeal initially to donors who wish to show their solidarity with *Charlie Hebdo* to ensure the financial sustainability of the newspaper. The Foundation will of course listen to any other initiative that the newspaper could take in this direction.

4. In addition to these actions of immediate support, it is essential that the commitment of GODF against all fanaticism, dogmatism, fundamentalism and communalism is more than ever at the heart of our work and our actions externalizing. To say that the barbarism will not pass is not enough, we must also unite a broad citizen movement to assert and defend on the ground republican principles, democratic and secular, unshakable foundations of our society. As such, the events devoted to debunking Anti-Masonry will be throughout the year as a messenger. Citizens, they are supposed to promote dialogue but they take enhanced sharpness in the current circumstances.

5. Finally, it is suggested in the extension of the national day of mourning that day that Loges open their future work with a minute of silence.[28]

A GODF programme was drafted around the *Charlie Hebdo* shootings including a call to man the figurative barricades in defence of republicanism. Keller wrote of 'barbarism' as though *Charlie Hebdo* stood for anything but the most pathological of the decaying West's sickness. However, the Grand Orient has always been a primary carrier for culture-pathogens, and images of Jesus sodomising God etc. would be regarded as the legacy of Voltaire, et al., and the values of Jacobin Republicanism. Hence, given that the center of world cultural contagion shifted to the

28   Keller, *ibid.*

USA generations ago, the National Endowment for Democracy (NED), the globalist version of the Comintern, but far more subversive, issued 'a statement of solidarity with the people of France', with luminaries from Republican and Demcoratic parties, labour and international finance (the omnipresent Goldman Sachs).[29]

Marie Harf, speaking for the U.S. State Department, declared that the U.S. 'absolutely supports' *Charlie Hebdo*.[30] Harf condemned a Turkish court for blocking internet sites from publishing the *Charlie Hebdo* cartoon of Muhammad, and she also condemned Turkish government officials for their criticism of the *Charlie Hebdo* cartoon as a provocation.[31]

While plans were underway to make *Charlie Hebdo* a journal of significance, the funeral of the late editor, 'Charb', was conducted to the tunes of L'Internationale, as clenched fists were raised, while speakers exhorted the crowd to defend the Republic.[32] *L'Humanite*, newspaper of France's Communist Party, editorialised of their *Charlie Hebdo* 'comrades':

> No words can name the horrible attack perpetrated yesterday in the middle of Paris, eliminating our friends, our comrades at *Charlie Hebdo*, one by one, in cold blood during a conference. A newspaper, its journalists, its cartoonists were shot down by forces of terror. Others were wounded. Faced with these militants, they only had their pens to defend themselves.

29   National Endowment for Democracy, 'Statement of Solidarity'.

30   'U.S. State Dept., supports *Charlie Hebdo* magazine's right to publish freely', *Sputnik International,* January 14 2015, http://sputniknews.com/politics/20150114/1016863398.html

31   'U. S. slams Turkey over ban on publishing *Charlie Hebdo* cover', Today's Zaman, January 15 2015, http://www.todayszaman.com/diplomacy_us-slams-turkey-over-ban-on-publishing-charlie-hebdo-cover_369893.html

32   'Farewell for 'Charb' the last of the funerals for the *Charlie Hebdo* attack', Euronews, January 16 2015, http://www.euronews.com/2015/01/16/farewell-for-charb-the-last-of-the-funerals-of-charlie-hebdo-attack/

Families will be in bereavement forever. We provide them assurance of our compassion, our solidarity. Beyond the death of our comrades, it is an attack against intelligence, the act of creating, and the right to think. Against freedom and democracy, as was the case in our history's darkest and most tragic hours. Terror and death are the weapons wielded against fraternity, culture, debate, and any inclination to free oneself from a reactionary and obscurantist project. This we must admit.

The targets are the Republic, its values, history, enlightenment, and secularism. This is a republic of tolerance, of respect for the other. No matter what you think, *Charlie Hebdo's* writing, drawings, and caricatures reveal hidden faces of this world's turpitude and its agents. To be able to publish these things as well as to dispute their contents is an integral part of the democratic debate. A united Republic must immediately express its views with the strength and dignity required under these circumstances. We will support any initiative which will allow united, assembled citizens this form of expression. ...

Dear George Wolinski, Cabu, Charb, Tignous, Honoré, and all the others, we cry for you and we will never forget you, faithful to the subversive power of your art which cost you your life. This terrible drama and these lives that were stolen away command us to defend the values of freedom, tolerance, fraternity and equality every step of the way. In these tragic hours, in a context where tension keeps mounting, the Republic, indivisible, tolerant, secular, and social, must become more tenacious than ever. It must resist and face up to these cowards and these barbarians.[33]

Again, from the Communists, there are the clear echoes of the GODF, with a very perverted perception of 'values'. The

---

33   Patrick Le Hyarick, 'Barbarians', *L'Humanite*, January 10, 2015, http://www. humaniteinenglish.com/spip.php?article2621

close relationship between *L'Humanité* and *Charlie Hebdo* was described by the French communists:

> Most of the cartoons published by *L'Humanité* are by Charlie's cartoonists. We followed the same path in work, and in friendship. They are one of us. A long companionship has grown, over the years, between the teams of *Charlie Hebdo* and of *L'Humanité*. Its conductor was Charb, communist, insolent, and a rigorous professional, who obtained from his crew of rebels the cartoon that enlivens our daily's last page. Jul, Luz, Babouze, and Charb himself never missed the weekly appointments, nor did Coco and Besse, who draw for *L'Humanité* Dimanche. On the eve of the Fête de l'Humanité, one year, Charlie's editorial team took over the entire iconography of the next day's issue, spreading over the pages an invigorating and harmless insolence, and their priceless creations that clarified, in a few strokes, the day's events. Charb was even one day's editor-in-chief for *L'Humanité*. … They were one of us, and we have raised our glasses together more than once. On the weekend of the Fête de l'Humanité at the Courneuve, where their booth, each year, was shared with Cuba Si…[1]

In a pathetic display of self-negation by the Church the bells of Notre Dame Cathedral rang in honour of *Charlie Hebdo*. In return the Charlies editorialised in the first issue since the January 7 attack, the issue subsidised by Rothschild, Google, GODF and the French tax payer:

> What made us laugh the most is that the bells of Notre Dame rang in our honor. We would like to send a message to Pope Francis – who also was Charlie this week: We will only accept the bells of Notre Dame ringing in our honor when it is Femen who make them ring.[2]

---

1   Henry Crapo, Isabelle Métral, 'They are one of us', *l'Humanité*, January 8, 2015, http://www.humaniteinenglish.com/spip.php?article2618

2   '*Charlie Hebdo* rejects Catholic support', *Catholic World News*, January 15, 2015, http://

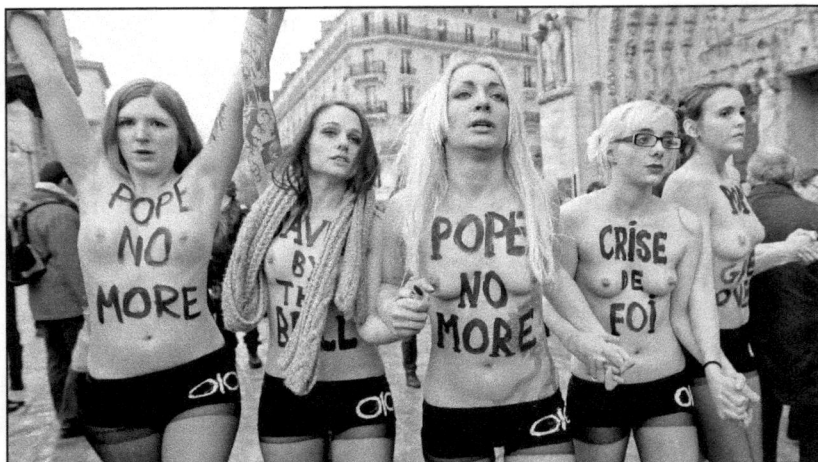

Femen protestors at the Notre Dame Cathedral in Paris.

Femen is an interesting, but not surprising choice by *Charlie Hebdo*. Like the Charlies, they are among the most puerile of Culture-retarders. Their antics go beyond several topless demonstrations in Europe. Founded in the Ukraine in 2008, it is based in Paris. It is an extreme feminist group, calling itself 'sextremist', aimed at faith and tradition, and therefore the type of organisation one would expect to be getting backing from the globalist power-elite. The original aim was laudable, opposing the trickery used to lure Ukrainian women abroad and then held as prostitutes. By far the largest component running this white slave trade are Israelis,[3] but Femen notably excludes Israel from its protests. As with *Charlie Hebdo*, Femen has been embraced by President Hollande who chose Femen activist Inna Shevchenko as one of the models for Marianne, the symbol of France of a woman wearing the Jacobin Phrygian cap.[4] The funding for the

angelqueen.org/2015/01/15/charlie-hebdo-rejects-catholic-support/

3   Ted Pike, "Israel whorehouse of the Middle East," http://www.goodnewsaboutgod.com/studies/political/jews/whorehouse.htm

R. Hovel, 'Three Israelis indicted for importing prostitutes from Ukraine', Haaretz, August 2, 2013, http://www.haaretz.com/news/national/three-israelis-indicted-for-importing-prostitutes-from-ukraine.premium-1.502212

4   'Femen's Inna Shevchenko inspired France's Marianne stamp', BBC News, July 15, 2013.

well-paid activists has come from Jed Sunden, a Brooklyn-born Jewish media magnate with newspaper interests in the Ukraine, who gave them their initial publicity in his *KyivPost*. His newspaper, since sold, reports its former owner's involvement, quoting Femen founder Anna Hutsol:

> In 2008, when topless protests were a novelty in Ukraine, Hutsol got a call from publisher Jed Sunden, the owner of KP Media. 'Jed was the very first influential person who noticed us, helped us with all the resources he had, gave us some useful advice, generously donated and said we were special. Jed was the very first person who helped us in organization's promotion and the creation of our website. We used to call him a 'Femen Post' [a play off of the *KyivPost* newspaper, which Sunden sold last year],' Hutsol said. Sunden acknowledged he is more than a fan of Femen. 'I confirm that I do give money to Femen,' Sunden said. 'I will not state the amount. After meeting with Anna Hutsol, I was impressed with her ideas and have been a supporter. I believe Anna is a young, independent voice in Ukraine. While I do not agree with all of her positions, I believe it is important to give her, and groups like hers, support'.[5]

KyivPost, continuing their publicity for Femen, reported in 2013 that a Femen disrupted Christmas Mass at Kolner Dom, the main Cathedral in Cologne, climbing topless atop the altar, her body painted with I am God'.[6] On November 25, 2014, a topless Femen entered Strasbourg Cathedral just prior to the scheduled visit of Pope Francis, dancing atop the altar.[7]

5   'Femen wants to move from public exposure to political power', *KyivPost*, April 29, 2010, http://www.kyivpost.com/content/politics/femen-wants-to-move-from-public-exposure-to-politi-65379.html

6   'Topless FEMEN activist climbs altar in Cologne cathedral during Christmas mass', *KyivPost*, December 25, 2013, http://www.kyivpost.com/content/world/topless-femen-activist-climbs-altar-in-cologne-cathedral-during-christmas-mass-334252.html

7   'Femen desecrate Strasbourg Cathedral', *Gallia Watch*, http://galliawatch.blogspot.co.nz/2014/11/femen-desecrate-strasbourg-cathedral.html

It is certainly understandable why the Charlies are so admiring of Femen, and why President Hollande would choose a Femen to model as Marianne. It is reminiscent of the Jacobin crowning of an actress as 'The Goddess of Reason', who was enthroned on the altar of Notre Dame and worshipped by the enlightened revolutionists. This is what the Charlies, Hollande, the GODF, Google, NED, U.S. State Department, and so on mean by 'Western values', and the 'secular Europe'. When Femen anarchists ring the bells of Notre Dame, as per the Charlie fantasy, then this pathogenic conglomerate of diseased cells on the body of the Western culture-organism will rightly proclaim that their disease has triumphed over the entire world.

'Principle of Conflict'

While the dialectical approach to history, expounded by Hegel, is best known as being applied as both a metaphysical doctrine conversely and a materialstic tactic by Marxism, called 'dialectical materialism', expressed as 'class war'; dialectics are also applied by globalist oligarchs.[1]

Dialectics postulates a thesis, or the germination of an idea, within which is contained its opposite or antithesis, the clash of the two opposites leading to a synthesis which combines (i.e. synthesises) the elements of thesis and antithesis into something different that goes beyond both. In Marxism the current historical process is expressed as capitalism (thesis) + socialism (antithesis) = communism. In the historical epoch prior to the present capitalist stage of development, the dialectical process ran as: feudalism (thesis) + commerce (antithesis) = capitalism (synthesis). In the capitalist historical epoch history as 'class struggle' is played out by the conflict between capitalist and proletariat, and from this struggle the majority (proletariat) emerges victorious, expropriates capitalist property and establishes socialism which evolves to pure communism. In the previous feudal epoch, the agents of 'class struggle' were the new middle class (bourgeois) conflicting with feudal nobility from out of which arises capitalism on the ruins of feudalism. The bourgeois hence becomes the new ruling class and the struggle proceeds with the proletariat being the new agency of dialectical 'progress'.

I have shown in my recent book *Revolution from Above* that the capitalists operate a similar scenario, however, they utilise socialism as the antithesis against rural and traditional societies

---

1   Bolton, *Revolution from Above*, pp. 9-14.

that are regarded as anachronistic in a New World Order, and that socialism is a quick method of pushing a traditional society through to the capitalist and industrial stage.

There is an historical nexus between the two supposed deadlydialectical opposites: Socialism and Capitalism, which find common cause in their opposition to Tradition. As Marx stated, dialectically socialism emerges from capitalism, hence it has the characteristics of capitalism. Oswald Spengler pointed this out in *The Decline of The West* and *The Hour of Decision* when he said that there is not a socialist movement that does not operate in the interests of Money.[2]

An early and significant example of this Money nexus using revolution is that of the French Revolution, where free market commerce was established on the ruins of the old feudal order and the abolition of the guilds in the name of 'The People'. The economic premises established by the revolutionist Declaration of on the Rights of Man & the Citizen guaranteed capitalistic property relations and free market commerce in the name of 'human rights'. Hence, socialism does not seek to transcend capitalism, but to make the proletariat the new capitalists. Under such a situation, the 'masses' are easily manipulated. Present-day examples are the 'colour revolutions' promoted by the currency speculator George Soros and agencies such as the Congressionally-funded National Endowment for Democracy. In France the 'rights' secured for 'man and the citizen' were those concerned with the liberty to trade without the burden of Christian ethics imposed by the old feudal system and the guilds.

From out of the Enlightenment doctrines of Jacobin France arose both Communism and Free Trade Liberalism. As we have seen, the secret societies had a definitive influence on these doctrines and it is logical that dialectics is part of the theory and practice of the cabals today aiming to establish a New World Order.

---

2   Bolton, *Ibid.*, pp. 22-23.

Cosmic Polarities

The Counter-Tradition applies dialectics in the form of the esoteric doctrine of cosmic polarities, which might be more readily recognised in the Oriental symbol of Yin and Yang, where each concept contains a seed of its own opposite. Something of this character can be seen in Marx's oft quoted 'capitalism contains the seeds of its own destruction'.

The Hermetic and Alchemical doctrine of the anima and animus as interacting polarities united in the Androgyne or Hermaphrodite, is a mystical expression of dialectics. In Hinduism the universe is activated by the comic interplay of the polarities represented by Shakti and Shiva united in Brahma. The cosmology of the Pythagoreans is based on the interaction of ten polarities emanating from Apeiron, reminiscent of the Cabalistic Tree of Life. In the Cabalistic Tree of Life, a type of cosmic map descending from the Godhead, polarities depicted as spheres (sephira) emanate from Left and Right Pillars, representing the female and male principles respectively. Binah and Chokma are male and female, positive and negative, anima and animus, synthesised in the Middle Pillar. The Cabalistic principles of Binah and Chokma are represented in the Masonic Temple as columns.[3] Such doctrines as alchemy and Cabbalism form important elements in Masonry and other secret societies, and have been appropriated by the Counter-Tradition.

This cosmic dialectic is explained in the 32° of the Scottish Rite. This is the Degree of the Sublime Prince of the Royal Secret, using the allegories of occult law on the interaction of polarities. Albert Pike writes in his instructions for this Degree:

> It is the fine dream of the greatest of the Poets, that Hell, become useless, is to be closed at length, by the aggrandizement of Heaven; that the problem of Evil is to receive its final solution, and Good alone, necessary and triumphant, is to reign in Eternity. So the Persian dogma

3   Butler, p. 10.

taught that AHRIMAN and his subordinate ministers of Evil were at last, by means of a Redeemer and Mediator, to be reconciled with Deity, and all Evil to end.[4]

The occult doctrine that there is no light without darkness is explained. The movement of contraries activates the cosmos:

> But unfortunately, the philosopher forgets all the laws of equilibrium, and seeks to absorb the Light in a splendor without shadow, and movement in an absolute repose that would be the cessation of life. So long as there shall be a visible light, there will be a shadow proportional to this Light, and whatever is illuminated will cast its own of shadow. Repose will never be happiness, if it is not balanced by an analogous and contrary movement. This is the immutable law of Nature, the Eternal Will of the JUSTICE which is GOD.[5]

Evil is therefore a necessity in the cosmos to impel movement, without which there would be stagnation. Here the Luciferianism Gnosis of Illuminist doctrine is explained:

> The same reason necessitates Evil and Sorrow in Humanity, which renders indispensable the bitterness of the waters of the seas. Here also, Harmony can result only from the analogy of contraries, and what is above exists by reason of what is below. It is the depth that determines the height; and if the valleys are filled up, the mountains disappear: so, if the shadows are effaced, the Light is annulled, which is only visible by the graduated contrast of gloom and splendor, and universal obscurity will be produced by an immense dazzling. Even the colors in the Light only exist by the presence of the shadow: it is the threefold alliance of the day and night, the luminous image of the dogma, the Light made Shadow, as the Saviour is the Logos made

---

4   Pike, Chapter 32, p. 847.

5   Pike, p. 847.

man: and all this reposes on the same law, the primary law of creation, the single and absolute law of Nature, that of the distinction and harmonious ponderation of the contrary forces in the universal equipoise.[6]

The principle is related to the Cabala and the pillars in the Masonic Temple are equated with the pillars of the Cabalistic Tree of Life:

> The Infinite Wisdom of God foresees what each will do, and uses it as an instrument, by the exertion of His Infinite Power, which yet does not control the Human action so as to annihilate its freedom. The result is Harmony, the third column that up-holds the Lodge. The same Harmony results from the equipoise of Necessity and Liberty. The will of God is not for an instant defeated nor thwarted, and this is the Divine Victory; and yet He does not tempt nor constrain men to do Evil, and thus His Infinite Glory is unimpaired. The result is Stability, Cohesion, and Permanence in the Universe, and undivided Dominion and Autocracy in the Deity. And these, Victory, Glory, Stability, the Infinite Wisdom of God foresees what each will do, and uses it as an instrument, and Dominion, are the last four Sephiroth of the Kabalah.[7]

Pike returns to the interplay of contraries, of good and evil, light and darkness, indicating an endless struggle of cosmic polarities on the human plane:

> Of that Equilibrium between Good and Evil, and Light and Darkness in the world, which assures us that all is the work of the Infinite Wisdom and of an Infinite Love; and that there is no rebellious demon of Evil, or Principle of Darkness co-existent and in eternal controversy with God, or the Principle of Light and of Good: by attaining to the

6   Pike, p. 848.

7   Pike, *ibid.*

knowledge of which equilibrium we can, through Faith, see that the existence of Evil, Sin, Suffering, and Sorrow in the world, is consistent with the Infinite Goodness as well as with the Infinite Wisdom of the Almighty.

Sympathy and Antipathy, Attraction and Repulsion, each a Force of nature, are contraries, in the souls of men and in the Universe of spheres and worlds; and from the action and opposition of each against the other, result Harmony, and that Life of the Universe and the Soul alike.[8]

Principle of Conflict & the New World Order

This occult explanation of the cosmic interplay of polarities is an esoteric equivalent to political dialectics. It is what occultists such as Alice Bailey refer to as the 'principle of conflict'. Bailey stated that from out of the dialectical conflict of capitalistic democracy and Soviet communism would emerge a 'New World Order'. This World State is supposed to be ruled over by a 'World Teacher'. We have considered something of the character of this 'World Teacher', when Master Morya dispatched Roerich to send messages to the Bolsheviks congratulating them on their destruction of faith, churches, class enemies, property and all other foundations of Tradition; the same 'Hidden Master' that is claimed to have instructed Blavatksy.

Bailey explained that out of the Principle of Conflict of three systems - American 'melting pot' democracy, British parliamentarianism, and Soviet communism - a new synthesis would emerge as the New World Order, writing:

The point, however, which is of major importance to us is the recognition that each of these three nations is distinguished by:

• A similarity of problems.

8   Pike, pp. 859-60.

- A battleground, which is leading to, the formation of a triangle of relationships brought about through the Principle of Conflict.

The similarity of problems consists in the fact that each of these three nations is essentially composite in nature and is formed by an amalgamation of many nations, of many peoples speaking many different languages, and is consequently staging a great experiment in fusion.

- The U.K. is the nucleus or the living germ of the British Commonwealth of Nations wherein a great experiment in free government is being tried out
- The U.S.A. is a fusing center wherein all nationalities are represented and are being slowly blended into a miniature One Humanity. A great experiment in right relationships is being undertaken and is making real progress. A culture and a civilisation will emerge which will be the result of right human relations and which can provide a world pattern in relationships.

The U.S.S.R. is also seeking to blend and unite into one great national project many diverse nations and races - European and Asiatic - and the effort is still largely embryonic. In Russia a world ideology is being wrought out which (when proven) can be presented to the world as a model system; this, however, will not come as a result of dictatorship, nor can it be presented aggressively to the world.[9]

Here Bailey expressly uses the term 'New World Order' indicating the esoteric origin of the term that has been in common political parlance across the Earth since uttered by President Bush in 1991:

In these three great nations, therefore, the three major

---

9   Bailey, 1971, pp. 632-634.

divine aspects are being brought into manifestation, thus laying the foundation for the new world order. All three are of equal importance.[10]

Bailey sets out a goal towards a New World Order with reference to 'democracy' and 'human rights'. The same principles were made by Woodrow Wilson in proposing a new world order in the aftermath of World War I via the League of Nations and based on his 'Fourteen Points', and by both Presidents Bush in the dialectic of the 'War on Evil' that was supposed to usher the 'New World Order'. Bailey continues:

> The factor that must and will relate the Principle of Conflict to the expression of harmony and bring about the new world order, the new civilisation and culture, is the trend and the voice of public opinion, and the opportunity offered to people everywhere to bring about social security and right human relations.[11]

Bailey defined this new world order as being the ultimate goal of the highest occult adepts. She also referred to work being carried out by international agencies for the purpose of humanitarianism as being a part of the process. Here we are reminded of the contemporary universal catchphrase, *le droit humain* – 'human rights' – that emanated from the 18th century Lodges and has ever since been the rationalisation for all manner of violence and repression, including the present-day excuse for 'regime change' against any state that is reticent to join the New World Order, under the auspices of UNO and NATO bombs. Behind the bombs, what Bailey next states, is that adepts are performing occult rituals to inaugurate the Universal Republic:

> To reorganise world affairs and so initiate the new world order. This is definitely in the realm of ceremonial magic. It is evident in the universal interest in goodwill, leading

---

10   Bailey, 1971, p. 632.

11   Bailey, 1971, p. 632.

eventually to peace; this desire for peace may be based on individual or national selfishness, or upon a true desire to see a happier world wherein man can lead a fuller spiritual life and base his efforts on truer values; it can be seen in all the planning which is going on for a new world order, based on human liberty, belief in human rights and right human relations; it is demonstrating also in the work of the great humanitarian movements, the welfare organisations, and the widespread evocation of the human mind through the network of educational institutions throughout the world.[12]

From a more mundane perspective, Dr Antony Sutton of the Hoover Institute, in his study of Lodge 322, which, as we have seen, he regarded as a continuation of the Illuminati, described the process:

> From this axiom it follows that controlled conflict can create a predetermined history. The synthesis sought by the Establishment is called the New World Order. Without controlled conflict this New World Order will not come about. The operational history of The Order can only be understood within a framework of the Hegelian dialectic process. Quite simply this is the notion that conflict creates history.[13]

The Hidden Masters – if their existence is to be accepted – proceed through a dialectical merging of all states through the use of controlled conflict, tormenting the universal psyche with perpetual crises, until humanity screams out for peace at any price. That at any rate is the programme of the Black Adepts that has been unfolding for centuries. While Roerich raised his so-called 'Banner of Peace', as he consulted with Bolshevik Commissars and couriered to them messages of support from Master Morya, the dominant power around which the creation of the New World Order is centred is the USA. American fulfils

12   Bailey, 1971, p. 494.
13   Sutton, 1985a, i.

its 'mission' of creating the Universal Republic with the same types of slogans that have been used to construct the tyrannies of their predecessors, Jacobin France and the USSR – 'human brotherhood' and 'human rights', while bombing any resistant state into submission. Just what this 'goodwill' means in erecting the Novus Ordo Seclorum is shown by the regard Alice Bailey had for the USA which she said, 'expresses the will-to-love....It is [here]...that people are most sensitive to the influence of the Hierarchy'. Hence, it is through the power of the USA that the world state is to be achieved.[14]

New World Order – Motto for the New Age

Although the motto Novus Ordo Seclorum on the Great Seal of the USA is often mistranslated as 'New World Order' it is 'A New Order of the Ages'. The meaning, however, is the same.

President Franklin Roosevelt 32°, and Vice President Henry Wallace 32°, considered that the USA had a manifest destiny to lead the world in establishing this 'new order of the ages'. The Masonic 'work' for the 'perfectibility of humanity' is represented by the placing of the capstone upon the Great Pyramid that is depicted on the US Great Seal. Henry Wallace wrote of this:

> It will take a more definite recognition of the Great Architect of the Universe before the apex stone [capstone of the pyramid] is finally fitted into place and this nation in the full strength of its power is in position to assume leadership among the nations in inaugurating 'the New Order of the Ages'.[15]

A comparison of the Wallace quote with statements made by both presidents Bush shows a similarity that suggests a common origin. It is notable that George W Bush specifically refers to both the New World Order and the 'new order of the ages', citing the

14   Bailey, 1934, p. 131.
15   Wallace, pp. 78-79.

belief of the Founding Fathers, in his inaugural address: 'When our Fathers declared a 'new order of the ages', they were acting on an ancient hope which is meant to be fulfilled'.[16] George H W Bush, in his State of the Union Address, declared:

> What is at stake is more than one small country, it is a big idea a new world order, where diverse nations are drawn together in common cause to achieve the universal aspirations of mankind: peace and security, freedom, and the rule of law. The world can therefore seize this opportunity to fulfil the long-held promise of a new world order where brutality will go unrewarded, and aggression will meet collective resistance.[17]

Before U.S. Congress President George H W Bush stated on 6 March 1991:

> Now, we can see a new world coming into view. A world in which there is the very real prospect of a new world order. In the words of Winston Churchill, a 'world order' in which 'the principles of justice and fair play ... protect the weak against the strong'. A world where the United Nations, freed from Cold War stalemate, is poised to fulfil the historic vision of its founders. A world in which freedom and respect for human rights find a home among all nations.

Esoteric Cult of the UNO

Gustavo Raffi, Grand Master of the Grand Orient of Italy has previously been cited as stating that Masonry acts through institutions such as the United Nations Organisations, and prior to that, the League of Nations. Much importance is attached to the UNO by New Age bodies, some of which are given official status by the UNO as NGO observers. One of these is the

---

16   Bush, 2005.

17   Bush, 1991.

Aquarian Age Community (AAC), which holds meetings in the
U.N. conference room, and whose website is sponsored by the
UNO. The AAC states that it exerts covert influence over well-
placed functionaries throughout the U.N.:

> We have an informal network at the UN, a humanity
> underground. It consists of those who are committed, aware,
> and striving to bring the New World to birth. It consists of
> people in high places and in low - of the patient secretary
> who has been 30 years with the UN, but lives with the vision
> and the spirit; of the professionals, and undersecretaries and
> heads of departments who are acting out the imperatives
> that their own inner vision gives them. Some few are
> conscious of the sources of their inspiration; most are not.
> They are the Karma Yogis of our time - those whose path
> of spirituality is to achieve through doing - to grow through
> serving. They are found not only in the secretariat but also
> in the delegations to the UN, among the diplomats and their
> staffs, and also among folks like us, representatives of non-
> governmental organizations around the UN.[18]

The aim of this organisation is that of Theosophy, and of the
Roerich movement: to prepare the way for the universal rule of
a World Teacher and the Hidden Masters, who have espoused
Bolshevik methods of mass murder and enslavement, or as the
AAC puts it, to 'cooperate and collaborate with the worldwide
community that is actively preparing the way for the reappearance
of the World-Teacher – the Christ (Anointed) One, the true
Aquarian'. Note that when the New Age and Theosophically-
derived cabals speak of returning 'Christ' they are referring to an
'Anointed One', not the Christian conception of Jesus. Through
the UNO the AAC hopes to see the fulfilment of the universalistic
Illuminist creed: 'Recognition of the One Humanity [that] can
be created through religious unification and realization of the
One Divinity'.[19] Here is the meaning of the syncretic religion.

18   Aquarian Age Community, 'About the AAC', http://www.aquaac.org/about/about.html
19   Aquarian Age Community, *ibid.*

AAC describes this doctrine as one of 'universality and synthesis', its first duty being 'alignment' with the 'Spiritual Beings who inspire the evolution of life on planet Earth'. One might wonder what the UNO is doing sponsoring such an organisation. The AAC explains that this is the cycle for which the 'Masters of the wisdom, the Teachers of humanity' have waited[20] to ascend to lordship over the world. The New World Order will be based upon what the AAC terms spiritual values: 'liberty, fraternity and equality'; that is, the very same slogan of the Grand Orient. Following the list of esoteric principles of the ACC is the final action of 'promoting the work of the United Nations'. The AAC claims to work along the path of Blavatksy and Bailey, and in the service of the Hidden Masters, including the Bolshevik-lauding Master Morya, Bailey's Mahatma Master Djwhal Khul (DK), and Blavatsky's Koot Hoomi.[21]

The AAC reminds us, in its description of the UNO that the name 'United Nations' was devised by President Franklin D Roosevelt in 1942, whom it should be recalled was a 32° Mason; that is to say, a high initiate of the Scottish Rite, who had previously recognised the manifest destiny of the USA in inaugurating a new world order. Vice President Henry Wallace 32° pointed out the Masonic symbolism of the Great Seal to Roosevelt. Wallace's personal guru was Nicholas Roerich.

According to the esoteric proponents of the new world order, Master/Commissar Morya gave a message to Alice Bailey in regard to the U.N. founding conference at San Francisco in 1945:

> Not for nothing is this conference being held during the five days of the Weak Full Moon. It will be a time of supreme difficulty, in which the Forces of Light will face the forces of selfishness and separativeness.[22]

---

20   Aquarian Age Community, *ibid*.

21   Aquarian Age Community, *ibid*.

22   Bailey, cited by Urso.

According to the Hidden Masters, the astrological alignments were right for the creation of this globalist organisation that would usher forth the New World Order, making the denizens of Shambhala supreme:

> The Hierarchy kept a keen vigilance over the events of this period and especially over the conference in San Francisco, which was of such significance that it called forth the attention of those great lives in Shambhala. ... In 1945, a supreme effort was made during the five days of the Full Moon from April 25 to April 30.[23]

The Master Morya told Bailey that this time was a test of power for them: 'The conference was also under the subjective influence of the Hierarchy who we are told were facing a major test of Their hierarchical power - not a test of their love, but of their power'.[24] Perhaps this 'major test' is a reference to the Axis that the 'United Nations' had just fought, or to the USSR, as Stalin, their former ally, was about to reject the scheme for a World Government through the UNO.[25]

23   Bailey/Urso, *ibid.*

24   Bailey/Urso, *ibid.*

25   Bolton, 'Origins of the Cold War and How Stalin Foiled a New World Order', *Foreign Policy Journal*, 31 May 2010.

Universal Syncretic Religion

To establish a World Government a world religion is essential. The Counter-Tradition has formulated this religion, which is known as syncretism. Included are those who claim to be Traditionalists but who are fulfilling the agenda of the Black Adepts. Of course, there are also many well-meaning 'fellow travellers'. Wherever the Black Adepts have gained sufficient authority over the State they have sought to erect a new cult on the ruins of traditional faith and custom. The Jacobins created new cults of civic religion and public worship based on 'reason' and 'nature', where the most irrational and unnatural excesses of fanaticism turned France into a madhouse of bedlam. Calles tried to create a 'Patriotic Church' in Mexico while repressing the Catholic Church. Even the Bolsheviks erected a pyramid to entomb a mummified Lenin. Today's new universal cult embodies the illuminist doctrine of *le droit humain* as a sacred creed with the United National Declaration on Human Rights forming the central core of Holy Writ around which subsidiary creedal documents are created and enforced.

Adam Weishaupt stated that he was creating a new cult under the guise of Christianity. The same process is taking place today, with cults forming around a concept of 'Christ' – The Anointed One – not the Jesus of Christian faith, but one of the so-called Hidden Masters. Weishaupt stated of the syncretic religion he was creating, referred to as 'Christian' in the lower degrees of the Illuminati:

> One would almost imagine, that this degree, as I have managed it, is genuine Christianity, and that its end was to free the Jews from slavery. I say, that Free Masonry is concealed Christianity. My explanation of the

hieroglyphics, at least, proceeds from this supposition; and as I explain things no man need be ashamed of being a Christian. Indeed I afterward throw away this name, and substitute Reason. But I assure you, this is no small affair; a new religion and a new state government, which so happily explain one and all of these symbols, and combines them in one degree.[1]

The above was the explanation given to the initiate of the 'priest degree', one of the higher degrees in the Illuminati.[2] Weishaupt explained that once the initiate moves up the higher degrees the veil of 'true Christianity' is discarded and the 'new religion' of 'Reason' is invoked. Weishaupt boasted that the explanation of the 'true sense of Christianity' in this Degree had beguiled a 'famous Protestant divine, who is now of the Order'. Weishaupt then stated, in a manner exposing his own amorality typical of those who proclaim themselves the prophets of human 'perfectibility': O MAN, MAN! TO WHAT MAY'ST THOU NOT BE PERSUADED. Who would imagine that I would be the founder of a new religion?'[3]

The Freemasonic doctrine of 'God' in the lower degrees is the Great Architect of the Universe – GAOTU – a godhead that can encompass all Gods, all religions and all creeds. It can be readily seen that the modern syncretic religion has emerged from this Masonic conception. Albert Pike also explained, in his Scottish Rite instructions, that Masonry is intended to be the incubator of a universal religion, and one, like the Illuminati, which would only be revealed – literally – by Degrees, while the bulk of humanity is kept in ignorance as to the true aims:

> Masonry, like all the Religions, all the Mysteries, Hermeticism and Alchemy, conceals its secrets from all except the Adepts and Sages, or the Elect, and uses false

1   Robison, p. 85.
2   Robison, p. 101.
3   Robison, p. 86.

explanations and misinterpretations of its symbols to mislead those who deserve only to be misled; to conceal the Truth, which it calls Light, from them, and to draw them away from it. Truth is not for those who are unworthy or unable to receive it, or would pervert it.

The truth must be kept secret, and the masses need a teaching proportioned to their imperfect reason.

Every man's conception of God must be proportioned to his mental cultivation and intellectual powers, and moral excellence. God is, as man conceives Him, the reflected image of man himself.[4]

The syncretic character of GAOTU, or the Supreme Being, is explained as follows by a present-day initiate of the Scottish Rite:

The Supreme Being. Masons believe that there is one God and that people employ many different ways to seek, and to express what they know of, God. Masonry primarily uses the appellation, 'Grand Architect of the Universe': and other non-sectarian titles, to address Deity. In this way, persons of different faiths may join together in prayer, concentrating on God, rather than differences among themselves. Masonry believes in religious freedom and that the relationship between the individual and God is personal, private, and sacred.[5]

The method in recent years has been ecumenicism in regard to Christian 'dialogue' with the world's faiths, and syncretism behind a façade of Tradition. Such 'interfaith dialogue' gives the superficial impression of representing the Perennial Tradition, but it is the antithesis. The result is not the preservation of Traditions but their bastardisation into a hotchpotch creed serving a globalist agenda.

4   Pike, pp. 104-105.

5   Bissey.

We are told of the aims of the Hidden Masters in regard to the ecumenical movement by Alice Bailey. According to Bailey, Master Djwhal Khul – or 'DK' – stated through her:

> The coming struggle will emerge within the churches themselves; it will be precipitated by the enlightened (progressive) elements...the fight will then spread to thinking men and women everywhere who - in a protesting revolt -have denied orthodox churchianity and theology.[6]

The impetus for this movement formally goes back to the 19th century when the first congress of the World's Parliament of Religions was held in Chicago in 1893.[7] Next, the World Fellowship of Faiths was co-founded by two Communists, K Das Gupta and Charles F Weller in the USA in 1924. Its first congress was held in 1933 under the co-chairmanship of Jane Addams, also a prominent Communist. She was an initiate of Co-Masonry, headed by Annie Besant, the Theosophical president. Addams was also an investor in Lenin's Russian-American Industrial Corporation and in the Communist Federation Press, and a member of the Federal Council of Churches,[8] U.S. constitute of the World Council of Churches whose 'Christianity' is ecumenical and communistic.[9]

Charles F Weller was a millionaire Communist whose organisation of the Fellowship of Faiths in the USA received the enthusiastic support of Zionist luminary, Supreme Court Justice Samuel Untermeyer, a confidante of President Woodrow Wilson.[10] The Fellowship Congress for 1936 was held in London. Freemasonry was taking an interest in this movement, as explained by The Speculative Mason:

---

6 Bailey, 1934, pp. 453-454.

7 World Congress of Faiths, 'The Beginnings', http://www.worldfaiths.org/TheBeginning.php

8 Hatonn, Vol. 1 p. 150.

9 H R Pike.

10 Hatonn, op. cit.

A different effort to promote world fellowship as seen in the Congress of Faiths. The plans were outlined by Sir Francis Younghusband. He pointed out that they were trying to set up a body of opinion that would form the basis for a new world order, which everyone now was wanting to see established, a spiritual basis for the League of Nations… Freemasons should make an effort to attend this unsectarian, non-political effort towards world unity.[11]

The reader will note the reference by Masonry, in 1936, to a 'new world order' in conjunction with the League of Nations, the failed predecessor of the United Nations Organisation, the concept of 'world unity' and the interests of Freemasonry. The front man for this movement was General Sir Francis Younghusband, who had led a British military expedition to Tibet in 1903-1904 and had become enamoured by Tibetan religion. He befriended Masonic luminary Manly P Hall when the latter was in London, and enabled him to study the restricted manuscripts in the British Museum.[12]

United Nations Meditation Room

The universal syncretic cult that is the stated aim of Masonry, Theosophists, and their derivatives, is embodied in a temple in the United Nations Building, the so-called U.N. Meditation Room. U.N. Secretary General Dag Hammarskjöld attached much importance to this U.N. meditation room. The New Age movement ascribes esoteric qualities to the U.N. temple. They also regard Hammarskjöld as an 'Adept'. According to Alice Bailey, Hammarskjöld was 'a leading disciple' who had been chosen for his world role as early as the 1930s. According to Donald Keys, speechwriter for U.N. Secretary General U Thant and founder of the Planetary Citizens organisation:

In one of Alice A. Bailey's books, written in the 1930's,

---

11   Quoted by Weston, Father of Lies.

12   Lodge Camden.

there is a statement that a leading Swedish disciple would soon be working in the world. A high Swedish initiate who was a friend of mine was once asked if the foretold one were he. His answer was 'no, it is Dag Hammarskjöld'.[13]

The following history and description of the U.N. Meditation Room is taken from the website of the UNO. It is stated that Hammarskjöld regarded the Meditation Room as a centre of religious contemplation above any established religion. Here again we see in this the Supreme Being, GAOTU, the syncretic God replacing the Traditional deities of all other faiths.

> In the original plan for the new Headquarters, a tiny room had been provided as a place dedicated to silence, where people could withdraw into themselves, regardless of their faith, creed or religion, but Dag Hammarskjöld wanted something more dignified. In his efforts he was supported by a group, composed of Christians, Jews, and Moslems, the 'Friends of the UN Meditation Room', who combined their efforts and provided the money for a room worthy of a world organization.

> The work on the room began, and Mr. Hammarskjöld personally planned and supervised in every detail the creation of the 'Meditation Room'.[14]

Like the final degrees of the Illuminati, the initiate is introduced to the inner teachings. Albert Pike discussed the manner by which Masons of all religious backgrounds can join the Lodge because each is able to define the symbols of Masonry according to his own religious background:

> Each of us makes such applications to his own faith and creed, of the symbols and ceremonies of this Degree, as seems to him proper. With these special interpretations we

---

13   Keys, ca. 1970s.

14   United Nations, 'A Room of Quiet'.

have here nothing to do. Like the legend of the Master Khūrūm, in which some see figured the condemnation and sufferings of Christ; others those of the unfortunate Grand Master of the Templars; others those of the first Charles, King of England; and others still the annual descent of the Sun at the winter Solstice to the regions of darkness, the basis of many an ancient legend; so the ceremonies of this Degree receive different explanations; each interpreting them for himself, and being offended at the interpretation of no other.

In no other way could Masonry possess its character of Universality; that character which has ever been peculiar to it from its origin; and which enables two Kings, worshippers of different Deities, to sit together as Masters, while the walls of the first temple arose; and the men of Gebal, bowing down to the Phœnician Gods, to work by the side of the Hebrews to whom those Gods were abomination; and to sit with them in the same Lodge as brethren.

You have already learned that these ceremonies have one general significance, to every one, of every faith, who believes in God and the soul's immortality.[15]

Hence, Pike explained, the Masonic approach to religion is that of syncretism, and in the lower degrees claims to be all things to all people. This is the syncretic doctrine that clearly inspired Hammarskjöld when he took such a personal interest in designing the U.N. Meditation Room as a Temple for a syncretic universal religion in which those bureaucrats working for a New World Order could worship, or attune their consciousness to the psychic powers that were supposedly being emanated by the adepts who serve the Hidden Masters. This U.N. Temple comprises primary features of a Masonic character, including:

---

15   Pike, pp. 276-277.

The Ashler.

The U.N. Meditation Room features an altar that is a large block of iron ore. The block suggests a Masonic Ashler. The Ashler takes the form of rough hewn and smoothed stone blocks. The rough hewn block represents humanity in its state of imperfection, while the smoothed block represented humanity's perfection by the reshaping of humanity though communistic social engineering - the purpose of Masonry, Illuminism and the New Age. The work of Hammarskjöld on this U.N. Temple is described:

> He banned chairs and replaced them with benches; in the center of the room he placed a six-and-half-ton rectangular block of iron ore, polished on the top and illuminated from above by a single spotlight. This block, which was a gift of the King of Sweden and a Swedish mining company, was the only symbol in the Room. Mr. Hammarskjöld described it as '...a meeting of the light, of the sky, and the earth... it is the altar to the God of all.... we want this massive altar to give the impression of something more than temporary...'[16]

In this passage there are a number of significant points:

1. Benches rather than chairs suggest a church.

2. The focus of a solid iron block represents Masonic-Illuminist perfectibilism.

3. The Temple is dedicated to the syncretic 'God of all'; the 'Supreme Being' or GAOTU of Masonry and Illuminism.

4. The single beam of light shining upon the altar unequivocally signifies Illuminism.

Albert Pike described the Ashler in instructions for the 1° Apprentice of the Scottish Rite:

---

16   United Nations, 'A Quiet Room'.

You will hear shortly of the Rough ASHLAR and the Perfect ASHLAR, as part of the jewels of the Lodge. The rough Ashlar is said to be 'a stone, as taken from the quarry, in its rude and natural state'. The perfect Ashlar is said to be 'a stone made ready by the hands of the workmen, to be adjusted by the working-tools of the Fellow-Craft'.

The rough Ashler is the PEOPLE, as a mass, rude and unorganized. The perfect Ashlar, or cubical stone, symbol of perfection, is the STATE, the rulers deriving their powers from the consent of the governed; the constitution and laws speaking the will of the people; the government harmonious, symmetrical, efficient, - its powers properly distributed and duly adjusted in equilibrium.[17]

If the block in the U.N. Meditation Room can be defined as an ashlar, then the Masonic interpretation is that of the U.N. as an embryonic world state shaping the masses to a state of 'Perfectibility'; the basis of all movements, such as communism, that aim to reshape humanity according to their own designs. This iron ore block at the centre of the room was a gift from King Gustaf VI Adolf,[18] Grand Master of Swedish Freemasonry. Swedish Kings assumed the position of Grand Master until King Gustaf VI Adolf's death in 1973, whereupon his successor declined to take up the role.[19]

The altar metal or stone in Masonic symbolism, according to Mackey, represents the Stone of Foundation placed within the foundations of the Temple of Solomon, which holds the key place in Masonic allegory. During the building of the second Temple it was said to have been taken to the Holy of Holies of the Israelites, and had the sacred and unutterable name of God transcribed in a Triangle.

---

17   Pike, Chapter 1, p. 7.

18   United Nations, 'A Quiet Room'.

19   Grand Lodge of BC & Yukon, 'Swedish Rite FAQ'.

All these elements are present in the U.N. Meditation Room.

The Eye in the Pyramid

The side walls of the room taper towards a mural taking up the entirety of the far wall. A central image on the mural suggests an iris. The shape of the Temple with the focus of an iris-shaped image at the end suggests the all Seeing Eye atop the uncapped Great Pyramid.

The Mural

The mural is the focus of meditation in the room. According to the U.N. account it is intended as a focus on the 'god of all'.

The predominant shape on the mural forms what can be readily seen as a large Hebrew letter Vau, the central letter of the esoteric name of God in Jewish mysticism known as Cabalism (an important component of Masonry and other exoteric systems): YHVH. Vau connects and inter-relates all 22 letters of the Hebrew alphabet, which is an esoteric alphabet at the basis of Western occultism including Masonry. Its esoteric meaning is that of 'a single line of light'. The single beam of light illuminating the altar, which Hammarskjöld characterised as a 'shaft of light striking the shimmering surface of solid rock', relates to the esoteric meaning of the letter Vau. Hebrew Cabalists confirm this meaning:

> In the beginning of Creation, when Infinite Light filled all reality, God contracted His Light to create hollow empty space, as it were, the 'place' necessary for the existence of finite worlds. Into this vacuum God drew down, figuratively speaking, a single line of light, from the Infinite Source. This ray of light is the secret of the [Hebrew] letter vav.[20]

Hammarskjöld refers to the 'symbol of how the light of the

20 Gal Einai Institute.

Wall Mural and Ashler in the U.N. Meditation Room.

spirit gives life to matter.' This is precisely the significance of Vau, as described above. It seems more than a coincidence that Hammarskjöld refers to a 'shaft of light', the stone block as an 'altar' and to 'the God of all.' Hammarskjöld uses terms that suggest him being an initiate of some system of occultism based on the Cabala. Hammarskjöld wrote of the U.N. Meditation Room as a Temple in which contact with what is clearly the astral realm could be gained through meditation on symbols of a universal type:

> People of many faiths will meet here, and for that reason none of the symbols to which we are accustomed in our meditation could be used. However, there are simple things, which speak to us all with the same language. We have sought for such things and we believe that we have found them in the shaft of light striking the shimmering surface of solid rock. So, in the middle of the room we see a symbol of how, daily, the light of the skies gives life to the earth on which we stand, a symbol to many of us of how the light of the spirit gives life to matter. But the stone in the middle of the room has more to tell us. We may see it

as an altar, empty not because there is no God, not because it is an altar to an unknown god, but because it is dedicated to the God whom man worships under many names and in many forms.[21]

The primary points of this description by Hammarskjöld are:

1. The use of universal symbols that can be tapped to connect with a syncretic godhead.

2. The shaft of light as the symbol of Illuminism.

3. An altar representing matter being infused with Illumination.

U.N. 'Holy of Holies'

The Lucis Trust, the organisation that was founded by Alice Bailey, is the guardian of the U.N. Meditation Room. Among the networks of the Bailey movement that spawned the preset-day New Age phenomenon, is the Seven Rays Institute. A spokesman for Seven Rays, Steven Nation, in an address on the 'spiritual' and esoteric significance of the UNO, including the U.N. Meditation Room, described the UNO as a focus for occultists. He began his address by leading his audience through a guided meditation, during which he termed the UN General Assembly a 'temple', and the Meditation Room as the 'Holy of Holies'. He alluded to the nature of the altar as being specifically 'Masonic', and described Hammarskjöld as a 'mystic and visionary'. U.N. activities are called occult rituals that are working on humanity on a subconscious level.

In the course of the address Mr Nation mentioned his own Masonic background. He was also a staff member for 20 years at the Lucis Trust H.Q. in London, and is founder of the Triangle Centres in New Zealand.

---

21   United Nations, 'A Quiet Room'.

It should be kept in mind that one of the primary activities of this esoteric network established by the Baileys is to co-ordinate adherents across the world to meditate on specific objectives towards the creation of a New World Order. Thus, the notion of an 'occult war' cannot be offhandedly dismissed as an unfounded 'conspiracy theory'. Even so, sceptics will ridicule the notion of occultists influencing the collective unconscious of humanity across the world, but one might consider two points that are scientifically grounded:

1. Carl Jung's theory of the collective unconscious.

2. Dr Rupert Sheldrake's theory of the morphic field and of morphic resonance, which is analogous to the occult concept of the astral plane or the akashic record.[22] Hence, where the occultist states that there is an akashic record that contains memories of a type of psyhic filing system, and what Jungians call archetypes, this is explained by Sheldrake as the means by which 'genetic memory' can be transmitted between organisms and through generations as an organising principle. He states in regard to the human organism and the part played by ritual and the so-called psychic:

Human societies have memories that are transmitted through the culture of the group, and are most explicitly communicated through the ritual re-enactment of a founding story or myth, as in the Jewish Passover celebration, the Christian Holy Communion and the American thanksgiving dinner, through which the past become present through a kind of resonance with those who have performed the same rituals before.

The morphic fields of social groups connect together members of the group even when they are many miles apart, and provide channels of communication through

22 For a definition of the akashic record in occultism and Theosophy see: Linda Howe, The Center for Akashic Studies.

which organisms can stay in touch at a distance. They help provide an explanation for telepathy. ... Telepathy is normal not paranormal, natural not supernatural, and is also common between people; especially people who know each other well.

The morphic fields of mental activity are not confined to the insides of our heads. They extend far beyond our brain though intention and attention. ... The fields of our minds extend far beyond our brains.[23]

Sheldrake offers empirical evidence that we might apply to explain how the intervention of occultists through co-ordinated worldwide meditation and ritual could result in mind manipulation on a mass, universal scale. It is against this background that we might give more serious attention to the co-ordinated global activities of occultists attempting to change human consciousness and usher a New World Order and the reign of their pro-Bolshevik Mahatmas. In such a context, we might consider Steven Nation's depiction of the U.N. General Assembly as a 'temple', serving as a world gathering point for esoteric worship:

And now imagine that the peoples of the world move back, there's a ritualistic movement they stand around the walls of the temple. Visualize them forming a vast circle. And in the midst of this great gathering of the world's people, within the great temple, picture another smaller temple, right at the center of the gathering, and imagine that this smaller temple takes a form through what we have all seen on television—it is the form of the General Assembly of the United Nations.[24]

Steven Nation referred to the U.N. as 'the Temple of Humanity' in the context of his Masonic background. Esoterically he has visions of the U.N. as the focus of occult rituals:

23   Sheldrake, 2005.

24   Nation, 2006.

Some of my most profound experiences in Freemasonry happened when I would sense the walls of the Masonic temple dissolving and feel as if I was witnessing and taking part in a ceremony within the General Assembly of the United Nations.[25]

Mr Nation regards the U.N. as the focus of the 'Avatar of Synthesis', the New Age 'messiah' or Hidden Master, the Anointed One or Maitreya, who is expected to establish the syncretic universal cult of the New World Order; hence the reference to 'synthesis'. The Lucis Trust and the myriad of groups springing therefrom were founded to prepare this syncretic cult and to pave the way for this 'avatar':

These experiences have always stayed with me and have been deeply reinforced upon occasions when I have been fortunate enough to visit the UN centres in Geneva, New York or Nairobi—to stand in the awesome space of the General Assembly or to sit in the UN meditation room … and feel the presence of the Avatar of Synthesis. [26]

The U.N. Meditation Room is given the status of the 'holy of holies', and it could be asked whether this is supposed to be the location for the earthly incarnation of this Avatar of Synthesis. Mr Nation places this on par with the Ark of the Covenant, as the dwelling place of God, speaking of the U.N. Meditation Room:

And whenever you go there, align with all of your co-workers from wherever you are in the world and feel their presence there with you. That room is like the holy of holies, the most sacred place in some of the most ancient temples.[27]

---

25   Nation, 2006.

26   Nation, 2006.

27   Nation, 2006.

Mr Nation gives special significance to the iron ore block altar and describes the importance attached to it by Hammarskjöld. He confirms the contention made above that the block is a Masonic altar:

> And just as in some of the Egyptian temples, there in the U.N. meditation room the dominant, powerful image is of this huge, wonderful block of iron ore. This rock was brought from Sweden by Dag Hammarskjöld. He was a mystic and a visionary who took such care in the quarrying of the stone. It was so heavy and difficult to ship to New York and the design of the building had to be changed and a whole new foundation built to accommodate the weight of that stone. When you go into the room you feel its presence. I always felt that because it is a diagonal shape it is incredibly Masonic because it is composed of squares.[28]

Mr Nation considers the gatherings of the U.N. to be the equivalent of collective magical rituals.

> Now I don't need to remind a group of esotericists that this view of UN activity as ritual involves the recognition that what's happening at a deep, unspoken level at these conferences is the invocation and evocation of energies.[29]

Again, we might consider this in conjunction with Sheldrake's theory of morphic resonance before such views are dismissed as the fantasies of a harmless crank. Regardless of how one considers these views, the important factor is, as always, how these beliefs are being actioned on a practical level. The question that might be asked is: Why does the administration of the U.N. permit a private network of occultists to play such an important role in this organisation, to the extent of being the custodians of the U.N. Meditation Room, that was considered of such importance to Hammarskjöld?

---

28   Nation, 2006.

29   Nation, 2006.

What types of mentalities are at work in a globally pervasive institution that can enforce its resolutions by an international army and its weapons of mass destruction that have rained terror upon reluctant states such as Syria, Iraq, Serbia and Libya?

The Role of the United Nations

Each epoch that we have considered previously has had a cult formulated by the Counter-Tradition that is suited for its times, under the auspices of a syncretic Supreme Being. The present epoch is described by Theosophical esotericists, including those of the New Age, as one of planetary change and planetary consciousness. The organisational focus is the U.N. but Masonry continues to be the inspiration.

Masonry: Religion of 'Those Who Should Wield Power'

Alice Bailey wrote of Masonry's role as the foundation of the religion of the New World Order, under the ever-watchful All Seeing Eye. She claimed to be writing as a spirit medium for one of the Hidden Masters, DK, in the legacy of Blavatsky, Roerich, and Besant. She candidly stated that the conception of the network of New Age adherents which she and her husband Foster founded, is dedicated to the establishment of a hierarchical World State over which there is an over-rulership of an elite:

> The Masonic Movement will meet the need of those who can, and should, wield power. It is the custodian of the law; it is the home of the Mysteries and the seat of initiation. It holds in its symbolism the ritual of Deity, and the way of salvation is pictorially preserved in its work. The methods of Deity are demonstrated in its Temples and under the All-Seeing Eye the work can go forward.[30]

Alice Bailey wrote that Masonry is a training school for advanced

30   Alice Bailey, 1934, pp. 511-513.

occultists and will prepare the way for the development of a new world religion, a new world church and a new priesthood:

> It is a far more occult organisation than can be realised and is intended to be the training school for the coming advanced occultists. In Masonry you have the three paths leading to initiation. As yet they are not used, and one of the things that will eventuate - when the new universal religion has sway and the nature of esotericism is understood - will be the utilisation of the banded esoteric organism, the Masonic organism and the Church organism as initiating centres. These three groups converge as their inner sanctuaries are approached. There is no dissociation between the One Universal Church, the sacred inner Lodge of all true Masons, and the inner-most circles of the esoteric societies.[31]

Foster Bailey alluded to the 'blotting out' of all religions that would occur to pave the way for a Masonic universal religion:

> Is it not possible from a contemplation of this side of Masonic teaching that it may provide all that is necessary for the formulation of a universal religion? May it not be true, as has been said, that if all religions and Scriptures were blotted out and only Masonry were left in the world we could still recover the great plan of salvation? Most earnestly should all true Masons consider this point.

> A revitalized Masonry, made up of Masons true to their obligations and realising the Mystic Tie that binds them all together in one true brotherhood, would also provide a platform so universal that it would meet the need of thinkers of all kinds and of every school of thought. It would thus not only meet a religious need by providing a universal religion, but would also satisfy the mental need felt by all broad-minded thinkers at this time.[32]

---

31 Bailey, *ibid.*

32 Foster Bailey, p. 109

Foster Bailey is stating that the world will not need any other religion than a universal Masonic religion, that can encompass both the mystically inclined and the agnostic and atheistic free thinkers and intellectuals; precisely the aim of Illuminism and the Grand Orient. Can one realistically imagine the devotees of Islam, Catholicism and Hinduism giving up their Traditional beliefs in favour of a universal, syncretic cult for the sake of a World State that blurs all distinctions in a nebulous 'Brotherhood of Man'? The Vendée in France did not think so, nor did the Cristeros in Mexico. Millions of faithful were exterminated in Russia, nuns raped and murdered in Spain, while the Jacobins, Bolsheviks and Masons attempted to illuminate humanity as to the beneficence of their Supreme Being; actions which Mahatma Morya – one of the ascended Masters who is supposed to rule the world - found laudable and necessary.

'Hidden Hierarchy' Working Through UNO

The leaders and founders of such Orders often claim to be only the 'outer chiefs' acting on the instructions of their Hidden Masters in fulfilling their commands for the destiny of humanity. We have already seen this in regard to Blavatsky, Bailey, Besant and Roerich. Of the UNO and the Hidden Masters Alice Bailey wrote:

> The Hierarchy is at this time attempting to channel the forces of reconstruction into the Assembly of the United Nations. The use of these impersonal energies is dependent on the quality and the nature of the recipient nation; on its measure of true enlightenment and on its point in evolution. Nations are the expression today of the massed self-centredness of a people and of their instinct to self-preservation. The main object of the Hierarchy is so to distribute these constructive energies that the theory of unity may slowly be turned into practice and the word 'United' may come to have a true significance and meaning. Also in The Reappearance of the Christ it is stated that the

one who works to produce at-one-ment, unification and fusion is generating a slowly growing will-to-unity within the Assembly of the United Nations. This being can only channel His energies through the mass consciousness or through a group conscious entity, such as the UN.[33]

33   Alice Bailey, 1979, p. 77. Emphasis added.

Jerusalem: World Capital

The basis of Masonic allegory is the rebuilding of the Temple of Solomon in Jerusalem. The fact that this is also the major goal of Messianic Zionists.[1] The Al Aqsa Mosque, the third holiest place for Islam, stands where the Temple once stood, is problematic and today has major consequences for the peace of the world. Nonetheless, the rebuilding of the Temple is an allegoric reflection of the aim of establishing Jerusalem as the capital of a Universal Republic. Whether this aim comes from Templar origins or Freemasonry does not concern us here; the concern is in regard to the practical fulfilment of this legend.

The creation of Israel was a seminal event for Masonry and for the Counter-Tradition. Of the Masonic interests in Israel, an Italian newspaper reported in 1993 that 'a celebration of political Masons was held in Jerusalem'. Tellingly entitled, 'Israel: There is a Pact Between Politicians and Masons', the article stated:

> The ceremony was attended by the Mayor of Jerusalem, Teddy Kollek, as well as by the Ashkenazi Chief Rabbi, Israel Meier Lau. Kollek told the gathered Masons, 'You do a great honour to Jerusalem. This is natural, considering that King Solomon was the great builder of the temple, which is at the roots of the Masonic idea, and that his workmen were the first Masons'.[2]

The purpose of the Knights Templar was to re-construct the Temple of Solomon. The building of the Temple of Solomon and its re-construction are the core of the ritual and the doctrines of Freemasonry, as Jerusalem's Mayor mentioned. Jerusalem

---

1   L. Dolphin, 'Preparations for a Third Jewish Temple'.

2   *La Republica*, October, 1993; cited by Golden, 2004.

is considered the centre of the world by both Masonry and Messianic Judaism.

The Myth of The Temple in Masonic Doctrine & Ritual

In explaining the 30° of Knight Kadosh, Albert Pike wrote that the Freemasons descend from the Knights Templar. Of the Knights Kadosh, Pike stated that the 'secret object [of the Knights Templar] was the re-building of the Temple of Solomon'.[3] Pike explained that the true aims of the secret societies are concealed until the initiate reaches the highest degrees. In this 30° of the Scottish Rite, the initiate is told that Freemasonry takes up the cause of the Templars in rebuilding the Temple of Solomon as the seat of a world empire:

> The Templars, like all other Secret Orders and Associations, had two doctrines, one concealed and reserved for the Masters, which was Johannism; the other public, which was the Roman Catholic. Thus they deceived the adversaries whom they sought to supplant.[4]

Leon Zeldis 33°[5] has traced the origins of Freemasonry in Israel and states that the Israeli Masons perform initiation rituals underneath the site of Solomon's Temple, writing:

> Jerusalem, the 'City of Peace', is the city of David, King of Israel, who, in the 10th century BCE, unified the Holy Land under his rule and established Jerusalem as his capital. His son, Solomon, King of Israel, built a Temple to the God of Israel, which became the archetypal Temple in Western thought and a central subject in Masonic tradition. King Solomon's Temple already appears in the Old Charges of

3   Pike, pp. 815-16.
4   Pike, *ibid.*
5   Supreme Council of the Scottish Rite for the State of Israel, Honorary Adjunct Grand Master.

Operative Masons used by medieval Lodges and many legendary and ritual features of various Masonic degrees are related to its construction and architecture.[6]

From the religious allegory of the guild masons of the Medieval era, the Freemasons adopted their craft allegory and wove an esoteric doctrine around it that culminates in the rebuilding of the Temple as the centre of a Universal Republic. Jerusalem has been regarded by the Tradition of Western Civilisation as the axis mundi, and the Crusaders believed it to be the nexus between Heaven and Earth. It is therefore a part of Tradition that has been usurped by Counter-Tradition via Freemasonry. Zeldis states:

> For both Christians and Jews, Jerusalem is the focal point of the world, the place where heaven and earth touch each other (Heavenly and Earthly Jerusalem). In the Middle Ages, some maps show Jerusalem as the center of the world, with Europe, Asia, and Africa radiating from it like the petals of a flower.[7]

Zeldis states that Masonry has been using a cavern beneath the site of the Temple since 1868, and that the ceremonies draw Masons from around the world:

> Beneath the wall encircling the Old City, there is a deep cavern known as King Solomon's Quarries. This was used in old times to quarry the characteristic yellow Jerusalem stone. In this cave took place, on May 13, 1868, the first recorded Masonic ceremony in the Holy Land. A group of Freemasons led by Robert Morris (Past Grand Master of Kentucky) held a meeting in the Secret Monitor Degree. At present, the cave is used to hold a Mark Master degree once or twice a year, usually conducted in English and attended by numerous Brethren from abroad.[8]

---

6   Zeldis, 'Jerusalem - Symbolic Cradle of Freemasonry'.

7   Zeldis, *ibid.*

8   Zeldis, *ibid.*

Aerial view of the Israeli Supreme Court showing the Masonic Pyramid.

Masonry has staked its mark on the borders of Israel. On the Egypt-Israel border a border marker has been erected by Masonry, consisting of a pyramid, the Masonic insignia and two columns representing Binah and Chokmah of the Cabalistic 'Tree of Life', a feature of Masonic Temples.[9] The edifice is of considerable size, carved from rock and is positioned within paved, radiating circles.

Supreme Court, Jerusalem: Masonic Symbolism

The ideal of Jerusalem as capital of the world has an overt symbolic manifestation in the Supreme Court building in Jerusalem. Like the U.N. Meditation Room, it is replete with occult symbolism that does not appear to offer any explanation for Israel's centre for legal deliberation other than that it was designed with an occult purpose. Photographs and descriptions of the Supreme Court Building have been published by J Golden, a Jewish convert to Christianity, resident in Israel.

---

9   A photograph of the marker can be viewed at: The Golden Report, 23 February 23, 2005: http://www.thegoldenreport.com/asp/jerrysnewsmanager/anmviewer.asp?a=863

The All Seeing Eye

While conspiracy theorists routinely state that the Rothschild banking dynasty has been the hidden rulership behind Freemasonry and the Illuminati this seems to be based on assumption without offering concrete evidence. However, the Rothschild involvement in this overtly Masonic construction is evidence of a Rothschild connection with Masonry. Golden noted:

> The Engineers who were chosen for this job by the Rothschild's were the grandson and granddaughter of Ben-Zion Guine from Turkey who worked for Baron Rothschild, Ram Kurmi, born in Jerusalem in 1931, and Ada Karmi-Melanede born in Tel-Aviv in 1936.[10]

A plaque dedicated to the Rothschilds has been placed on the Supreme Court, so the Rothschild involvement is beyond doubt. The emblem at the top left of the plaque is a radiating All Seeing Eye. On the roof of the Supreme Court building there is a pyramid affixed with the image of an eye. Golden states of this, 'The first thing you will notice is the pyramid with the All Seeing Eye just like the one you will see on the American dollar bill; it sits in a circle to the left'.[11]

The Rothschilds were intimately involved with the construction of the Supreme Court Building. They were responsible for the site of the building. A picture honouring Lord Rothschild et al adorns the entrance of the building. Golden states:

> The Rothschilds made several stipulations with the Israeli Government before the building began, among them were: The Rothschilds would pick the plot of land to build the Supreme Court; they would use their own architects, and no one would ever know how much the building cost. It took them four years to build this structure with many secrets

10   Golden, 2004.

11   Golden, *ibid*.

built into it. After passing through security the first thing you will notice on the left wall is a large picture. From the left you will see Teddy Kollek, then Lord Rothschild, on the right standing you will see Shimon Peres, and sitting at the bottom left Yhzhak Rabin.[12]

Specifically it was Dorothy de Rothschild who mooted the idea in a letter to the Israeli Government, according to the official Jerusalem tourist guide.[13]

Golden describes the walk from shadow to the light shining through a large window. From out of the window there is the large eye and pyramid construction looming above. Here the motifs appear as illumination from darkness, as one ascends steps towards the All Seeing Eye and pyramid. The walk is reminiscent of a type of journey of initiation. It is also reminiscent of the U.N. Meditation Room, where the dimness is illuminated through a beam of light, and the shape of the room itself narrows to a mural, with the depiction of what is reminiscent of an iris and the letter Hebrew letter Vau, signifying a beam of light.

33 Degrees of Initiation

The interior of the building is replete with Masonic symbolism specific to the Scottish Rite. Thirty steps to the Supreme Court and three specialised libraries are reminiscent of the 33 Degrees of Scottish Rite Freemasonry.

Here it is very important to count the steps; there are three sets of 10 steps, making a total of 30. As you ascend these 30 steps you come from the darkness into the light. And from here you can see the world or in this case the city of Jerusalem like you haven't seen it before. It is also worth mentioning that on the left

12   Golden, *ibid.*

13   Jerusalem Insider's Guide. While this tourist website alludes sarcastically to 'Masonic conspiracy theories', and mentions that the pyramid was inspired by the tombs of Zechariah and Absalom, the All Seeing Eye is not explained.

side you will see the old Jerusalem Stone, some even believe these same stones were used in the second Temple, but I have no way to prove that. On the other side you will see the smooth modern wall. There are 6 lamp stands going up that speak to man in his journey to gain knowledge and become illuminated. But once again I feel it necessary to tell you that it's very important to the ones who built this building that everything be perfect and in their order of things, even numerically.

For a moment let's go back to the top of the 30 steps, as we know there are 33 degrees in Free Masonry but the last three are the ones of higher learning.[14]

Are these references to 30 steps plus 3 libraries merely a juggling of numbers to reach 33 and thereby fit into Golden's theory that the steps and libraries together comprise 33 Masonic Degrees? Let us consider each of the factors.

As noted above, it is at the 30° where the Mason of the Scottish Rite learns of his origins from the Knights Templars and that the aim is the restoration of the Temple of Solomon as the centre of the world. Of the 33° of the Scottish Rite, Masonic authorities refer specifically and separately to the first 30. Pick writing of the conferring of the Scottish Rite Degrees in England, states that those above the 30th are sparingly conferred in London by the Supreme Council as distinctions for services to the Rite'.[15] Since there are 33 Degrees in the Scottish Rite, that leaves the three highest degrees considered as separated by higher forms of initiation. It would seem apt that three libraries would correspond to the three highest degrees of the Scottish Rite, and that moreover, those three libraries are themselves on separate levels. Golden states of the three libraries:

This is a very large and expensive Library, but there is something else about this one that should be mentioned.

14   Golden, 2004.

15   Pick, p. 239.

The first tier is 'only' for Lawyers; the second tier is 'only' for sitting Judges. The highest and third tier is 'only' for retired judges.[16]

Thus there is an indication of a level of initiation or knowledge that corresponds to each of the three libraries, graded exclusively for different levels within the legal profession. There are five courtrooms in the shape of a Jewish tomb, with three judges sitting in each room. 'Above the seats of the Judges there are smaller pyramids that shed light onto the Judges as they sit over those who are brought up from the prisons cells below'.[17] The light being shed on the judges emanates from crystals, which in occultism are regarded as 'batteries' for cosmic energies. These occult and Masonic correspondences suggest that the Supreme Court Building was constructed for purposes other than merely handing out sentences in the Israeli justice system. Such a building crowned with the pyramid and All Seeing Eye would accord with the requirements of a World Court for a New World Order. Masonic symbolism and architecture are features of states where Masonry has assumed political importance. This has been shown to be the case with Washington DC [18]and Paris.[19] Considering the central importance that Jerusalem has in the esoteric aim of creating a New World Order, the Supreme Court building in Jerusalem has been designed, in a fairly obvious manner, to display the doctrines and hierarchy of the Counter-Tradition.

---

16   Golden, 2004.

17   Golden, 2004.

18   Ovason, The Secret Zodiacs of Washington DC, which carries the recommendation of C F Kleinknecht 33° Sovereign Grand Commander, The Supreme Council 33° (Mother Council of the World) Southern Jurisdiction, Washington DC, of the Scottish Rite; who wrote the Preface.

19   Hancock, Bauval, *Talisman: Sacred Cities, Secret Faith.*

Conclusion

While much of what has been said might be dismissed by rationalists and sceptics as superstition, and the various societies as nothing more than the harmless delusions of bored dilettantes, there is no necessity to believe any of the myths and so-called superstitions that are the basis of the secret societies we have considered. What is important is that there have existed, and continue to exist, powerful societies and individuals committed to certain mythic beliefs which THEY seek to make reality.

Myth drives history. It is the basis of religion and has inspired wars, revolutions, and massacres, and on the other hand, the most sublime expressions of human culture. The value of a Myth is therefore not whether it is based on 'truth' in the present-day empirical, scientific sense. It is how the Myth is perceived and how it works out in history as enacted on the world stage by its believers.

The secret societies that have been referred to as working for or being the Black School of Magick, the Black Lodges, Black Adepts, adherents of Anti-Tradition and wire pullers of Counter-Tradition, are committed to making their Myths reality over the mundane world. We have seen how they have, with their supposed advanced state of spiritual enlightenment, been at the heart of rationalistic and communistic doctrines, have served in the bloody Cheka during the early years of the USSR, work within the very bowels of the UNO, and have been seminal influences in the creation of the European Union, and many revolutions, and have moulded the concept of the modern, secular nation-state. Most orthodox historians would have us dismiss all this as 'myth'; and 'myth' indeed it is, but no less real in its manifestations on the earthly plane.

Conclusion

An added problem as shown, is that there are those who seem to be Black Adepts, working for the Counter-Tradition, but who are Traditionalists; and those who appear to be Traditionalists, but conversely, must be judged by their actions to be working for the Counter-Tradition. Hence, for example, Nicholas Roerich, a world ambassador for the maintenance and exaltation of culture and spirituality, showed himself to be working for the Black Adepts when he followed their pro-Bolshevik position. Aleister Crowley, on the other hand, who was close to Anti-Traditionalist forms of Masonry, and referred to Weishaupt as a 'saint', showed himself to be working for Tradition, his doctrine of Thelema being anything but Illuminatist. Miguel Serrano, Chilean diplomat, author, and mystic, considered himself to be a 'luciferian', yet his beliefs were opposed the Illuminist doctrines or the Luciferians of Theosophy. Rene Guénon, one of the seminal thinkers of present-day Tradition was, like Crowley, close to some forms of the Anti-Tradition, but was also aware, again like Crowley, of how Masonry had been subverted, and was also unequivocal in his condemnation of Theosophy. Although Guénon saw Masonry as an important element of the Primordial Tradition he also attacked it as having become 'rationalist and anti-spiritual', collaborated with Clarin de la Rive, editor of the anti-Masonic paper *La France chrétienne antimaçonnique*, and there existed a mutual respect between Guénon and the anti-Masonic Rightist author Vicomte Léon de Poncin. Julius Evola's attitude towards Masonry remained much more critical than Guénon's.

As for the present, with the flourishing of various cults, revivals, neo-paganism, neo-traditions, many like Theosophy, based on syncretic artifices, with such a proliferation itself symptomatic of the spiritual crisis of Western Civilisation, they must be judged by their actions and motivations. There is a significant push towards 'interfaith dialogue', which often claims to be undertaken in the interests of preserving Tradition in a materialistic world, yet these efforts also include as a major element in their beliefs the creation of a world order. One should therefore be suspicious as to whether this 'interfaith dialogue' is intended to bring together Traditionalists to unite against the symptoms of the Kali Yuga, or whether they are acting in the interests of Counter-Tradition, promoting a syncretic world religion that would subsume all Traditional faiths into a new cult.

What is required is a dialogue between genuine Traditionalists who eschew any notion of syncretic amalgamation and a cynical 'world brotherhood' but who recognise the need for each to survive on the basis of distinctiveness.

References

Allen, G. None Dare Call It Conspiracy, California Concord Press, 1972.
The Rockefeller File, Ca., 76 Press, 1976.

American Atheists Inc.: http://www.atheists.org/Atheism/enligttnment/

Ancient & Primitive Rite of Memphis-Mizraim, Sovereign Sanctuary for Bulgaria, 'History', http://sites.google.com/site/memphismizraimbg/home

Aquarian Age Community, 'About the AAC', http://www.aquaac.org/about/about.html

Aston, N. Religion and Revolution in France, London, Macmillan Press, 2000.

Baigent, M., R Leigh, and H Lincoln. *The Holy Blood & The Holy Grail*, London, Corgi Books, 1983.
The Temple & the Lodge, London, Jonathan Cape, 1989.

Bailey, A. The Externalisation of the Hierarchy, New York, Lucis Trust, 1934.
The Rays and the Initiations, New York, Lucis Trust, 1971.
Reappearance of Christ, New York, Lucis Trust, 1979.

Bailey, F. (1957) The Spirit of Masonry, London, Lucis Press, 1996.

Bakunin, Mikhail. God & State, 1883; New York, Dover Publications, 1970.

Barruel, A. Memoire pur servir a l'histoire du jacobinisme, 1797. English translation: New York, Hudson & Goodwin, 1799. Hon. Robert Cofford, translator.

Baudelaire, C. 'Litany to Satan', Flowers of Evil, M and J Mathews (ed.) New York, New Directions, 1962.

Baxter, J. P. The Greatest of Literary Problems: Shakespeare, Boston, Houghton Mifflin, 1915.
'Rosicrucian Archive', www.crcsite.org/bacon.htm

BBC News, 'Italy school crucifixes "barred"'; 3 November 2009, http://news.bbc.co.uk/2/hi/8340411.stm

Belloc, H. (1920) Europe and the Faith (London: Black House Publishing, 2012).

References

Besant, A. Theosophy and Christianity, Adyar, Madras, Theosophical Publishing House, 1932.

Billington, J. H. Fire in the Minds of Men: Origins of the Revolutionary Faith, New Jersey, Transaction Publishers, 2011.

Bissey, W. K. 'G.A.O.T.U.', Indiana Freemason, Spring 1997; Scottish Rite Journal, August 1997, http://www.masonicworld.com/education/files/gaotuapr01.htm

Blavatsky, H. P. 'H P Blavatsky's Masonic Patent', The Franklin Resister, 8 February 1878, http://www.blavatsky.net/blavatsky/arts/HPBlavatskysMasonicPatent.htm
   1888. The Secret Doctrine, Adyar, The Theosophical Society, 1978.

Boehme, Jacob. Theosophishe Wercken, Amsterdam, 1682.

Bolton, K. R. 'Origins of the Cold War and How Stalin Foiled a New World Order', Foreign Policy Journal, 31 May 2010, http://www.foreignpolicyjournal.com/2010/05/31/origins-of-the-cold-war-how-stalin-foild-a-new-world-order/all/1
   'Aleister Crowley as Political Theorist', Crowley: Thoughts & Perspectives Vol. 2, T Southgate (ed.), London, Black Front Press, 2011a.
   Revolution from Above: Creating 'Dissent' in the New World Order, London, Arktos Media Ltd., 2011.

Brogan, D. W. Proudhon, London, Hamish Hamilton, 1934.

Brown, D. Angels & Demons, London, Random House, 2000.

Bullock, S. C. Revolutionary Brotherhood, Chapel Hill, University of North Carokina Press, 1996.

Burnett, T., and A Games, Who Really Runs the World?, London, Collins & Brown, 2005.

Burstein, D., and A Sura (ed.) Secrets of Angels & Demons – of Conspiracies & Conspirators, London, Orion, 2005.

Bush, G. H. W. United States Capitol, 29 January 1991. US Congress, 6 March 1991.

Bush, G. W. Second Inaugural Address, United States Capitol, 20 January 2005.

Buta, J. 'The Politics of Grand Lodge Foreign Relations', http://www.freemasons-freemasonry.com/masonic_foreign_recognitions.html

The Occult & Subversive Movements

Carducci, G. 1882. Hymn to Satan, Poetry Classics, All Poetry, http://allpoetry.com/poem/8492167-Hymn_To_Satan-by-Giosue_Carducci

Carson, R. 'Gnostics & Mandaeans', Blavatsky Net Foundation, http://www.blavatsky.net/newsletters/mandaeans.htm

Caryle, T. The French Revolution: A History, London, Lonodn, James Fraser, 1837.

Case, P Foster. *Oracle of The Tarot: A Course on Tarot Divination*, Chapter 6, 'The Major Trumps: 15. Le Diable', http://tarotinstitute.com/free/Oracle2.pdf.

Catholic Encyclopaedia, New York, Robert Appleton Company, 1910, Imprimatur. +John M. Farley, Archbishop of New York. Online Edition 2003 by K. Knight. Article: "Masonry", Vol. IX, http://www.newadvent.org/cathen/09771a.htm

CBS 60 Minutes: 'Bush's Skull & Bones Society', CBS News, Alex Jones' Prison Planet, http://www.prisonplanet.com/111803skullandbones.html

Churchill, W. S. 'Zionism vs. Bolshevism', *Illustrated Sunday Herald*, 8 February 1920.

Churton, *T. Aleister Crowley: The Biography,* London, Watkins Publishing, 2011.

Cohn, N. *Warrant for Genocide*, London, Pelican Books,1967.

Conway, D. *A Farewell to Marx*, Penguin Books, Harmondsworth, 1987.

Cousins, N. *In God We Trust: Religious Beliefs of the Founding Fathers*, New York, Harpers, 1958.

Cox, S. *Dan Brown Companion*, Edinburgh, Mainstream Publishing Co., 2006.

Cramer D., *The True Society of Jesus & the Rosy Cross*, Frankfurt, 1617.

Crowley, Aleister, Magick Without Tears, Phoenix, Falcon Press, 1983.
    The Confessions of Aleister Crowley, London, Routledge & Kegan Paul, 1986.

Cutler, R. M. (ed. & transl.). *The Basic Bakunin: Writings 1869-1871* Buffalo, Prometheus Books, 1992.

Cumbey, C. Hidden *Dangers of the Rainbow,* Lafayette, Huntington House Inc., 1983.

Cyran, Olivier. 'La liberté d'expression selon *Charlie Hebdo*', March 4 2006, http://lmsi.net/L-opinion-du-Patron

Cyran, Olivier. '*Charlie Hebdo* Pas Racciste Si Vou Le Dites', Aricle11, December 2013, http://www.article11.info/?Charlie-Hebdo-pas-raciste-Si-vous

References

Davy, Ted G. 'Early Canadian Theosophists & Social Reform', www.
theosophycanada.com/fohat_early.htm

Declaration of the Rights of Man and the Citizen (August 1789), The History
Guide, Lectures on Modern European Intellectual History. www.historyguide.org/
intellect/lecture12a.html

DeFur, Emily. 'Satan in Literature', Loquemur Honors Journal, 2004, Christian
Brothers University, Memphis, Tennessee, http://www.cbu.edu/Academics/honors/
honorsjournal2k4.htm#contents

Delpech, A. Compte-redu Grand Orient de France, Paris, 1902.

Denslow, W. R. and H S Truman, *10,000 Famous Freemasons from A-J*, Part 1,
Missouri Lodge of Research, 1957,

DePoncins, Vicomte L. *The Secret Powers Behind Revolution*, Hawthorne, California,
Christian Book Club of America, n.d.

De Rougemont, D. *The Idea of Europe*, New York, Macmillan Co., 1966.

Drayer, R. 'The Book Wayfarers: The Spiritual Journeys of Nicholas and Helena
Roerich', Living Ethics in the World, 24 November 2004, http://lebendige-ethik.
net/engl/4-Wayfarers.html
    Nicholas & Helena Roerich: The Spiritual Jourey of Two Great Artists & Peace-
    makers, Quest Books, 2005.

Dolphin, L. 'Preparations for a Third Jewish Temple', http://www.templemount.org/
tempprep.html

Dunn, Dr C. W. 'The Roots of American Humanism', *The Humanist Threat*,
Greenville, South Carolina, UP Publications, 1987.

Egerton, F. C. C. *Salazar: Rebuilder of Portugal*, London, Hodder & Stoughton, 1943.

Ehler, S. Z. *Church & State Through the Centuries*, Biblo & Tannen Publishers, 1988.

Eisenhower, D. 'Farewell Address', 1961, http://www.h-net.org/~hst306/documents/
indust.html

Eringer, R. The Global Manipulators: The Bilderberg Group ... the Trilateral
Commission... covert power groups of the West, Bristol, Pentacle Books, 1980.
Europa Press Releases Rapid, 'Presidents of Commission and Parliament meet
European philosophical non-confessional organisations, Brussels', 26 June 2009.

Evans, H. 'Masonry and Magic in the Eighteenth Century', The Master Mason,
June 1927.

Evola, J. *Revolt Against the Modern World,* Rochester, Inner Traditions, 1995.
   Ride the Tiger, Vermont, Inner Traditions, 2003.
   Men Among the Ruins, Vermont, Inner Traditions, 2002.

Federal Citizens Information Center, 'The Great Seal of the US', http://www.
pueblo.gsa.gov/cic_text/misc/ourflag/greatseal.htm

Fischer, B. B. 'Okhrana: The Paris Operations of the Russian Imperial Police',
Central Intelligence Agency, 1997, https://www.cia.gov/library/center-for-the-
study-of-intelligence/csi-publications/books-and-monographs/okhrana-the-paris-
operations-of-the-russian-imperial-police/5474-1.html

Fludd, R. Tractatus apologeticus integritutem Societatis Rosea Cruce defendum,
Leiden, 1617.
   Ultrjusqae Cosmi Maioris, Frankfurt, 1621.

Fox, V. and R Allyn, *Revolution of Hope,* Viking, 2007.

France Diplomatie, 'The Symbols of the Republic', http://www.diplomatie.gouv.fr/
en/france_159/institutions-and-politics_6814/the-symbols-of-the-republic_2002/
the-declaration-of-the-rights-of-man-and-the-citizen_1505.html

Free Legal Dictionary, 'Conspiracy', http://legal-dictionary.thefreedictionary.com/
conspiracy

Gal Einai Institute, 'Mystical Significance of the Hebrew Letters', http://www.inner.
org/HEBLETER/vav.htm

Ginsberg, B. *The Fatal Embrace: Jews and the State*, University of Chicago Press, 1993.

Goeringer, C. 'The Enlightenment, Freemasonry, and The Illuminati, Part I - The
Enlightenment', http://www.atheists.org/Atheism/roots/enlightenment/

Goncalves, A. M. 'Breve historical da Maconaria em Portugal', Pel Irmao Mestre
Macom, R L Anderson No 16 Grande Loja Regular de Portugal/GLLP, 14° Grau
do Rito Escoces Antigo e Aceite. 'A shortened History of Freemasonry in Portugal',
English translation by W. Bro. Don Falconer, Pietre-Stones Review of Freemasonry,
http://www.freemasons-freemasonry.com/arnaldoGeng.html

Golden, J. 'Masons making a move in Israel, and a closer look at the Road Map',
Jerry Golden Report: February 23, 2005, http://thegoldenreport.com
   'Masonic Supreme Court in Jerusalem – Seat of the New World Order',
   November 09, 2004, ww.thegoldenreport.com/asp/jerrysnewsmanager/anmviewer.

Grand Lodge of British Columbia & Yukon: http://freemaosnry.bcy.ca.
   What is the Skull & Bones? Anti-Masonry Frequently Asked Questions, Section
   1, Version 2.9.

References

Grand Lodge BC & Yukon, 'Freemasonry & Nineteenth Century Revolution', http://freemasonry.bcy.ca/history/revolution/index.html

Grand Lodge BC & Yukon, 'Annie Wood Besant', http://freemasonry.bcy.ca/biography/esoterica/besant_a/besant_a.html

Grand Lodge of BC & Yukon, 'Swedish Rite FAQ', http://freemasonry.bcy.ca/texts/swedish_faq.html

Grand Lodge Pennsylvania, 'Masonic Presidents', http://www.pagrandlodge.org/mlam/presidents/froosevelt.html

Grand Orient de France: 'History', http://www.godf.org/foreign/uk/histoire_uk.html

Grand Orient de France: 'Masons killed in *Charlie Hebdo* attack', Masoneria 357, http://masoneria357.com/2015/01/10/masons-killed-in-charlie-hebdo-attack/

Gruner, Fr. N. 'Historical Context of Portugal,1910-1917 - Religious, Political, Social', http://fatima.org/essentials/facts/

Guénon, R. The Reign of Quantity and the Signs of the Times, New York, Sophia Perrenis, 2001.
    Theosophy: History of a Pseudo-Religion, New York, Sophia Perennis, 2004.
    The Spiritist Fallacy, New York: Sophia Perennis, 2004.

Gullette, A. 'A Brief Biographical-Character Sketch of Jiddu Krishnamurti', 1980, http://alangullette.com/essays/philo/k_bio.htm

Hackett, L. 'The Age of Enlightenment', History World International, 1992, http://history-world.org/age_of_enlightenment.htm

Hagger, N. *The Secret Founding of America*, London, Watkins Publishing, 2007.

Hall, Manly P. Rosicrucian & Masonic Origins, LA, Hall Publishing Co.,1929a.
    Lectures on Ancient Philosophy, LA, Hall Publishing Co., 1929.
    The Secret Destiny of America, LA, The Philosophical Research Society, Inc., 1944.
    America's Assignment With Destiny, LA, The Philosophical Research Society,1951. (See: http://www.sirbacon.org/raleighall.html)

Hancock, G. and R. Bauval, *Talisman: Sacred Cities, Secret Faith*, London, Penguin Books, 2005.

Harrington G. F. 'Masonic Heroes of the American Revolution', http://www.srmason-sj.org/council/journal/jul01/harrington.html

Hatonn, G. C. *Tangled Webs*, Nevada, America West Publishers, 1992.

Holtman, R. B. *The Napoleonic Revolution*, New York, J B Lippincott Co., 1967.

Howard, M. 'The Enlightened Ones: The Illuminati & the New World Order', Melbourne, *New Dawn*, Special Issue No. 11, Autumn 2010.

Howe, L. Center for Akashic Studies, http://www.akashicstudies.com/

Iancu, C. Masonic Forum, http://www.masonicforum.ro/en/nr10/ci.html

Icke, D. *The Biggest Secret*, Mo., Bridge of Love Publications, 2001.

International Order of Co-Freemasonry La Broti Humain, British Federation, http://www.droit-humain.org/uk/index.html

Jackson, A. C. F. Rose Croix: *A History of the Ancient & Accepted Rite for England and Wales*, London, Lewis Masonic, 1987.

James, R. Secret Societies and the Labour Movement, Biennial Conference of the Australian Society for the Study of Labour History, Wollongong, 1999. Reproduced online at Radical Tradition, www.takver.com/history/secsoc01.htm - 21

Jerusalem Insider's Guide, 'The Israeli Supreme Court: Landmark of Jerusalem Architecture', http://www.jerusalem-insiders-guide.com/israeli-supreme-court.html

Johnstone, M. *The Freemasons: The Illustrated Book of an Ancient Brotherhood*, London, Arcturus Publishing, 2006.

Jolly, J. 'Aguste Delpech', Dictionary of French Parliamentarians, 1977, http://www.senat.fr/senateur-3eme-republique/delpech_auguste0187r3.html

Kalergi, R. N. C. *Pan Europe*, Vienna, Pan Europa Verlag, 1923.

Katinka H. 'Famous People and the impact of the Theosophical Society, Inventory of the Influence of the Theosophical Society', http://www.katinkahesselink.net/2006

Keller, Daniel. Grand Master, Circular of the Grand Master of the GODF, January 8, 2015.

Kelley, Bishop F. C. Blood Drenched Altars, Milwaukee, The Bruce Publishing Co., 1935.

Keys, D. 'Spirituality at the United Nations', Aquarian Age Community, http://www.aquaac.org/un/sprtatun.html

Knight, S. *The Brotherhood*, London, Granada Publishing, 1985.

Lause, M. A. 'Walking Like an Egyptian: The American Destinies of a

References

Revolutionary French Secret Society', www.geocities.com/CollegePark/Quad/6460/WalkingEgyptian4.html - 81k

LaVey, A. S. *Satanic Bible*, New York, Avon Books, 1969.

Layiktez, C. Past Grand Master No. 146 Grand Lodge of Turkey, 'History of Freemasonry in Turkey', Pietre-Stones Review of Freemasonry, 9 April 2001, http://www.freemasons-freemasonry.com/layiktez.html

Lazare, B. 1894. *Antisemitism, Its History And Causes*, London, Britons Publishing Co., 1967.

Lelibre, O. 'The Cristeros: 20th Century Mexico's Catholic Uprising', The Angelus, Volume 15, no. 1, January 2002.

Leo XIII, Humanum Genus, April 6, 1884. Reprinted in Rodriguez, *Mystery of Freemasonry Unveiled.*

Levi E, *The History of Magic*, translated by A E Waite, 1913; London, Rider, 1982.

Lodge Camden # 297 United Grand Lodge of NSW & ACT, 'Manly P Hall: The 20th Century Masonic Philosopher'. 10 September 2008, http://www.lodgecamden.org/index.php?option=com_content&view=article&id=15:manly-p-hall-20th-centuary-masonic-philosopher&catid=9:esoterica&Itemid=17

Lord, J. 'Skull and Crossbones', Making History, Beyond the Broadcast, BBCUK, http://www.bbc.co.uk/education/beyond/factsheets/makhist/makhist4_prog3a.shtml

Lucis Trust, www.lucistrust.org/).

Mackey, A.G. An Encyclopaedia of Freemasonry, 1912. Text online at: http://www.phoenixmasonry.org/mackeys_encyclopedia/a.htm

Malevolti, G. 'Poetry Before San Guido: Brother Carducci', Pietre-Stones Review of Freemasonry, http://translate.google.com/translate?hl=en&ie=UTF8&prev=_t&sl=it&tl=en&u=http://www.freemasons-freemasonry.com/carducci.html

Maltsev, Y. N. ed. Requiem for Marx, Auburn, Alabama, Praxeology Press, Auburn University, 1993.

Manifold, D. *Fatima & The Great Conspiracy*, New York, The Militia of Our Immaculate Mother, 1992.

Manly P Hall Archive & Memorial, 'About', http://www.manlyphall.org/

Marrs, T. *Codex Magica: Secret Signs, Mysterious Symbols And Hidden Codes Of The Illuminati*, Texas, River Crest, 2006.

Marsaudon, Y. L'oecuménisme vu par un franc-maçon de tradition, Vitiano, 1964.

Marx, K. *Early Works of Karl Marx*: Book of Verse, 1837, http://www.marxists.org/archive/marx/works/1837-pre/verse/index.htm
   The Communist Manifesto, 1848. Moscow, Progress Publishers, 1975.

Masson, S. 'Remembering the Vendée', LewRockwell.com, http://www.lewrockwell.com/orig5/masson1.html

McCalman, I. *The Seven Ordeals of Count Cagliostro*, London, Arrow Books, 2004.

McGregor, M. I. 'The History and the Persecutions of Spanish Freemasonry', 19 July 2009, Pietre-Stones Review of Freemasonry
http://www.freemasons-freemasonry.com/history-spanish-freemasonry.html

Melanson, T. 'Owl of Wisdom', Illuminati Archive, http://www.conspiracyarchive.com/Articles/Owl_of_Minerva.htm

Mihaila, M. 'European Union and Freemasonry', Masonic Forum, http://www.masonicforum.ro/en/nr27/european.html#b_22

Miller, E. S., *The Lady Queenborough* (1933), Occult Theocracy, Hawthorne, California, The Christian Book Club of America, 1980.

Mirabello, M. Secret Societies: A Brief Essay, http://www.markmirabello.com/uploads/3/9/5/9/395973/secret_societies_a_brief_essay.pdf

Nation, S. 'The United Nations and the Temple of Humanity', Journal of Esoteric Psychology, vol 2 #1 2006, http://www.unmeditation.org/)

National Endowment for Demcoracy, 'Board of Directors of the NED issues statement of solidarity with the people of France', http://www.ned.org/board-of-directors-of-the-national-endowment-for-democracy-issues-statement-of-solidar/

New York Times, 'Religion: Catholics vs. Daniels', 29 October 1934.

Ng, Ronald Paul. 'The Age of Enlightenment and Freemasonry', Pietre-Stones Review of Freemasonry, UGL lecture, 2007, http://www.freemasons-freemasonry.com/freemasonry_enlightenment.html

Nicolaevsky, B. I. 'Secret Societies and the First International', *The Revolutionary Internationals, 1864-1943*, Milorad M. Drachkovitch ed., Stanford, Stanford University Press for the Hoover Institution on War, Revolution, and Peace, 1966. http://libcom.org/library/secret-societies-and-first-international-boris-i-nicolaevsky

Oldenerg, D. 'Bush, Kerry Share Tippy-Top Secret', Washington Post, 4 April 2004, http://www.washingtonpost.com/ac2/wp-dyn/A48358-2004Apr3?language=printer

References

Ovason, D. *The Secret Zodiacs of Washington DC : Was the City of Stars Planned by Masons?*, London, Arrow Books, 2000.

Oxford Dictionaries, 'Conspiracy', http://oxforddictionaries.com/definition/conspiracy

Pagels, E. *The Gnostic Gospels*, Harmondsworth, Penguin Books, 1986.

Partner, P. *The Murdered Magicians – The Templars & Their Myth*, Crucible Press, 1987.

Payne, R. *The Unknown Marx*, New York, New York University Press, 1971.

Penn State University Press, http://www.psupress.org/books/titles/978-0-271-03525-3.html

Phillips, P. M. A Relative Advantage: Sociology of the San Francisco Bohemian Club, Doctoral Dissertation, University of California, 1994, http://library.sonoma.edu/regional/faculty/phillips/bohemianindex.php

Pick F. L., and G. N. Knight, *The Pocket Book of Freemasonry*, London, Hutchison, 1992.

Pike, A. Morals & Dogma of the Ancient and Accepted Scottish Rite of Freemasonry, Supreme Council of the Thirty Third Degree, Southern Jurisdiction USA, Charleston, 1871. http://www.freemasons-freemasonry.com/apikefr.html

Pike, H. R. Religion Red & Rotten: A documentary examination of the liberal-leftist ecumenical movement, The Christian Mission to Europe, Johannesburg, 1974.

Pini, G. The Official Life of Benito Mussolini, London, Hutchison & Co., 1939.

Porter, L. *Who Are the Illuminati? Exploring the Myth of the Secret Society*, London, Collins & Brown, 2005.

Priahin, Andrei. Noteworthy members Of the Grand Orient of France in Russia and the Supreme Council of the Grand Orient of Russia's People, http://freemasonry.bcy.ca/texts/russia/russian_masons.html

Protocols of the Meetings of the Learned Elders of Zion, Russia, ca. 1905; Chulmleigh, Britain, Britons Publishing Co., 1972.

Raffi, G. Grande Oriente d'Italia, http://www.masonicforum.ro/en/nr19/raffi.html

Raleigh, W. History of the World, 1614, http://www.clements.umich.edu/exhibits/online/bannedbooks/entry3.html

Read, W. The Church of Rome & Freemasonry, Ars Quatuor Coronatorium, Transactions of Lodge No. 2076, Vol. 104, 1991.

Redd, M. 'The Swan & The Serpent', Rosicrucian Digest, Vol. 82, No. 1, 2004, http://www.scribd.com/doc/53073600/fama-fraternatatis-digest-vol-82-1

Rhoda, R. L. 'Freemasonry in Russia', 20 June, 1996, http://www.mastermason.com/hempstead749/RussiaMas.htm

Ridley, J. *The Freemasons: A History of the World's Most Powerful Secret Society*, New York, Arcade Publishing, 2011.

Rivista, Rome, 1909, p 44, quoted in the *Catholic Encyclopaedia*, 1910.

Robbins, A. *Secrets of the Tomb,* New York, Little, Brown, 2003.

Roberts, J. M. *The Mythology of the Secret Societies*, London, Secker & Warburg,:1972.

Robinson, John J. *Born in Blood – the Lost Secrets of Freemasonry,* London, Arrow Books, 1989.

Robison, John. *Proofs of a Conspiracy,* 1798; Mass., Western Islands, 1967.

Rodriguez, Cardinal Caro y. *The Mystery of Freemasonry Unveiled*, Hawthorne, Ca., Christian Book Club of America, 1980.

Roerich, N. Heart of Asia, http://www.roerich.org/HoA.html

Roerich, N. 'Banner of Peace', *New York Times*, 11 March 1930, http://www.roerich.org/realm.html

Rose Croix Martinist Order of Ontario, Canada, www3.sympatico.ca/mtronics/rcmo/

Rosov, V. Nikolas Roerich: The Messenger of Zwenigorod. Archives of the Ministry of Foreign Affairs: AWP RF. F. Otdel Dalnego Wostoka. NKID, on. 1, papka 4, portfel 35, l. 7-8., a typewritten copy.

Rushdoony, Rousas J. *Law & Liberty*, Ca., Ross House Books, 1984.

Salinas, O. J. 'Mexican Masonry – Politics & Religion: Mexican Free masonries- Encounters with Religion and Politics', Tucson, Arizona, 10 September 1999, Estados Unidos Mexicanos, http://yorkrite.com/gcmx/os1999.html

Schlesinger Jr., Ar. 'Who Was Henry A Wallace?' *Los Angeles Times*, 12 March 2000.

Scottish Rite Creed, http://scottishrite.org/

References

Sheldrake, R. 'Rupert Sheldrake: Biologist & Author', http://www.sheldrake.org/homepage.html
  'Morphic Resonance & Morphic Fields: An Introduction', February 2005, http://www.sheldrake.org/Articles&Papers/papers/morphic/morphic_intro.html

Singer, R. C. 'Masonry & the Statue of Liberty', MasonicWorld.com, http://www.masonicworld.com/education/articles/Masonry-and-the-statue-of-liberty.htm

Singh, G. Mystic Pages, The Rosicrucian Museum hosts a new show of rare of esoteric volumes, Metro_ ("Silicon Valley's Weekly Newspaper"), 24-31 March 2004.

Smith, Barry. Final Notice, Barry Smith Family Evangelism, Havelock, NZ, ca. 1989.

Sovereign Sanctuary for Bulgaria, Ancient & Primitive Rite of Memphis Misraim, Martinist Masonic Order, http://sites.google.com/site/memphismizraimbg/martinist

Spence, R. 'The Magus was a Spy: Aleister Crowley and the Curious Connections Between Intelligence and the Occult', Melbourne, New Dawn, No. 105, November-December 2007.
  'Red Star Over Shambhala', New Dawn (Melbourne), No. 109, July-August 2008.

Spence, L. An Encyclopaedia of Occultism, New Jersey, Citadel Press, 1960.

Spengler, O. Decline of The West, London, George Allen & Unwin, 1971.
  The Hour of Decision, New York, Alfred A Knopf, 1934.

Stafyla, A. 'The Masonic Landmarks' Pietre Stones Review of Masonry, http://www.freemasons-freemasonry.com/athena1.html

Stanton, D. E. Mystery 666, Lockridge, Western Australia, Marantha Revival Crusade, 1982.

Starr, Martin P. The Unknown God: W T Smith and the Thelemites (Bolingbrook, Illinois: The Teitan Press, 2003.

Steiner, R. 'The Work of the Secret Societies in the World', Berlin, 23 December 1904, http://wn.rsarchive.org/Lectures/19041223p02.html

Steiner, R. 'The Karma of Untruthfulness', 'Rudolf Steiner Archive, GA 173', 18 December 1916, http://www.rsarchive.org/Lectures/GA/index.php?ga=GA0173

Steiner, R.'Karma of Untruthfulness, Part II', GA 174, 8 January 1917, http://www.rsarchive.org/GA/index.php?ga=GA0174

Steiner, R. 'The Ahrimanic Deception', Zurich, 27 October 1919, http://wn.rsarchive.org/Lectures/AhrDec_index.html

Steiner, R. *The History & Actuality of Imperialism*, Dornach, Switzerland, 21 February 1920.

Stocks, D. 'Russian Freemasonry', http://www.casebook.org/dissertations/freemasonry/russianfm.html

Stoddard, *Light Bearers of Darkness*, London, 1930.
　　The Trail of the Serpent, ca. 1935; California, Omni Christian Book Club, 1982.

Sutton, A. C. National Suicide – Military Aid to the Soviet Union, Melbourne, League of Rights, 1973.
　　An Introduction to the Order, W. Australia, Veritas Publishing Co., 1983.
　　How the Order Creates War & Revolution, Veritas, 1985a.
　　How the Order Controls Education, Veritas, 1985b.
　　Secret Cult of the Order, Veritas, 1986.

Taylor, M. Francis Bacon Secret Societies: Francis Bacon 1561-1626, The Secret Bard, http://www.themystica.com/mystica/articles/b/bacon_francis.html

Theosophical Society, 'Early History', http://www.ts-adyar.org/content/early-history

Theosophical Society, 'Objects', http://www.ts-adyar.org/content/objects

Till, F. 'The Christian Nation Myth', http://66.102.7.104/search?q=cache:ONYuW_HgAQsJ:www.infidels.org/library/modern/farrell_till/myth.html+washington+%2B+deist+%2B+abercrombie+%2B+wilson&hl=en&gl=nz&ct=clnk&cd=1

Traditional Martinist Order, The Light of Martinism, New South Wales, http://www.amorc.org.au/admin200/pdflibrary/lightofmartinism.pdf

Trotsky, L. 'The Workers' State, Thermidor & Bonapartism', New York, New International, Vol., 2, No.4, July 1935, ppp.116-122.

United Nations. 'A Room of Quiet. The Meditation Room. United Nations Headquarters', http://www.un.org/depts/dhl/dag/meditationroom.htm

United Nations meditation room: http://www.un.org/depts/dhl/dag/meditiationroom.htm

Urso, I. Arcane School Conference, New York City, 13 May 13, 1995, http://www.aquaac.org/un/impulse.html

Uzzel, L. 'Henry Agard Wallace 32 Degree – Prophet of Agrarianism'. www.srmason-sj.org/council/journal/uzzel.html
　　'Freemasons and the Knights of Labor, Scottish Rite Journal, August 1999, Vaihinger, H. *The Philosophy of As If*

References

Val, Philippe, et al. 'The Twelve's Manifesto: Together Against the New Totalitarianism', *L'Express*, March 2006.

Vaughn, T. (transl.) 'Fama Fraternatatis or, A Discovery of the Most Laudable Order of the Rosy Cross, *Rosicrucian Digest*, Vol. 84, No. 1, 2004, http://www.scribd.com/doc/53073600/fama-fraternatatis-digest-vol-82-1

Walker, B. G. *Woman's Encyclopaedia of Myths & Secrets,* New York, Harper & Rowe, 1983.

Walker, J. 'Masonic Symbols in a $1 Bill', Washington, The New Age, Official organ of the Supreme Council 33 Degree, Ancient & Accepted Scottish Rite of Freemasonry Southern Jurisdiction, April 1960.

Wallace, Henry A. *Statesmanship and Religion.* New York, Round Table Press, 1934.

Washington, G. *The Writings of George Washington* U.S. George Washington Bicentennial Commission, U.S. Government Printing Office, 1941.

Waterfield, R. *René Guénon & the Future of the West,* New York, Sophia Perennis, 2002.

Webster, N. H. (1924) *Secret Societies & Subversive Movements*, London, Britons Publishing Co., 1964.
   (1921) *World Revolution*, London, Constable, Devon, Britons Publishing Co., 1971.

Welch, R. *The Blue Book of the John Birch Society,* Belmont, Mass., Western Islands, 1961.
   The Truth in Time, Belmont, Mass., *American Opinion*, 1966.

Weston, W. *Father of Lies,* Omni (?), ca. 1980s. First published Britain, ca. 1930s.

Wilson, D. B. *Seeking Nature's Logic: Natural Philosophy in the Scottish Enlightenment*, Pennsylvania, Penn State University Press, 2009.

Wisdom Lodge 202, 'Famous Masons: France', http://www.wisdomlodge202.org/famous_masons.htm

World Congress of Faiths, 'The Beginnings', http://www.worldfaiths.org/TheBeginning.php

Wright, D. 'Co-Masonry', *The Builder*, November 1920.

Wurmbrand, R. *Marx – Prophet of Darkness,* London, Marshall Morgan & Scott Publications Ltd., 1986.

Yarker, J. *Freemasonry Universal,* Vol. V, Part 2, Autumn Equinox, 1929.

Yorke, O. *The Secret History of the International Working Men's Association*, Geneva, 1871.

Zangwill, I. *London Times*, 18 August, 1921.

Zarnitsky, S. and L. Trofimova, 'The Way to the Native Country', *International Life*, 1965.

Zeana, C. 'The European Union – a Masonic Accomplishment', Masonic Forum, http://www.masonicforum.ro/en/nr20/zeana.html

Zeldis, L. 'Jerusalem - Symbolic Cradle of Freemasonry', http://www.freemasonry.org/leonzeldis/

www.ingramcontent.com/pod-product-compliance
Lightning Source LLC
Chambersburg PA
CBHW071048280326
41928CB00050B/2000